S0-ASU-956

Glimmer of a New Leviathan

Glimmer of a New Leviathan

Total War in the Realism of Niebuhr, Morgenthau, and Waltz

Campbell Craig

COLUMBIA UNIVERSITY PRESS NEW YORK

COLORADO COLLEGE LIBRARY
COLORADO SPRINGS
COLORADO

COLUMBIA UNIVERSITY PRESS
Publishers Since 1893
New York, Chichester, West Sussex
Copyright © 2003 Columbia University Press
All rights Reserved

Library of Congress Cataloging-in-Publication Data

Craig, Campbell, 1964-
    Glimmer of a new Leviathan : total war in the realism of Niebuhr, Morgenthau,
and Waltz / Campbell Craig
        p. cm.
    Includes bibliographical references (p.) and index
    ISBN 0–231-12348-5 (cloth : alk. paper)
    1. Nuclear warfare — Moral and eithical aspects. 2. Realism — Political aspects.
3. Niebuhr, Reinhold, 1892-1971. 4. Morgenthau, Hans Joachim, 1904– 5. Waltz,
Kenneth Neal, 1924- 6. World politics — 20th century. I. Title.
U263.C73 2003
355′.001 — dc21   2003055087

Columbia University Press books are
printed on permanent and durable acid-free paper
Printed in the United States of America

c 10 9 8 7 6 5 4 3 2 1

All the citations to information derived from the World Wide Web
were accurate at the time of writing. Neither the author nor
Columbia University Press is responsible for web sites that have
changed or expired since the time of publication.

J
63
C73
2003

For Miles Fairburn

Contents

Preface

The idea that thermonuclear war can put an end to every-thing plays a strikingly small part in the history of formal American thinking about international politics. There is not a large body of literature on that topic, but in the few histories currently available, nuclear war occupies a minor role.[1]

---

1. The LSU series on political realism founded by Kenneth Thompson has brought us three important histories of postwar American thought about international politics: Michael Joseph Smith, *Realism from Weber to Kissinger* (Baton Rouge: Louisiana State University Press, 1986); Greg Russell, *Hans J. Morgenthau and the Ethics of American Statecraft* (Baton Rouge: Louisiana State University Press, 1990); and Joel Rosenthal, *Righteous Realists: Political Realism, Responsible Power, and American Culture in the Nuclear Age* (Baton Rouge: Louisiana State University Press, 1991). The works by Smith and Russell do not address the nuclear question at any length, however, while Joel Rosenthal's treatment of five Realists' views in his chapter on "usable and unusable force" is suggestively brilliant but too brief to provide a full story. Jonathan Haslam's encompassing history of Realism since Machiavelli, *No Virtue Like Necessity* (New Haven: Yale University Press, 2002) barely touches upon the problem of nuclear war, even though its final chapter addresses the shift in American realism from *Realpolitik* to neorealism in the 1950s and 1960s. There are a number of "history of the discipline" pieces written by (and usually for) political scientists, the most important of which remains Stanley Hoffmann's essay "An American Social Science: International Relations," *Daedalus* 106 (Summer 1977). A more recent disciplinary recounting is K. J. Holsti, "Scholarship in an era of Anxiety: the study of international politics during the Cold War," *Review of International Studies* 24 (1998), pp. 17–46. A terrific history of American IR thought before the Second

Even more surprising, perhaps, is the fact that few contemporary theorists of international politics pay much attention at all to the problem of thermonuclear war. Daniel Deudney and Robert Jervis have emerged as the leading theorists who have wondered how nuclear weaponry can be reconciled with the political philosophy of modern Realism. Jervis has shown how the advent of thermonuclear weapons makes modern great war unwinnable, a conclusion that obviously undermines certain basic Realist assumptions.[2] Deudney goes even further to suggest that thermonuclear weapons have made the nation-state obsolete, which not only undermines state-centric Realism, as it is currently understood, but pretty much destroys it.[3] But Jervis and Deudney seem to be among the only prominent American social scientists who have made the question of thermonuclear war central to their comprehension of international politics. Most of today's leading scholars exclude it from their primary inquiries.

The politically eradicative possibilities raised by the prospect of thermonuclear war (leaving aside for the moment the human eradicative possibilities) make it reasonable to ask why few intellectual historians and theorists of international politics have placed it at the center of their work. Speaking as a historian, I would suggest that the answer to the first half of the query is fairly obvious. To deal seriously with the history of American thinking about international politics and thermonuclear war, one must become familiar with the immense body of contemporary scholarship on international relations (IR) theory and on nuclear strategy, a task neither easy nor historiographically fashionable. Crossing into the world of political science is an adventure that is not going to appeal to most practicing historians.[4]

World War can be found in Brian Schmidt, *The Political Discourse of Anarchy: A Disciplinary History of International Relations* (Albany: SUNY Press, 1998). Torbjørn Knutsen's *A History of International Relations Theory* 2nd ed. (Manchester: University of Manchester Press, 1997) is the best overall survey of IR thinking since the Classical period.

2. See in particular his *The Illogic of American Nuclear Strategy* (Ithaca: Cornell University Press, 1984). Jervis's ideas are discussed at greater length in chapter 1.

3. Deudney aims to develop a variant of Realist thinking he calls "Nuclear one worldism," which shows how Realism points toward a kind of world state. His latest expression of this thinking, "Regrounding Realism: Anarchy, Security, and Changing Material Contexts," *Security Studies* 10 (Autumn 2000), pp. 1–42, has had a major influence upon my own conclusions.

4. Discussion of this barrier can be found in Colin Elman and Mirian Elman, eds., *Bridges and Boundaries: Historians, Political Scientists, and the Study of International Relations* (Cambridge: MIT Press, 2001)

The second half of the query is therefore more puzzling, and indeed bears more directly upon larger arguments in this book. As Jervis and Deudney have shown, the implications of the thermonuclear revolution apply deeply and unarguably to basic theorizing about international politics, and yet major books and articles about that topic dismiss it as an uninteresting or irrelevant concern.[5]

There are probably several reasons for this, including the general, and self-defeating, unwillingness of many non-Realist IR scholars to take questions of security and military power seriously, and perhaps also a general human inclination to avoid thinking too much about thermonuclear omnicide.[6] But I would attribute the contemporary theoretical indifference to the thermonuclear revolution, especially among scholars not contemptuous of security issues, primarily to the widespread belief that nuclear deterrence has largely eliminated the possibility of thermonuclear war. According to this belief, nations will avoid nuclear war at almost all costs, by rationally fashioning their foreign policies around the general aim of avoiding major war with nuclear-armed nations, and, perhaps, by developing deterrent nuclear arsenals of their own. As a consequence, the prospect of thermonuclear war has become simply a hypothetical problem, akin perhaps to an outbreak of the black plague: abstractly terrifying, but not currently likely, and relatively easy to prevent. The serious conflicts in contemporary international politics now take place beneath, or outside of, the specter of nuclear holocaust.[7]

As I shall argue at greater length in the conclusion, I regard this confidence in deterrence to be flawed, at least insofar as it is based upon an understanding of the past. I have written elsewhere[8] that deterring nuclear

---

5. Three recent major theoretical studies of international politics consign the problem of nuclear war to the margins. These are Barry Buzan and Richard Little, *International Systems in World History* (Oxford: Oxford University Press, 2000); John Mearsheimer, *The Tragedy of Great Power Politics* (New York: Norton, 2001); and Alexander Wendt, *Social Theory of International Politics* (Cambridge: Cambridge University Press, 1999).

6. On this former point see Daniel Deudney, "Geopolitics as Theory: Historical Security Materialism," *European Journal of International Relations* 6 (Winter, 2000), pp. 79, 93. On the latter, see Martin Amis, *Einstein's Monsters* (London: Jonathan Cape, 1987), p. 11.

7. This appears to be Mearsheimer's general attitude. *Tragedy of Great Power Politics*.

8. Campbell Craig, *Destroying the Village: Eisenhower and Thermonuclear War* (New York: Columbia University Press, 1998).

war during the Cold War was much harder than many theorists seem to believe, an argument that other recent work on Cold War history bears out. During the 1957–62 crisis period the United States and the Soviet Union almost went to war over minor issues on several occasions, despite both having had large deterrent arsenals, and despite both nations' stable position as international superpowers.[9] Even though nations today may not be able to boast such advantages, a remarkable confidence in deterrence remains, permitting the specter of nuclear war to be pushed into the background.

A nice symmetry thus emerges. Historians have avoided dealing with thinking about the nuclear question because it requires arduous forays into the realm of social science. Many theorists have avoided it by adopting an optimistic, almost utopian, view of nuclear deterrence[10] that will not withstand a reading of recent works on the history of the Cold War. The difficulties inherent in interdisciplinary study have contributed to the evasion of a topic that ought to be central to both historians and theorists. This book seeks to redress that problem.

Method

What follows is an historical account of Realist theoretical analysis and the problem of nuclear war, not a new work of theory. Since the end of the Cold War political scientists have embarked upon a new, "second-order" debate about Realism and international relations, a debate, in other words, which is concerned primarily with methodology rather than with the analysis of major problems in world politics.[11] Though I have tried vainly to keep up

---

9. Indeed recent scholarship shows how a nuclear war came close to occurring well after the 1957–62 crisis period. See Jeremi Suri and Scott Sagan, "The Madman Nuclear Alert: Secrecy, Signaling and Safety in the October 1969 crises," *International Security* 27 (Spring 2003), forthcoming.

10. See Peter D. Feaver, "Neooptimists and the Enduring Problem of Nuclear Proliferation," *Security Studies* 6 (Summer 1997), pp. 93-125, and Matthew Woods, "Reflections on nuclear optimism: Waltz, Burke and proliferation," *Review of International Studies* 28 (2002), pp. 163–89.

11. The output of "second order" writing in major IR journals lately is truly staggering. For a review, i.e. a "third order" analysis, see Gerald Holden, "Who Contextualizes the Contextualizers? Disciplinary History and the Discourse About IR Discourse," *Review of*

with this debate, and indeed nourish the hope that this book will affect it, I do not pretend to write as a theorist.[12]

Instead, what I have tried to do is write a traditional history of ideas. By this I mean that I have concentrated mostly on the published writings of my three thinkers, proceeding from the assumption that their most important ideas can be better gleaned from what they wrote publicly than from their private correspondence, from psychological analysis, or from an extensive treatment of their particular personal circumstances. There is no attempt here, in other words, to develop a biography of the three Realists. Certain aspects of their personal lives are surely relevant to the story, not least of which may be that all three of them grew up in German-speaking environments, but I have decided not to emphasize such things. The sparkling biographies of Niebuhr by Richard Wightman Fox, and of Morgenthau by Christophe Frei, have, I think, relieved me of this duty, and I can heartily recommend them to readers interested in the personal lives and general intellectual development of the first two thinkers analyzed here.[13] There is no biography of Ken Waltz yet, but, if intellectual importance means anything, there will be one sometime.

My focus on published writing and relative inattention to biography raises the possibility that this book is a kind of theoretical analysis in disguise. My defense against such a charge is, actually, quite important. A primary difference between the history of political thought and its more abstract analysis is context — the placement of ideas within a discrete historical period, and the identification of their particular public purposes. I intend, as Quentin Skinner puts it, to understand Realist works by trying "to characterise what

---

International Studies 28 (2002), pp. 253-70. Also see Robert M. A. Crawford, *Idealism and Realism in International Relations* (London: Routledge, 2000).

12. I would also agree with Brian Schmidt that much of the attention to history one can find in this "second order" debate is "largely done for 'presentist' purposes rather than with the intention of actually reconstructing the past. The primary concern of many disciplinary histories of international relations, like those in political science, is really to say something authoritative about the field's current character." Schmidt, *Political Discourse of Anarchy*, p. 31.

13. Indeed, as Frei reveals, Morgenthau formulated his thinking about international politics well before he even arrived in the United States. I have focused here on Morgenthau's American writing, rather than his earlier work, because it was what shaped American realist thought.

their authors were *doing* in writing them."[14] The three authors analyzed here were writing during the height of the Cold War confrontation between the United States and the Soviet Union, a time when both superpowers developed huge arsenals of thermonuclear weapons. It is my historical judgment that the purpose of their political philosophy — what, finally, they were trying *to do* — became the aim of finding some way, any way, to fit their Realist conception of international politics within a broader opposition to the use of those arsenals in a global war. Their articulation of this purpose occurred not instantaneously, in the turning of a textbook page, but over time, in the inconclusive and messy fashion that always characterizes intellectual upheaval in history.

Readers may ask why I chose to focus upon Niebuhr, Morgenthau, and Waltz, and not other prominent Realists. To repeat the words of Richard Hofstadter, whose study of three American historians served as a kind of model for this more slender work, my criterion was, above all, influence.[15] The English writer E. H. Carr inaugurated the Realist study of modern international relations with his epochal 1939 book *The Twenty Years' Crisis*, and those familiar with that book will recognize how substantially it has affected my own views. But the fact remains that Carr did not develop new and influential ideas about international politics after the Second World War — perhaps, I would say, because his country played a lesser part in those affairs than it had in the prewar era.[16] The topic at hand, I will reiterate, is the development of the political philosophy of modern *American* Realism and its engagement with the problem of total war. Conceivably, a non-American might be shown to have had a decisive influence upon that subject, but I do not think so in this case. Thus I have also chosen not to examine the ideas of another influential Realist, the French scholar Raymond Aron, even though he arrived at similar conclusions to those of Niebuhr and Morgenthau. I judge the contributions of other early American Realists, such as Nicholas Spykman and Arnold Wolfers, to be fundamentally less influ-

---

14. Quentin Skinner, *The Foundations of Modern Political Thought*, vol. 1 (Cambridge: Cambridge University Press, 1978), p. xiii. Emphasis is in the original.

15. Hofstadter, *The Progressive Historians: Turner, Beard, Parrington* (New York: Alfred A. Knopf, 1968).

16. See Charles Jones, *E. H. Carr and International Relations: A Duty to Lie* (Cambridge: Cambridge University Press, 1998), pp. 112–120.

ential than those of my three writers, and I would say the same about Walter Lippmann and George Kennan. Both of these men wielded an enormous influence on U.S. Cold War policy, Lippmann as a powerful Washington journalist and Kennan as a policymaker, and Kennan as a matter of fact went on to revisit his Realism in the face of nuclear weapons in a manner strikingly similar to that of Niebuhr and Morgenthau. But I think that neither one of them shaped the formal articulation of postwar American Realism in an original way, which is what I mean here by influence. The most difficult omission was John Herz, whose early writings on the security dilemma paved the way for a more systematic Realist explanation of major war, and whose 1959 book *International Politics in the Atomic Age* articulated the Realist nuclear dilemma more comprehensively than any contemporary writing by my three authors. In the end, however, I decided to restrict myself to the study of those thinkers who developed the philosophical foundations of post-war American Realism as we know it — those thinkers, in other words, without whom that political philosophy in its present incarnation would not exist. *Sine quibus non.* In my view, this must be said of Niebuhr, Morgenthau, and Waltz, and probably not of anyone else. It was a judgment call.

A Note on the Title

Thomas Hobbes's evocation of the Leviathan, of an all-powerful state, a "mortal God" who restrains us from descending into anarchy and violence in exchange for total subjugation — this is one of the most powerful images in political thought, and it is natural to assume that by "New Leviathan" I mean to suggest that the three Realists envisaged a global super-state, a trans-national version of the kind of government Hobbes called for at the national level. I will state clearly now that this is not what I mean by "New Leviathan," and that none of the three Realists promoted such a state. As we shall see, Niebuhr and Morgenthau were deeply skeptical of plans for the constitutional development of a world government, and Kenneth Waltz continues to argue that such a super-state would likely become a worldwide tyranny, and that indeed the very possibility of such a state coming into existence would constitute an "invitation to commence global civil war."

What, then, does the title mean? Hobbes believed that permanent civil peace could be obtained when citizens came to realize that their most basic interest, the avoidance of violent death, justified acceptance of a powerful, even tyrannical state that could eliminate anarchy.[17] He worried, however, about a threat to this permanent peace. Citizens might decide that since the fear of death is absurd, as everybody dies eventually anyway, it is better to live dangerously and freely, to value honor, than to wallow under the repressive protection of the Leviathan. To quash such sentiments, public figures must embark upon a campaign of "instruction," to remind everyone of the abysmal miseries that come with the collapse of the state and the onset of anarchy, and to highlight the death-avoidance that can be assured by the development of an effective Leviathan.[18]

In the late 1950s and early 1960s, the prospect of thermonuclear war led Reinhold Niebuhr and Hans Morgenthau to articulate, vaguely, this kind of "instruction," but in a manner shaped by the revolutionary consequences of such a war. The task facing Niebuhr and Morgenthau was different than that facing earlier Hobbesians. Advocates of the original Hobbesian domestic state — or even of a world state before 1945 — possessed a powerful advantage over their nuclear successors, because they were not limited simply to issuing warnings about the dangers of anarchy: instead, they could point to the actual strife and war besetting societies lacking a powerful state to protect them. They could show that it is possible to pick up the pieces after such strife, for a population to learn from its mistakes, and then go on to establish the Leviathan. Indeed, this is one of Hobbes's main demands.[19] It is up to the "instructors" to drive this point home to those who value honor over personal security.

---

17. This section relies upon Peter Ahrensdorf, "The Fear of Death and the Longing for Immortality: Hobbes and Thucydides on Human Nature and the Problem of Anarchy," *American Political Science Review* 94 (September 2000), pp. 580–87, Deudney, "Regrounding Realism," pp. 13–15, and David Gauthier, *The Logic of Leviathan: The Moral and Political Theory of Thomas Hobbes* (London: Oxford University Press, 1969), pp. 207–12. I am grateful to Professor Ahrensdorf for his assistance on Hobbe's notion of "instruction."

18. Ahrensdorf, pp. 582–83.

19. ". . . it belongs of right to whatsoever man or assembly that has the sovereignty to be judge both of the means of peace and defense and also of the hindrances and disturbances of the same, and to do whatsoever he shall think necessary to be done, both beforehand, for the preserving of peace and security by prevention of discord at home and hostilities from abroad, and, when peace and security are lost, for the recovery of the same." Thomas Hobbes, *Leviathan* chapter 18 (New York: Bobbs-Merrill, 1958), p. 147.

The possibility of omnicide that thermonuclear weaponry raises led Niebuhr and Morgenthau to realize that this option is not reliably available to nations underneath the nuclear specter, for if war occurs no one may be left to point out how bad the war was, and then call for the construction of a state that could have prevented it. That turn of thought led them to glimpse — not to design, to glimpse — a *new*, that is, unforeseen, political process whereby a condition of anarchy evolves into a new Leviathan: a world state that comes into being merely because of the *prospect* of a nuclear war of all against all. Such an evolution may be dismissed as fanciful by many contemporary Realists. But in their dismissals they provide no rebuttal to the statistical certainty of a global thermonuclear war occurring as long as interstate anarchy and nuclear arsenals persist — a war after which anyone still left alive would not find their arguments against a world state convincing. Proponents of the Realist status quo have no means of denying this; as Martin Amis notes, "the trouble with deterrence is that it can't last out the necessary timespan, which is roughly between now and the death of the sun."[20] It was this understanding, grasped dimly and gradually by Niebuhr and Morgenthau, that led them to "instruct" the public about the dangers of accepting the perpetuation of international anarchy, and, correspondingly, to let go their earlier belief that a world state was neither desirable nor possible.

Kenneth Waltz, as I have mentioned, has not arrived at such a conclusion. I shall argue later that his writing nevertheless points in this direction.

A Final Note on Realism

This book is critical of the three Realists, or at least critical of them insofar as they maintained that a state-centered, anarchical Realism remains the most suitable form of international political order in a world that can be destroyed by interstate thermonuclear war. Yet, as the reader will perceive, I am hardly unsympathetic with the general political philosophy of Realism, in particular its emphasis upon collective fear and insecurity, its corresponding rejection of the Marxian claim that economic interests explain all poli-

---

20. Amis, *Einstein's Monsters*, pp. 16–17.

tics, and its presumption that idealistic, universal ideologies usually serve as a cover for the self-interests of powerful regimes.[21]

Yet there continues to be a widespread misconception, fostered perhaps by the polarization of American thought during the Cold War, that Realism is simply an ideology of heedless power maximization.[22] How difficult, really, is it to see that the Realist Cold War strategy of containing the Soviet Union, a strategy which very few anymore still energetically deplore, has little to do with the ideology of American expansion and adventurism today? Realism is concerned only with national survival in a dangerous world. All three Realists believed that Stalin's USSR posed a possible threat to that survival. Yet it was no accident that they all were early, and vocal, critics of the Vietnam War, and that Kenneth Waltz has opposed American adventurism consistently over the past forty years, including, along with many other prominent Realists, the recent war in Iraq.[23] All three understood that cynical self-interest lies behind the foreign policies of all states, not just the other ones, and that the tendency of nations to disbelieve that their universalist ideologies are invariably going to be regarded by others as imperialistic remains a root cause of major war. "Nations will always find it more difficult than individuals to behold the beam that is in their own eye," wrote Reinhold Niebuhr, "while they observe the mote that is in their brother's eye." This remains true even in the thermonuclear era.

---

21. This latter point is made forcefully by Carr, *The Twenty Years' Crisis*, and Mearsheimer, *The Tragedy of Great Power Politics*.

22. See Robert Gilpin, "The Richness of the Tradition of Political Realism," in Robert O. Keohane, ed., *Neorealism and its Critics* (New York: Columbia University Press, 1986), p. 319.

23. American IR realists were virtually unanimous in opposing a war against Iraq, as is evidenced by their advertisement on the op-ed page of *The New York Times*, September 26, 2002. Also see Nicholas Lemann, "The War on What?" *New Yorker*, September 16, 2002.

Acknowledgments

I have developed the ideas in this book over many years, and thus I would like first of all to acknowledge Ben Frankel and the late Ian Barbour of Carleton College, who introduced me to the problem of Realism and nuclear weaponry when I was an undergraduate. Alonzo Hamby and my doctoral mentor John Gaddis taught me how to attack this problem as a historian when I was a graduate student. It would be remiss of me not to take this opportunity to thank John as well for his continuing advice and support long after my dissertation was turned in. I'm grateful to John Mearsheimer, Stanley Hoffman, and Kenneth Thompson for agreeing to discuss the book project with me in its early stages.

My colleague Chris Connolly here at Canterbury kindly read and provided useful comments for chapter 1. I'm indebted to the University for a major grant and many minor ones that allowed me to conduct research far afield. Andrew Conway provided crucial research assistance even though I always ask him when he's busiest. Terry Austrin helped me out with Weber and Durkheim. Peter Field lent me several books from his formidable library, repressing his horror as I rifled through them looking only for the bits I wanted.

My old friend Tim Spiekerman of Kenyon College went far beyond the call of duty in reading and critiquing the first chapter. His insights on irrationality and twentieth-century Realism compelled to me to rethink chapter 1 and in a sense the book's larger thesis. Participants in seminars I gave on the book at Canterbury, Massey, Columbia, Yale, and Princeton Universities,

and the University of Virginia, forced me to revisit some of the more speculative arguments I make in the conclusion.

Akira Iriye of Harvard and Bob Jervis of Columbia read the manuscript
and provided me with innumerable helpful suggestions. I'm grateful to Akira
for encouraging my interest in intellectual history since our days at the University of Chicago, and for pushing me to regard American Realism as a
discrete intellectual episode rather than an all-encompassing worldview. Bob
Jervis has influenced this book more than anyone else: formally, as the
world's leading theorist of the thermonuclear revolution; informally, as a
friend and adviser helping to me hammer out the many distortions that occur
when a historian tries to write a book about theory. I can't see how the book
would have gotten anywhere without his assistance. Daniel Deudney of
Johns Hopkins read the manuscript as well and provided dozens and dozens
of valuable criticisms, based upon his own pioneering work on political
philosophy and the thermonuclear revolution.

Kenneth Waltz agreed to sit for two interviews in the (northern) spring
of 2000; he provided me with background papers and old articles and re-
views; he and his wife treated me graciously when I visited him in New York.
All of this even though he cannot have doubted that my book would criticize
his work. That's a testimony to the self-assuredness of someone who knows
his place at the top of the scholarly world. I hope he will see my criticisms
as those of an admirer who sees inconsistency over time, and not of a cynic
bent only on ahistorical attack.

My wife Christine edited the manuscript in early 2002 and patiently
accommodated my disappearance just about every evening throughout that
summer. Sylvie and Elise are now used to their father's odd behavior. My
parents, Bruce and Andrea Craig, uncomplainingly photocopied and sent
me old essays from the *Bulletin of Atomic Scientists* and *Christianity and
Crisis* from their enviable perch in New York. The other New Yorkers I'd
like to acknowledge are Peter Dimock, Anne Routon, and Leslie Bialler of
Columbia University Press, who have cheerfully supported this project since
its inception.

Sections of chapter 4 were originally published in the *Journal of the History of Ideas*; I'd like to thank that journal's editors for allowing me to re-
publish them here.

Campbell Craig
May 2003

Fear of a nuclear death provides the common interest which alone can provide nations with a basis for common action.

— David Gauthier,
The Logic of Leviathan

The man with the cocked gun in his mouth may boast that he never thinks about the cocked gun. But he tastes it, all the time.

— Martin Amis
Einstein's Monsters

Glimmer of a New Leviathan

1 The Historical Setting of Modern American Realism and the Thermonuclear Revolution

The dilemma facing American Realists during the nuclear age finds its origins in three histories. The first is the history of the general idea, or ideology, of modern Realism, which was not invented by Cold War American thinkers but rather passed to them along a relay of Western political thought which, as this chapter suggests, spent its formative years in turn-of-the-century Germany. The second is the diplomatic history of the United States during the Second World War, when America underwent an extremely rapid transformation from an isolated, continental nation with no threats to its security to a global superpower contending with Nazi Germany, and then the Soviet Union. The third history is of the technology of modern warfare, of the development of long-range bombers, missiles, and fission and fusion bombs which, combined together in a modern arsenal, are capable of overcoming any known defense and destroying a nation beyond repair: a history, in other words, of the advent of the thermonuclear revolution. Because these three histories are far from uncontested, this introductory chapter puts forward a brief, interpretative overview of them.

1. The Pessimistic Turn of Twentieth Century Realism

As Jonathan Haslam has shown, European philosophers and statesmen from the medieval period to the industrial revolution developed concepts that would become central to the twentieth-century version of Realism, and hence to the thinking of American Cold War Realists. Haslam extracts from centuries of European diplomacy and writing three premises: the primacy of the state, the notion of the balance of power, and the widespread belief that the conduct of foreign policy "should be unconstricted by moral values."[1] It was according to these fundamental premises, he demonstrates, that European leaders fashioned the modern state system, and by so doing established the historical setting for contemporary Realist understanding.

One of the most important points Haslam makes in his account of the rise of Realism is to show that the thinkers and leaders responsible for its development came at their subject from varying political and philosophical perspectives, amidst an evolving historical setting. The pessimistic and even cynical writing of Machiavelli and Hobbes contributed essentially to the rise of Realist thought, but so did the more idealistic work of Kant and Rousseau, the legally oriented writings of Botero and Pufendorf, the political economy of Smith and List, and the contingent foreign-policy-making of Richelieu, Cavour, Metternich, and dozens of other lesser-known statesmen. It would be the height of ahistoricism to identify a Realist "school" of thought in pre–World War One Europe: what Haslam describes instead is a more organic, or at least unselfconscious, establishment of traditions and ideas that came to affect the way European leaders conceived of foreign policy and interacted with one another. There was no coherent theoretical argument, no scholarly consensus, because there was no "field" of international relations before the twentieth century.[2]

That being said, it is possible to place the development of these premises within that broader European philosophical tradition we call the Enlightenment. Taking a very wide view, we may regard the development of the modern, secular state, the idea of the balance of power, and the distinction

---

1. Haslam, *No Virtue Like Necessity: Realist Thought in International Relations Since Machiavelli* (New Haven: Yale University Press, 2002), p. 11. Also see Torbjørn Knutsen, *A History of International Relations Theory* 2nd ed. (Manchester: Manchester University Press, 1997), especially chapters 2 and 4; Brian Schmidt, *The Political Discourse of Anarchy: A Disciplinary History of International Relations* (Albany: SUNY Press, 1998), chapter 2; Stefano Guzzini, *Realism in International Relations and International Political Economy* (London: Routledge, 1998), chapter 2.

2. Compare, to take a recent example, Jack Donnelly, *Realism and International Relations* (Cambridge: Cambridge University Press, 2000), which pays little attention to the development of the idea within the context of international history.

between private and diplomatic affairs all as manifestations of the rise of rational, social scientific thought which began in Europe in the sixteenth and seventeenth centuries. European political leaders and philosophers since the time of Machiavelli came to subscribe to the notion that reason ought to prevail over superstition and arbitrary tradition in the political sphere, and that by applying reason to political and social problems, such as anarchy, conflict, and war, it would be possible to construct a better world. The modern secular state emerged as an alternative to the transnational domination of the church, on one hand, and the chaos of feuding principalities and fiefdoms, on the other. The idea of the balance of power derived directly from scientific notions of equilibrium, from the Newtonian vision of a world governed by a kind of mechanistic logic: indeed, the balance of power epitomizes the Enlightenment worldview, the "assumption," E. H. Carr writes, "of the eighteenth century rationalists that man would infallibly conform to the moral law of nature once its content had been rationally determined."[3] Similarly, the distinction between private and public morality represents a blow to the premodern supposition that absolute moral commandments apply everywhere and to everyone: the overriding importance of the survival of the state — *Raison d'Etat* — allows statesmen to play by different rules, or, to put it more accurately, no rules at all.

The two coherent challenges to the traditional state system that arose in the nineteenth century, Liberal universalism and Marxism, fell also into this broad enlightenment tradition. The advent of industrial capitalism exacerbated and intensified the problems inherent in the old tradition of international relations: as industrial nations scrambled desperately for new markets and resources, the balance of European power became unstable. Liberals believed that international war stemmed from unenlightened restrictions upon international trade and upon the primitive anarchism of the balance of power. By establishing international forms of governance, under which the capitalist nations could resolve their disputes rationally and govern their empires peacefully, and by creating a system of free international capitalist trade, the sources of great war would be eliminated.[4]

---

3. E. H. Carr, *The Twenty Years' Crisis, 1919–1939: An Introduction to the Study of International Relations* (New York: Harper, 1984 [1939]), p. 23.
4. The best treatment of 19th- and early 20th-century liberal views about international relations may well remain Carr, ibid., chapter 3. Also see Knutsen, *History of International Relations Theory*, chapter 6.

Overtly, the Marxian view could not have differed more from the liberal idea. Karl Marx, Friedrich Engels, and their followers in the nineteenth and early twentieth centuries regarded the capitalist system as the cause, rather than the solution, of major war. Loathe to compel capitalist industries to distribute surplus goods to the masses, or to pay laborers higher wages, imperial governments insatiably sought new sources of cheap labor and materials in overseas colonies; their competition for these colonies pushed them inexorably into conflict. Marx and his successors called for the overthrow of capitalist regimes, for a global social revolution that they believed would usher in the age of international socialism. With the establishment of socialist regimes throughout Europe and the rest of the industrialized world, the imperial quest for overseas markets and resources would come to an end, and with it great-power war.[5]

The state of Western thinking about international relations at the end of the nineteenth century was, therefore, in flux. The centuries-old tradition of balance of power and state-centrism remained central to the worldviews of statesmen in Europe, but this tradition was coming under severe pressure from the new ideas of liberalism and Marxism. In their respective campaigns to defeat the old way of thinking, both the liberals and the Marxists possessed two important advantages. First, both schools incorporated the new economic realities of modern capitalism and the methodologies of social science to forge coherent *ideologies*, systematic approaches to contemporary international relations that the loose philosophical tradition of Realism could not hope to match. Second, and perhaps the more important, both the liberals and the Marxists contended with the old Realist tradition on the latter's own terms. The idea of the Enlightenment, the thread that connects the disparate founders of Realism to one another, was the conviction that reason, conveyed to and then applied by enlightened rulers, could overcome the social and political miseries that had affected Western civilization. Yet the greatest misery of all, large-scale war, had not been overcome, despite the efforts of statesmen and thinkers over the previous four centuries. The secular logic of Enlightenment thinking — ideas are judged by how well they work — clearly revealed that the balance of power system was unsuccessful, that it was time to use reason to develop an alternative mode of international

---

5. A nice recent treatment is in Guzzini, *Realism and International Relations*, pp. 82–86.

relations that which could foreseeably prevent wars that the "old false theories" could not. It was an unanswerable point, and the onrush of liberal and Marxian writing during the latter part of the nineteenth century and up to 1914 consistently hammered it home.[6]

Jonathan Haslam argues that the Realist answer to this challenge manifested itself in the rise of Geopolitics, and it is here that his story and the present one part ways.[7] The Geopoliticians — including Mahan, Haushofer, and above all Mackinder — responded to the liberal and Marxian riposte by attempting to develop a more systematic approach to international politics, by trying, in other words, to develop a new Realist ideology that incorporated the old ideas into a more formal, and even scientific, study of global conflict and warfare. Geopolitics became, for a while, a major school within the nascent field of international relations, and it is true that geopolitical ideas influenced the thinking of some of the later American realists, including certainly that of Hans Morgenthau.[8]

But there was another intellectual response to the rise of liberalism and Marxism in the late nineteenth century that shaped American Realism in a considerably more profound way than did geopolitics. This was the more modern thinking of the German intellectuals Max Weber and Friedrich Nietzsche, whose response to these seemingly unanswerable claims of liberalism and Marxism was simply to reject the premise that reason could reliably apply to an understanding of international politics and warfare.

Max Weber

Weber's writing about power politics is, perhaps, not as well known among scholars today as his sociological inquiries into modern society and capitalism, but the former may well have wielded a greater influence upon

---

6. Classic British examples are, respectively, Norman Angell, *The Great Illusion* (London: Heinemann, 1913), see especially part II, chapter 2: "The Psychological Case for Peace," pp. 173–99; and J. A. Hobson, *Imperialism: A Study* 3rd ed., rev. (London: Allen & Unwin, 1938), chapter 6, pp. 71–93. The quotation, "old false theories," is from Angell, p. 341.

7. Haslam, *No Virtue Like Necessity*, pp. 164–65.

8. On turn-of-the-century geopolitics, see Daniel Deudney, "Greater Britain, or Greater Synthesis," *Review of International Studies* 27 (2001), pp. 187–208.

twentieth-century thought. For in addressing the international situation facing Wilhelmine Germany, Weber put forward two arguments that underlie contemporary Realism.[9]

International power politics, Weber believed, was a struggle among major powers to determine whose national culture would prevail over the rest. Nations could choose to withdraw from this struggle, by doing so resigning themselves to the domination of a larger power's culture and interest. A nation that feared the domination of another state, that wished to preserve its culture from outside influence, would have to contend with other large powers in the international arena. To do so, it would have to accumulate military might and be prepared to wage great war.[10]

Like the earlier Realists, Weber directed his writing to his own nation. Power politics meant above all the means with which Germany must contend in the struggle to define European civilization. German disunity and weakness had allowed other powers to expand and impose their cultures throughout central Europe. If German culture were to survive in an increasingly powerful and contentious environment, the German nation would have to defend it from the advances of rival nations, particularly Russia.

To survive this Darwinian clash, Germany would have to cultivate its national power by enlarging its colonial empire, developing a professional bureaucracy, and preparing for great war against its enemies.[11] This was how Weber defined the policy of *Machtpolitik,* or power politics: in a world of perennial struggle and conflict, the survival of nations and cultures depends ultimately and irreducibly upon traditional forms of national power.[12] Weber, like many Europeans of his day, believed in the basic superiority of

9. For a recent discussion of Weber and contemporary Realism, see the companion pieces on Weber and Morgenthau by Tarak Barkawi. "Strategy as a Vocation: Weber, Morgenthau, and Modern Strategic Studies, " and Hans-Karl Pichler, "The Godfathers of 'Truth': Max Weber and Carl Schmitt in Morgenthau's Theory of Power Politics," in *Review of International Studies* 24 (1998), pp. 159–200.

10. Weber makes this point most dramatically in his inaugural lecture at the University of Freiburg, "The Nation-State and Economic Policy," in Max Weber, *Political Writings,* Peter Lassman and Ronald Speirs, eds. (Cambridge: Cambridge University Press, 1994). Also see H. H Gerth and C. Wright Mills, eds., *From Max Weber: Essays in Sociology* (London: Routledge, 1991), pp. 35–36.

11. Raymond Aron, "Max Weber and Power Politics," in Otto Stammer, ed., *Max Weber and Sociology Today* tr. Kathleen Morris (Oxford: Blackwell, 1971), pp. 84–90.

12. See Michael Joseph Smith, *Realist Thought from Weber to Kissinger* (Baton Rouge: LSU Press, 1986), p. 27.

his nation's culture, particularly when contrasted to Anglo-Saxon "conventionalism," Latin (i.e. French) *"raison,"* and the "Russian knout." Unless Germany wielded its power on an international scale, the lesser cultures to its west and (especially) east would prevail. Weber's *Machtpolitik* thus combined a superior view of German culture with a defensive attitude toward international politics. Preventing the domination of central Europe by the Anglo-Saxons or the Russians required the subordination of politics to the general end of national power.[13]

Central to Weber's understanding of national power — and this is where he departs from the enlightenment Realists — is the belief that a transnational discrimination between legitimate and illegitimate states cannot be achieved. The statesman or citizen cannot demonstrate to the satisfaction of some universal body that the objectives and culture of his state are superior to that of his neighbor, thus justifying a belligerent foreign policy. There is no such universal body, just as there is no universal agreement about what constitutes moral or immoral policy. Because of this, the statesman and citizens must have a *faith* in the superiority of their nation, a conviction that its culture must be preserved over those of its rivals, if their nation is to contend successfully in the realm of international conflict. Reason is impotent to adjudge various national claims of superiority: these claims are sorted out in the irrational and brutal arena of international politics and war, an arena in which charisma and passion prevail over reason and moderation.[14]

A second aspect of Weber's body of writing relevant to the development of modern Realism was his rejection of economic interpretations of politics, and in particular Marxist ideology. Marxism was an especially dangerous rival to Weber's *Machtpolitik*, because it purported to provide the kind of objective, critical interpretation of modern life that Weber, a sociologist himself, sought to develop. Unlike liberalism, which made its preferences for how politics *ought* to be quite clear, Marxism's relentlessly materialist explanation of politics and culture provided an alternative sociological argument that Weber could not ignore. If modern Realism was to be a critical,

13. Karl Deutsch, "discussion," in Stammer, op cit., pp. 117–18; Also see Anthony Giddens, *Politics and Sociology in the thought of Max Weber* (London: MacMillan, 1972), p. 54.

14. See Gerth and Mills, eds., pp. 53–54. Also see Pichler, "The Godfathers of Truth," p. 191.

objective ideology, rather than an *ancienne idée* whispered into the ears of
princes, it had to deal forthrightly with the Marxist challenge.

In his inaugural Freiburg lecture of 1895, a manifesto for a new German
Machtpolitik, Weber reserved his most withering criticism for the "economic
way of looking at things." "In every sphere," Weber told his new university
colleagues,

> we find that the economic way of looking at things is on the advance.
> Social policy has superceded politics at the forefront of thinking, just
> as economic power-relations have replaced legal relations, and cultural
> and economic history have replaced political history. In the outstand-
> ing works of our colleagues in history we find that, where once they
> told us about the warlike deeds of our ancestors, they expatiate today
> on the monstrous notion of 'matriarchy,' while regulating to a subor-
> dinate clause the victory of the Huns on the Catalaunian Plain.[15]

Weber's main criticism of this view is central to the ideology of modern
Realism. To quote him again, at some length:

> it is one of the delusions which arise from the modern over-estimation
> of the 'economic' in the usual sense of the word when people assert
> that feelings of political community would be stretched beyond break-
> ing point by temporary divergences of economic interest, indeed that
> such feelings *merely* reflect the economic base underlying that shifting
> constellation of interests. . . . One thing is certainly true: where nations
> are not reminded daily of the dependence of their economic success
> on their position of political power (as happens in England[16]), the
> instinct for these specifically political interests does *not*, or at least not
> as a rule, dwell in the broad masses of the nation as they struggle with
> daily necessity, nor would it be fair to expect it of them. At great
> moments, in time of war, for example, their souls too become aware
> of the significance of national power, and at such times it becomes
> evident that the nation state rests on deeply rooted psychological foun-
> dations in the broad, economically subordinate strata of the nation as

15. Weber, "The Nation-State and Economic Policy," p. 17.
16. And, Weber might have added, the United States.

well, and that it is far from being a mere 'superstructure,' the organi-
sation of the ruling economic classes.[17]

Weber's polemic here resonated into the twentieth century. Materialist
interpretations of politics thrive in times of calm, when the broad mass of
citizens (and intellectuals, he was suggesting) begin to take the state for
granted and turn their political attention instead to issues of economic dis-
tribution and injustice. For nations that rarely experience national insecurity,
such as England, questions of domestic political economy become dominant, perhaps even exclusive. But that can change at any time. At the "great
moments" of international convulsion, when the national "soul" comes under threat, citizens shed their self-interested materialism and turn to the
emotional issue of national survival. According to Weber, these moments
reveal the ultimate dominance of politics over economics.[18]

As Raymond Aron has written, however, Weber's policy of *Machtpolitik*
failed to anticipate the Wilsonian alternative, a new order in which nation-
states could cultivate their own cultures *within* an internationalist liberal
framework, set up by rational political leaders. By subordinating *all* politics
to the interests of national power, and dismissing the possibility of perpetu-
ating national culture by means short of great war, Weber was helping to
promote a Darwinian ideology of absolute international struggle. This view,
Aron notes, justified not only the violent history of international relations
during the twentieth century but also, to put it delicately (as Aron did), the
particular course taken by the German nation. To contend with Aron's de-
murral, modern Realism must not only show how politics subsumes economics; it must also show how the quest for power overcomes reason — how
the establishment of an international order by means of reason and peaceable competition is impossible.

Friedrich Nietzsche

"No American uses such language."
— Raymond Aron

As we have just seen, Weber's departure from the enlightenment tradition
of Realist thought about international relations was partial rather than total.

---

17. Weber, "Nation-State and Economic Policy," p. 21.
18. See Gerth and Mills, eds., pp. 46–51.

In developing a rationale for German foreign policy based upon a defensive notion of cultural survival, Weber was following Hobbes's general claim that the basic quest for survival drives all politics, and that reason can allow people and states to perceive this and develop policies to perpetuate their existence.

Weber's contemporary Friedrich Nietzsche's departure from the enlightenment tradition was not partial. Nietzsche did not write about international relations. He is rarely mentioned in contemporary writing about that subject, and was, because of the Nazis' appropriation of many of his more extreme ideas, excluded from the bibliographies of writers who later drew upon his thinking. However, as U. E. Petersen and Christoph Frei have shown, Nietzsche's conception of the "will-to-power," taken as a general view of political nature, provided modern Realism with an explanation of permanent conflict, and therefore a rejoinder to the Liberal challenge as presented by Aron.[19]

The Darwinian view of international relations that Weber described was based on the idea of national survival — on the struggle among nations for existence. Why, then, do nations whose survival is not at risk embark upon war? If all nations are interested only in survival, why, indeed, is there any war at all? Nietzsche's answer was that conflict does not derive from a struggle for existence.[20] Rather, the dominant force in human nature, and thus in all human affairs, is the will-to-power, the desire to dominate others. The will-to-power is not one of several basic human drives, coexisting uneasily with the drive for food, sex, society; it is the only basic human drive, from which these other human desires derive.[21] "Physiologists," wrote Nietzsche in *Beyond Good and Evil*, "should think before putting down the instinct of self-preservation as the cardinal instinct of an organic being. A living thing seeks above all to discharge its strength — life itself is will to power; self-preservation is only one of the indirect and most frequent results."[22]

---

19. U.E. Petersen, "Breathing Nietzsche's Air," *Alternatives* 24 (1999), esp. pp. 87–95; Christoph Frei, *Hans J. Morgenthau, An Intellectual Biography* (Baton Rouge: Louisiana State University Press, 2001), pp. 102–08.

20. Aron calls Weber's *Machtpolitik* "Darwinian-Nietzschean," a clear contradiction in this context. "Max Weber and Power Politics," pp. 92–94.

21. Arthur Danto, *Nietzsche as Philosopher* (New York: Macmillan, 1965), pp. 215–23.

22. *Beyond Good and Evil* #13, in *Basic Writings of Nietzsche*, tr. and ed. Walter Kaufmann (New York: Random House, 1968), p. 211.

The application of Nietzsche's will-to-power to the problem of international conflict is obvious — even if Nietzsche himself did not emphasize it.
The desire to dominate and prevail manifests itself in any manner of social
interaction, but it reaches its most spectacular form in war. Nations wage
war not because of some pragmatically defined interest but because "grand
politics" stems from the "need of the feeling of power, which, not only in
the souls of the princes and the powerful, but not least in the lower orders
of the people, bursts forth from time to time out of inexhaustible wells."[23]
"Life itself," he maintained, is "overpowering what is alien and weaker; suppression, hardness, imposition of one's own forms, incorporation and, at
least, at its mildest, exploitation." Nietzsche himself glorified this feeling of
power, and the sort of *Übermensch* who sought it; but that is not relevant to
his philosophical contribution here. One need not revel in the lust for power
as Nietzsche does to believe that it can dominate human affairs. "Something
might be true," he wrote, "while being harmful and dangerous in the highest
degree."[24]

Nietzsche's will-to-power undermines the enlightenment approach to international relations — i.e., traditional Realism, and its Marxian and especially Liberal successors — in two fundamental ways. Nietzsche led the way
in rejecting the rationalism of Enlightenment — the presumption that peace,
affluence, and order can be had because rational people prefer these to war,
sacrifice, and chaos. By claiming that irrational, destructive lusts for power
dictate human affairs, Nietzsche is ruling out reason, at least as the traditional Realists understood it, *a priori*. Furthermore, Nietzsche explains
where Weber had not why wars occur. Weber had portrayed Germany as a
defensive regime; yet if Germany were defensive, then it was not preposter-
ous to conclude that all other nations might be, which left unanswered the
question as to why major war occurs. For Nietzsche there is no mystery at
all: wars occur because people lust for them.[25]

---

23. Nietzsche, *Daybreak, Thoughts on the Prejudices of Morality* tr. R. J. Hollingdale
(Cambridge: Cambridge University Press, 1982), p. 110.
24. *Beyond Good and Evil* # 39, in *Basic Writings of Nietzsche*, p. 235.
25. Indeed, if Weber has a difficult time explaining why wars occur, Nietzsche cannot
easily explain peace. This distinction predicts uncannily the contemporary debate between offensive and defensive Realists in American international relations theorizing. In
fact, I would go as far as to say that Weber and Nietzsche may be regarded as the respective
founders of defensive and offensive Realism.

The pessimistic understanding of human nature and international politics articulated by Weber and Nietzsche can initially be discerned by examining the reaction of Western thought about international relations to the
First World War. What could possibly explain the willingness of the sup-
posedly civilized nations of the world to embark upon a four-year descent
into the barbarism and wholesale carnage of trench warfare? The old Realist
tradition had no answer to this question at all, insofar as it became implausible, if not obscene, to argue after 1918 that the Great War was a most
reasonable and enlightened way to maintain the European balance of power;
that the trenches fit into a kind of moral historical progress from darkness
to light. World War One "made an end," as Carr put it, of traditional
Realism.[26]

As the historian N. Gordon Levin shows, both liberals and Marxians
viewed the Great War in this way, and hence regarded the postwar era as
the moment of global struggle between the two ideologies to define a new
world order. With the tradition of balance-of-power politics now discredited,
or even dead, the stage was set for a contest between liberalism and Marxism,
represented respectively by the United States and the new Soviet Union,
and even personally, as Levin argues, by the "messianic political thinkers"
Woodrow Wilson and Vladimir Lenin.[27]

There was another way of understanding the carnage of the Great War,
however, and when the Wilsonian and Leninist experiments began to unravel
in the 1920s and 1930s, allowing for the emergence of figures like Hitler and
Stalin, the premise that irrational forces played a greater role in international
relations than the liberals or Marxists believed became sensible to a new
generation of thinkers. The chaotic collapse of international order in the
1930s "did not seem to conform to the world-view of idealism," as Stefano
Guzzini gently puts it.[28] As we will see, this world-view began to unravel in
even that most rationalistic and progressive of nations, the United States.

26. Carr, *Twenty Years' Crisis*, p. 1. Also see Paul Fussell, *The Great War and Modern Memory* (New York: Oxford University Press, 1975).

27. N. Gordon Levin, Jr., *Woodrow Wilson and World Politics* (New York: Oxford University Press, 1968),

28. Guzzini, *Realism in International Relations*, p. 18.

2. The End of American Free Security

In 1939, a year which saw the Japanese intensify their war of conquest against China, a nonaggression treaty signed between the USSR of Joseph Stalin and Adolf Hitler's Nazi Germany, the German invasion of Poland and the outbreak of the Second World War, the establishment of a formal military alliance between Germany, Italy, and Japan, and dozens of other international events any one of which would today trigger a rapid and expensive American reaction, polls taken in the United States indicated that the American public would oppose any government policy designed to involve America in the world conflict. Preoccupied with the continuing weakness of the economy, still bitter about the failed intervention in the First World War, most American citizens and most American intellectuals opposed going to war under almost any circumstances.[29] In accord with this opposition, the U.S. government remained formally neutral; in the 1940 election both major party candidates, Democrat Franklin Roosevelt and Republican Wendell Willkie, campaigned upon a promise not to enter the war.

As the past sixty years have shown, the American aversion to becoming involved in major international war before 1941 was not due to an inherent pacifism, or ingrained indifference to world affairs, lodged within the American psyche. It was due, primarily, instead to the United States' geographical position. Americans paid little attention to power politics and thus to ideologies concerned with power politics because the United States, at least after the British withdrawal from the War of 1812, had become physically invulnerable to invasion. America's transformation from an isolated nation, largely indifferent to even the most convulsive power politics, to a superpower bestriding much of the planet took place within a decade, making the hasty ascension of Bismarck's Germany seem ponderous in comparison. There were many proximate causes of this transformation; all derive from the collapse of American invulnerability — the demise of America's free security.[30]

---

29. On American neutrality before the Second World War, see Hadley Cantril and Mildred Strunk, eds., *Public Opinion 1935–1946* (Princeton: Princeton University Press, 1951), pp. 966–70.

30. I regard the idea of free security as essential to an understanding of American foreign relations: see Campbell Craig, "The Not-So-Strange Career of Charles Beard," *Diplo-*

The Capricious Nature of U.S. Foreign Relations Before 1940

Like several other industrial powers, the United States experienced acute economic and social crises in its growth to industrial might after the Civil War. Unlike these other nations, America did not have to worry at the same time about its position in an increasingly dangerous world of international power politics. As a consequence, U.S. political thought and action during the period 1870–1940 focused primarily upon problems of domestic political economy. American foreign policy during this period was parochial, a series of unsustained actions stemming from domestic economic imperatives.[31] Two examples illustrate.

In 1898, President William McKinley initiated a war with Spain for the purposes of seizing the Spanish colonies of Cuba, Puerto Rico, and, most important, the Philippines. McKinley claimed that he initiated the war in order to rid the Cubans, Puerto Ricans, and Filipinos of Spanish colonial rule; he also implied that the United States needed to acquire overseas bases to contend with the European powers. The administration was also, however, motivated by its desire to obtain overseas markets and resources for American industries hit hard by the depression of the mid-1890s. The seizure of the Philippines, in particular, was taken in order to obtain American access to the "China market," as was demonstrated by Secretary of State John Hay's "Open Door" notes of 1899 and 1900. Hay demanded that the European powers respect American economic penetration of China, a request buttressed by President Theodore Roosevelt's seizure of Panama in 1903 and subsequent building of the Panama Canal.

The easy manner with which the McKinley administration and succeeding administrations let its victory over Spain dwindle away reveals the capriciousness of its 1898 wartime ideology. How did the United States follow through on its objectives in its war with Spain? It rid the three colonies of Spanish colonial rule, stressing its aim to end old-world imperialism, only to replace it with unpopular American colonial rule. It established minor

matic History 25 (Spring, 2001), esp. p. 253. C. Vann Woodward, in "The Age of Reinterpretation," *American Historical Review* 66 (October, 1960), pp. 2–8, coined the expression. Also see Robert Jervis, "Cooperation under the Security Dilemma," *World Politics* 30 (January 1978), pp. 184–85; Arnold Wolfers, *Discord and Collaboration* (Baltimore: Johns Hopkins Press, 1962), pp. 247, 250; and Carr, *Twenty Years' Crisis*, p. 159.
31. Carr, *Twenty Years' Crisis*, p. 1.

military bases on Cuba and the Philippines which served to raise America's geopolitical stature in the eyes of other world powers to the level of, say, Belgium. And, most striking, despite its brutal five year war to subdue the Filipinos the United States made no serious attempt to pursue the China market in the first part of the twentieth century. The revival of the American economy in the 1900s, together with the collapse of the Chinese political system, diminished the appeal of an American empire in Asia, and the China market went largely ignored by American politicians and businessmen until the 1930s.[32]

In a similar fashion, as we have already suggested, pressing economic problems lay behind the next American entry into old world power politics — intervention in the Great War. Despite clear warnings from advisers such as Secretary of State William Jennings Bryan, Wilson allowed American manufacturers to sell war goods to Great Britain and France, and he allowed American banks to finance these purchases to the tune, by the end of 1916, of more than $2 billion. That decision obviously benefited the American economy, but it also tied it utterly to the fates of those two nations: defeat would mean Entente default and an American economic tailspin. In calling for American entry into the war in 1917, Wilson asserted that the United States would join the battle only for idealistic reasons: to make the world "safe for democracy," to rescue the defunct Europeans from themselves, to prevent a victory of German autocracy. That a German victory would mean almost certain economic collapse was not mentioned.

As was the case with the 1898 war, the vital interests of the American nation with respect to the First World War may be discerned by observing its behavior afterwards. The American congress and people quickly lost interest in Wilsonian ideals after 1918, particularly after Wilson decided to make compromises with Realists like David Lloyd-George and Georges Clemençeau at the Paris Peace talks. In a move that epitomized the capricious nature of American foreign policy before 1941, in 1919 the American congress actually rejected American entry into the very League of Nations that Wilson had founded. In other words, the U.S. congress disallowed American

---

32. See Thomas McCormick, *China Market* (Chicago: Ivan Dee, 1990), William Appleman Williams, *The Tragedy of American Diplomacy* 2nd ed., (New York: Delta, 1959), chapter 1; and Walter LaFeber, *The New Empire: An Interpretation of American Expansion, 1860–98* (Ithaca: Cornell University Press, 1963), chapter 8.

participation in the establishment of idealist international institutions, even though that was the declared reason for American entry into the war. Not only would the American decision to stay out of the League of Nations prevent the U.S. from reshaping European politics along Wilsonian lines; it would also allow it to ignore the rejuvenation of German power in the 1930s. The U.S. response to victory in the First World War was to divorce itself from serious international politics.

Rarely do nations participate in a major war, come out on the winning side, and then decline to follow through on the objectives they used to justify their involvement. The reasons for this American diffidence are apparent. American entry into the war accomplished its economic objective: there was no collapse such as would likely have followed a German victory. Indeed, relatively unscathed by the war, and prosperous from its lucrative trade with the Entente powers, the United States experienced an economic boom after 1918. As with the abortive empire in Asia, American leaders and the broader public lost interest in Wilson's plans to reform international politics, and in particular his objective to involve the U.S. in the old world cauldron of European affairs.[33] As Harry Truman, an artillery captain during the war, put it, most of his comrades "don't give a whoop (to put it mildly) whether Russia has a Red government or no government and if the King of the Lollipops wants to slaughter his subjects or his Prime Minister it's all the same to us."[34]

Initially, the American response to the onset of the Great Depression in 1929 was to learn from these errors — to resist foreign adventurism as a means of dealing with an economic problem. The progressive historian Charles Beard famously called for an American policy of "cultivating our own garden," of looking to markets and resources within the vast expanse of the North American continent rather than pursuing economic opportunities in dangerous and warlike foreign lands. President Franklin Roosevelt initially embraced this idea. He had responded to the Depression by socializing much of the American economy, maintaining cool relations with the European powers, and officially ignoring the growing world crisis. One of

---

33. See Akira Iriye, *Cambridge History of American Foreign Relations* volume III (Cambridge: Cambridge University Press), pp. 68–72.
34. Quoted in Robert Ferrell, *Woodrow Wilson and World War One* (New York: HarperCollins, 1985), p. 180.

Roosevelt's first foreign policy decisions was to quit the London Conference in 1933, a clear indication of his determination to turn his back on great-power politics. By 1937, however, Roosevelt began to direct his government's attention away from the domestic economy, and toward events in Asia and Europe. Beard, and other supporters of his social-democratic isolationism, accused Roosevelt of seeking a foreign policy solution to a domestic problem, like McKinley and Wilson had before him.

United States foreign policy before 1940 was shaped by the absence of serious consequences.[35] America could pick a fight with Spain over Cuba and then seize the Philippines, intervene in the First World War only at the last moment, call for a League of Nations then decline membership in it, pay little attention to the convulsive international aftermath of the First World War all without suffering any major repercussions. As a prominent political scientist concludes: the "absence of threat permits policy to become capricious."[36] Foreign affairs in American life were fleeting; Americans interested in politics cared about the domestic economy. What Beard, his colleagues, and the broad mass of the American public did not see was that this luxury of looking inward was reaching its end, because of two developments, occurring simultaneously, over which the United States had no control.

Decline, Part One: Collapse of the European Balance

From 1815 to 1914 the balance of European power had remained in "equilibrium," which is to say that since the era of Napoleon no state, or alliance of states, had accumulated enough power to be able to dominate the continent. This balance allowed the United States to pay little attention to European power politics. There was no serious threat: for a European power to consider attacking the United States — particularly after the burst of American industrialization and growth in the late nineteenth century — it would have to be in control of Europe, not opposed in its quest by other European states that might ally themselves with the Americans, as the British

---

35. For a similar argument also see Stanley Hoffmann, "An American Social Science: International Relations," *Daedalus* 106 (Summer, 1977), p. 42.

36. Kenneth Waltz, "Realism after the Cold War," address to American Political Science Association, Boston, 1998.

discovered during the War for Independence. Moreover, when the balance of power in Europe failed, after 1914, neither side came close to achieving the kind of victory that would have allowed it even to conceive of transoceanic expansion. Pouring their wealth and young men into the trenches for year after year, none of the major belligerents — Britain, France, Germany, Russia — were in any position to threaten the United States when it declared war in April 1917.[37] Indeed, it is hard to imagine a time when the nation was physically safer than during the latter stages of the First World War. After the war, a semblance of a new balance of power reemerged, but not for long.

Over a period of about two years Nazi Germany approached a dominance over the European continent that had not been seen since Napoleon. In August 1939 Hitler signed a nonaggression pact with his fellow dictator Joseph Stalin, thereby gaining a free hand to invade Poland. This he immediately did, and after a delay during the winter of 1939–40 Nazi forces swept through northwestern Europe, capturing the low countries, much of Scandanavia, and, by June 1940, France. After an abortive attempt to bombard Great Britain into neutrality, Hitler in June 1941 invaded the Soviet Union. By the end of that year Nazi forces had penetrated much of Russia. Europe from the Atlantic to the Urals was on the verge of falling totally under German domination.

It is important to consider this development as it appeared at the time. Germany's easy victories over the western European nations and, to that

---

37. John Mearsheimer, in his recent book *The Tragedy of Great Power Politics*, argues that the United States entered the First World War for security reasons, in order to prevent the rise of an unchallenged hegemon — Germany — on the European continent. American security policy, he contends, has always sought to maintain a balance of power in Europe, and has fought there when that balance is threatened. This is a dubious argument on two historical grounds: first, the likelihood of a total German victory in 1916 and 1917, when the United States government decided to go to war, was not apparent; no one perceiving the course of the war at this time could have believed that either side was close to attaining victory, and certainly not the kind of victory that would allow it to challenge the United States. Had the United States been motivated by this concern, it surely would have entered the war much earlier, when the possibility of a quick and overwhelming victory by Germany was still imaginable. Second, Mearsheimer's theory would have the United States going to war to oppose Napoleon's conquest of Europe in the early nineteenth century. Yet in the War of 1812 America instead fought Great Britain, by then Napoleon's most important adversary. See Mearsheimer, *The Tragedy of Great Power Politics* (New York: Norton, 2001), pp. 252–54.

point, the Soviet Union made it entirely foreseeable that within a short
period of time Hitler's totalitarian regime would be in control over the industries and populations of all continental Europe. Hitler's stated objective
was world domination, and he had shown no qualms about ruthlessly using
the material and people under his control toward that end. Simple, objective
indices of power indicated that Germany was on the way toward creating
the kind of superstate that would be capable of conquering the United
States.

Decline, Part Two: The Shrinking of the Oceans

Had Hitler been in command of Europe in 1930, rather than 1940, the
great distance between his European empire and the United States would
have made an invasion of America, even if geopolitically feasible, militarily
implausible. Before the late 1930s, any nation envisioning an attack on the
United States would have had to assemble a gigantic Naval fleet, equip it
with weaponry and manpower sufficient to sustain a prolonged invasion of
an entire continent, and then sail it across the Atlantic or, worse, the Pacific.
In the meantime, an America bristling with industrial potential and manpower would have ample time to prepare its defenses.

By 1940, however, the time between the decision to launch such an
invasion and its execution on American shores had shrunk to days, in some
respects even hours. During the 1930s, innovations in aviation design made
it possible to build bombers capable of carrying large payloads over continental distances. Suddenly, a nation deploying a modern air force could
bombard the cities of a distant nation, something which many strategists
believed could disable the enemy badly. As the historian John Buckley notes,
by the mid-1930s Great Britain, for a millennium protected by its Navy and
the Channel, "was no longer secure from direct attack."[38] Any continental
power with enough airplanes could bombard every major British city.

Adding to the bomber's range was another recent development, the aircraft carrier. Like the bomber, carriers had improved in design and reliability

---

38. John Buckley, *Air Power in the Age of Total War* (London: UCL Press, 1999), p. 112.
An interesting biography of the British architect of such thinking is Charles Messenger,
'Bomber' Harris and the Strategic Bombing Offensive, 1939–1945 (London: Leventhal,
1984).

during the 1930s. What the carrier allowed a nation to do, simply enough, was to deploy bombers (or other aircraft) as far forward as its naval power would allow. This basic fact brought the United States into the scope of the Second World War. Bombers could not yet fly from land bases in Europe or Asia, attack American cities, and return home. But they could do so from carriers. Nothing could change the distance between the American continent and the Eurasian landmass, but the mastery of the seas with aircraft carriers could make that distance less important. An enemy in control of large parts of the Pacific or the Atlantic could get within bombing range of major American cities.

Many Americans were not indifferent to the threat of German superpower. President Roosevelt had pushed for a stronger alliance with Great Britain since 1937, and by 1941 was actively trying to manipulate the nation into declaring war on Germany. Interventionist groups such as the Committee to Defend America by Aiding the Allies warned Americans daily about the Nazi threat; the scientist Albert Einstein, no war-monger, went so far as to urge Roosevelt in 1939 to launch a program to build an atomic bomb. The reasoning was simple: Germany had a similar program, and a Germany with sole possession of an atomic bomb could pound, or intimidate, the United States into submission. In 1941, with German control over Europe at its zenith, Roosevelt initiated the Manhattan project.[39]

Still, the American public and its representatives in Washington opposed going to war against Germany. By supporting Great Britain (and, after June 1941, the Soviet Union) with economic and military aid, the United States could keep Germany at bay without having to send its armies to Europe. Even as late as the fall of 1941 most Americans, polling data shows, did not believe that Nazi Germany posed a threat to American survival. The protective oceans lingered in the American consciousness.

The Japanese attack on the U.S. naval base at Pearl Harbor put an end to that. The surprise attack by Japanese bombers, launched from invisible carriers just over the Pacific horizon, demonstrated to the United States in a way only violence can that the era of Free Security was over. If the Japanese could attack Hawaii, then it was simple to see that German bombers in the

---

39. See Richard Rhodes, *The Making of the Atomic Bomb* (New York: Touchstone, 1986), pp. 378–79.

Atlantic could attack Washington and New York. Military technology had overcome the oceans.

The Demise of Free Security and the Origins of the Cold War

By the time of the German surrender in May 1945 many of the world's traditional great powers were left prone. Germany, obviously, was completely defenseless at the war's end, as was Japan. Great Britain and France were beaten down by the war: their populations war-weary and depleted, their economies unstable, their overseas empires precarious, and, in the case of France, her morale shattered. Far more powerful at the end of the war were the United States and the Soviet Union. Though the latter had suffered grievously during the war, in the process of repelling the German invasion Russian armies had passed through, and now stood in control of, much of Central and Eastern Europe. No European power could have hoped to stop it had the USSR sought to extend its domination of the continent westward.[40] What is more, the nationalist government in China was on the verge of collapse, undermined both by its feeble response to Japanese conquest over the past decade and a growing communist revolutionary movement in the north. Having agreed to participate in the war on Japan, Stalin would have to send his armies through China. By the summer of 1945, the Soviet Union was in a position to gain predominant power over the Eurasian continent, a prospect that would appeal to any nation, not least one that subscribed to an ideology of historical destiny.

The American government, under the new President Harry S Truman, had to decide whether it could accept such an outcome. No one could be certain that the Soviet Union would indeed bid for Eurasian dominance, but it was equally impossible to be sure that it would not. In the history of international politics, powerful nations had tended to project their power into areas where military resistance was unlikely. The Soviet Premier, Joseph

---

40. On American perceptions of the USSR's position in Europe at the end of the Second World War, the best treatment is John Lewis Gaddis, *The Long Peace: Inquiries into the History of the Cold War* (New York: Oxford, 1987), chapter two. Recent scholarship from Soviet archives suggests that Stalin hoped to consolidate and retrench rather than expand. There was no way that the Americans could have known this; furthermore, a conspicuous US decision to quit western Europe might well have changed Stalin's mind.

Stalin, had demonstrated very clearly his grasp of this historical tendency.[41] Were the United States to return to its policy of isolation from great-power politics, it was reasonable to believe that the USSR would fill the gaping power vacuum that was Eurasia.

Had a war similar in its geopolitical outcomes to those of the Second World War ended in 1930, not 1945, the United States might well have left the old world to its fate. A Soviet Union in control of the Eurasian landmass could not, given the state of military technology in 1930, have threatened the United States. Isolation would have allowed America to preserve its culture, its national existence, irrespective of Soviet power. Life under Stalin's brand of totalitarian communism might have been miserable for its new minions; American civilization, nevertheless, would remain unthreatened in its part of the world, at least for the time being.

In 1945, however, Americans could not be so sanguine. Were the Soviet Union to take control of the Eurasian continent, seizing the industrial capabilities of Europe and Asia as Germany and Japan had tried to do, it could create a superstate *capable of* traversing the oceans and attacking the United States. Such a capability, in and of itself, would put American existence at risk, just as Hitler's domination of Europe did.

As Weber had argued a half-century earlier, a budding power must choose to either become a great power and practice power politics, or run the risk of allowing another great power's civilization to prevail over it. The United States in 1945 faced such a decision. It was not certain that the Soviet Union would to try to impose its civilization upon the rest of the world. But if the United States retreated from power politics, returning to its Western hemispheric realm, nothing could stop the Soviet Union from attempting such conquest. No longer immune from the ramifications of such a possibility, the United States chose to confront the Soviet Union in Europe and East Asia.

3. The Thermonuclear Revolution

By dropping two atomic bombs on the Japanese cities of Hiroshima and Nagasaki, the United States was able to shorten its war with Japan, thereby avoiding further American casualties and preventing the Soviet Union from

---

41. See Robert C. Tucker, *Stalin in Power: The Revolution from Above, 1928–1941* (New York: Norton, 1990), especially chapter 10.

participating in the postwar occupation with one stroke. But the scale and scope of the atomic bombings portended something new. Bernard Brodie wrote in 1946 that "thus far the chief purpose of our military establishment has been to win wars. From now on its chief purpose must be to avert them. It can have almost no other useful purpose."[42] With this statement, Brodie articulated the idea of the nuclear revolution in its barest sense. The American establishment, he was suggesting, would have to avert all future major warfare, for a war between nations possessing atomic bombs, waged in the total manner of the Second World War, threatened to unleash destruction far beyond what even Germany and Japan had experienced — not to mention the United States. As prescient as Brodie was, he was of course unable to foresee the advent of thermonuclear weapons and intercontinental missiles, a phenomenon that transformed the prospect of total war beyond the cataclysm Brodie imagined into something qualitatively worse.

Total War and the Atom Bomb

Brodie's fears stemmed not only from the nature of atomic weaponry *per se* but also from the experience of the Second World War. Before 1939, the idea that a war between the major powers would invariably involve the dropping of large bombs upon urban centers, culminating in the kind of cataclysm Brodie envisioned, would have shocked many Western leaders. The Just War tradition, to which political leaders and military academies alike paid regular homage, forbade the direct and intentional killing of civilians.[43] This tradition lay behind the widespread condemnation of Italian atrocities in Ethiopia, for example, and of the bombing of republican strongholds such as Guernica by Franco's air force during the Spanish civil war. Roosevelt, in his first public statement following the outbreak of the war in Europe, made America's position plain: he urged all belligerents to refrain from "bombardment from the air of civilian populations or of unfortified cities."[44]

All of this was soon abandoned. Viewing the war against Germany and

---

42. Bernard Brodie, ed., *The Absolute Weapon* (New York: Harcourt, Brace, 1946), p. 76.
43. On the Just War tradition, see William O'Brien, *The Conduct of Just and Limited War* (New York: Praeger, 1981) and James Turner Johnson, *The Just War Tradition and the Restraint of War* (Princeton: Princeton University Press, 1981).
44. Quoted in David Kennedy, *Freedom From Fear* (New York: Oxford University Press, 1999), p. 426.

Japan as a total war, one that must be won by whatever means, the United States (along with the less squeamish British) gradually adopted a strategy of city-bombardment. By destroying German and Japanese urban centers, American and British leaders believed that they were diminishing the enemy's industrial output, terrorizing and demoralizing its inhabitants, and paving the way for a quicker end to the war. Strategic bombing also was a way of avoiding attrition warfare on the ground, and it played to American beliefs, as the historian Michael Sherry notes, in the superiority of American technology. Thus the American Army Air Force and the British RAF bombed dozens of German cities into rubble, often using incendiary bombs on urban targets made up predominantly of wooden buildings. Fire-bombing of cities like Hamburg and Essen killed tens of thousands of civilians in a matter of days; in February 1945, by which time the fate of Germany was well decided, American and British airplanes fire-bombed Dresden, incinerating some 35,000 people over the space of four days. As for Japan, the U.S. Army Air Force was even more ruthless, bombing defenseless Japanese cities at will in 1944 and 1945. The incendiary raids on Tokyo, in early March 1945, killed as many as 100,000 civilians and set the city's canals aboil.[45]

In one sense, then, the atomic bombings of Hiroshima and Nagasaki were merely a continuation of existing practice. The fire-bombing of Tokyo killed more than either atomic bombing did, and equally indiscriminately. For the hypothetical Japanese civilian, the atomic bombings may not initially have seemed any worse than what happened to Tokyo. However, as Brodie perceived, there was a profound difference. It took the firestorms three or four days, coming as a result of hundreds of sorties, to decimate the populations of Dresden and Tokyo;[46] in Hiroshima and Nagasaki, one plane dropping one bomb managed to kill tens of thousands of civilians in each city instantaneously. The firepower and explosive scale of the two atomic bombs dropped on Japan was of a magnitude roughly one thousand times greater than that of the largest existing conventional bomb.[47] The radioactive fallout

---

45. Michael Sherry, *The Rise of American Air Power: The Creation of Armageddon* (New Haven: Yale University Press, 1987), pp. 261–82.
46. On the Tokyo raids, see Kenneth P. Werrell, *Blankets of Fire: U.S. Bombers over Japan during World War II* (Washington: Smithsonian Institution Press, 1996), pp. 160–61.
47. See Sidney Drell, "Nuclear Weapons," in John Whiteclay Chambers, et al, eds.,

an atomic explosion produces, moreover, can kill thousands more. Indeed, a nation in possession of several hundred atomic bombs and a large bomber force could hypothetically level every major city in any enemy nation. What had been done to German and Japanese cities over several years could now be accomplished in a few minutes, and to American cities as well. This was the sort of warfare Brodie wanted to avert.

In 1946, however, it was possible to imagine how such warfare could be ameliorated. The destructive power of the atomic bomb, while colossal, was — at least for a geographically large nation like the United States, or the Soviet Union — evadable: by dispersing city-dwellers into the countryside, it would be possible for American or Russian civil authorities to spare large parts of their populations from even an all-out atomic attack. The bomb dropped on Hiroshima instantly incinerated virtually all citizens found within a radius of about one kilometer from the target's epicenter.[48] To destroy reliably a dispersed population in America or Russia, hundreds of thousands of such bombs would be required.

Moreover, in 1946 there was only one reliable way to bomb cities — by manned airplane. In preparing for atomic attack, surely nations would dedicate massive efforts toward the building of extensive anti-aircraft defenses and the training of fighter pilots. To put it another way, in the bomber age military skill — anti-aircraft fire, combat in the air — could have a real effect on the outcome of an atomic war. By dispersing its populations, building solid air defenses, and skillfully shooting bombers out of the sky, the United States could meaningfully survive an all-out atomic attack. Brodie's scenario was, in this respect, premature when he presented it in 1946: the American military establishment could still win a war in the atomic age.

Thermonuclear War

Hopes that total war in the atomic age could be ameliorated by effective forms of defense were, and remain, shattered by the development in the 1950s of the thermonuclear bomb and the intercontinental ballistic missile.

An atomic explosion occurs as the result of the splitting, or fission, of an

---

Oxford Companion to American Military History (New York: Oxford University Press, 1999), p. 510.
48. See Rhodes, *Making of the Atomic Bomb*, pp. 714–15.

atom. Early in the atomic age American nuclear scientists, led by the vocal Edward Teller, speculated that the merging, or fusion, of two atomic nuclei into one might create an explosion that could dwarf even that of an atomic bomb. Just as Roosevelt initiated the atomic program for fear that Germany might get the bomb first, Truman initiated the thermonuclear program in order to build this new kind of weapon before the Soviets did. The Soviet Union had built and tested an atomic bomb in 1949, much sooner than the American administration had expected. They were able to do so with the important help of a spy network within the American nuclear program. Alarmed, the Truman administration rushed to build the "super bomb," and tested its first one in 1952. The Soviet Union followed suit a year later.[49]

The destructive capabilities of atomic bombs are measured in terms of kilotons, i.e., thousands of tons of dynamite. The thermonuclear weapons that the United States and the Soviet Union rushed to build in the 1950s and thereafter are measured in megatons — millions of tons. Early weapons reached the level of one megaton. Later, both sides deployed bombs of ten or twenty megatons. The USSR is known to have built a sixty-megaton bomb, and is supposed to have developed one of 100 megatons.[50] A bomb of ten megatons is capable, depending upon wind and topography, of killing everyone within fifty square miles of ground zero, and producing a radioactive cloud that can spread over hundreds of square miles.[51] Whereas the atomic bomb dropped on Hiroshima, with a metropolitan population of about 300,000, left a mile-wide ring of devastation in its center, killing roughly 40,000 people immediately and a total of about 70,000, a ten-megaton thermonuclear bomb dropped over a city of its size would obliterate it, killing all of its citizens and irradiating the surrounding areas.[52] The effect of a ten-megaton bomb dropped upon a dense metropolis, like New York City or Hong Kong, would, of course, be spectacularly worse.

Furthermore, the development of intercontinental ballistic missiles (ICBMs) by both Cold War superpowers made defense against a thermonuclear attack hopeless.[53] Not only was (and is) it almost impossible to shoot

49. The best history of the development of the H-Bomb is Richard Rhodes, *Dark Sun* (New York: Simon and Schuster, 1995).

50. See Freedman, *The Evolution of Nuclear Strategy*, p. 266.

51. Fred Kaplan, *The Wizards of Armageddon* (New York: Simon and Schuster, 1984), pp. 77–79.

52. Rhodes, *Making of the Atomic Bomb*, p. 713.

53. The United States developed a triad of land, sea, and air based ICBMs in the late

down ballistic missiles, which are relatively small in size and travel at speeds up to 10,000 miles an hour, the speed with which a missile attack can occur makes the preparation of civil defense and dispersal extremely difficult.[54] In the atomic/bomber age, urban populations might have several hours to get away from the likely targets in their midst. That would make for a chaotic process, but the removal of large numbers of people only a few miles — walking distance — from an urban center might well save most of their lives. In the thermonuclear/missile age, urban populations will likely have less than one hour to get at least ten miles from a likely target. Unlike bombers, all, or almost all, of the missiles would get through, and in many parts of the country those people who somehow managed to travel ten miles to escape one likely target would only find themselves near another. Populations in urbanized nations cannot be adequately protected from a general ICBM attack, which is one reason why both the United States and the Soviet Union abandoned serious programs of civil defense during the Cold War.

What would a general thermonuclear attack on the United States then entail? A Soviet missile attack consisting of, say, 3,000 one-to-ten-megaton warheads, aiming at maximum civilian casualties, could easily have obliterated America's 500 largest cities, killing perhaps 100 million people outright. The destruction of transportation, communication, and medical facilities would leave little hope for the injured, nor anything for those facing deadly radioactive clouds and rain, not to mention a second wave of missiles. In a more fundamental sense, the existence of the U.S. as a sovereign state and distinctive national society would come to an end. The chaos, anarchy, destruction, misery, and governmental collapse following a nuclear attack would have succeeded in eliminating American civilization as it is commonly regarded. Representative government, free markets, American values, norms and cultures — all would have disappeared, only to return, if at all,

---

1950s and early 1960s comprising several thousand thermonuclear warheads. The Soviet Union lagged behind, not developing a comparable arsenal until the mid-1960s. The lay observer in the 1950s could not have known about Soviet missile inferiority, and indeed after the "missile gap" rhetoric of the 1960 election campaign few would have believed it. More important, the Realists who perceived the advent of a "thermonuclear revolution" in the late 1950s were not thinking of the consequences of an imminent war but rather of total war between the nuclear superpowers in general.

54. Information on missile technology can be found in Thomas B. Cochran, William M. Arkin, and Milton M. Hoenig, *Nuclear Weapons Databook, vol. 1e: U.S. Nuclear Forces and Capabilities* (Cambridge MA: Ballinger, 1984), pp. 111ff.

in a distant future and imposed by outside forces. A nation devastated by nuclear attack is totally vulnerable to invasion and occupation, something that would likely occur, under any number of pretexts, after the radioactive clouds had dissipated.[55]

In thinking about the revolutionary effects of thermonuclear warfare, it is important to keep in mind above all else its *duration*. Societies have recovered from devastating wars, but these wars have occurred over the space of years, giving people and governments time to rebuild, and to adjust and adapt to the misery and violence. As Daniel Deudney writes, now

> nuclear science and technology have given us the capability to wreak violence at an unprecedented scale and speed. To find historical analogies for a full-scale nuclear war one must look to great cataclysms like the Fall of Rome, the Mongol Invasions, the Black Plague, the European Invasion of the Americas, and the World Wars and imagine several of them occurring at once and greatly compressed in time, perhaps into a single afternoon.[56]

Existing societies are not equipped to withstand the kind of disaster Deudney describes. American society — urbanized, highly dependent upon modern infrastructures, and with no experience of war on its own soil — could hardly be regarded as an exception to this rule. A general thermonuclear attack on the United States would destroy it; American society, its government and institutions, would rapidly crumble and disappear.

The Realist *Ultima Ratio* and the Thermonuclear Revolution

The Realist ideology, deriving from traditional political ideas, enhanced by modern political thinking, and — as we shall see — developed by American scholars into a systematic approach to international relations, is based

---

55. Nuclear war scenarios can be found in these two very different books: Jonathan Schell, *The Fate of the Earth* (New York: Avon, 1982) and Herman Kahn, *On Thermonuclear War* (Princeton: Princeton University Press, 1960).
56. Daniel Deudney, "Nuclear Weapons and the Waning of the *Real*-State," *Daedalus* 124 (Spring, 1995), p. 210.

ultimately upon a great power's readiness to wage major war. A great power engages in power politics by contending with other great powers in an anarchical international environment, in which the threat of war is always the ultimate recourse. According to all conventional Realist thinking, a great power cannot rely upon a supranational authority to protect it from other great powers. Nations can use international organizations and institutions to advance their interests in the international arena. A powerful state determined to get what it wants, however, can bypass these institutions, knowing that in the end the institutions possess no capability to stop it. The only thing that can stop a great power in an anarchical environment is the threat of major war posed by another great power.

This line of thinking defined American policy toward the Soviet Union after the Second World War. Determined to maintain and extend American society and institutions, the United States concluded that it could not rely upon international organizations like the United Nations to stop Soviet power.[57] The primary military means used by the United States to dissuade the Soviet Union from aggression was, of course, its nuclear arsenal. To prevent the Soviet Union from moving into Central Europe or Japan, the United States threatened it with thermonuclear attack.

By the late 1950s, the American *ultima ratio* of great war was becoming absurd. This is to say, as American and Soviet thermonuclear arsenals grew, major war to stop potential Soviet aggression appeared likely to bring such destruction to the United States as to destroy its society indefinitely. In defending American culture from its Soviet rival, a major war threatened to put an end to it. The advent of secure, second-strike retaliatory forces meant that even if the United States were to launch a first strike against the Soviet Union, enough Soviet missiles would get through in the counter-attack to destroy America beyond repair. This new state of affairs is called the *thermonuclear revolution*: whereby the unique destructive capabilities of ther-

---

57. The U.S. could conceivably have equipped the United Nations with great war-making power after World War Two, as it considering doing in 1946. For classic Realist reasons — namely, that it could not be absolutely sure that the Soviet Union would not somehow co-opt UN power — it chose not to. Had the U.S. plan, rewritten to accommodate these fears, to equip the UN with its atomic weapons been accepted, the UN would have become an arm of the United States. Such an outcome would not have refuted the Realist argument, and in any event was rejected by the Soviet Union — for its own, obvious, Realist reasons.

monuclear weaponry make it impossible to win a great war in a meaningful sense.

Is the thermonuclear revolution inescapable? If new techniques of warfare could conceivably limit the destruction of an atomic war, why could not similar techniques do the same for a thermonuclear war? In the 1950s and early 1960s, dozens of the most brilliant academicians in the United States dedicated themselves to finding a means of escape from the dilemma: a strategy for winning a nuclear war. But as Robert Jervis has shown, nuclear strategy cannot work. Once both sides acquire an arsenal of invulnerable, retaliatory missiles — an arsenal that cannot reliably be destroyed by a pre-emptive attack — it becomes extremely difficult to see how a war between the two powers can be prevented from escalating into total nuclear war. As World War Two demonstrated, even in an age of conventional weapons nations waged total war, unleashing their full military capabilities, bombing cities, sending entire armies to the slaughter, rather than running the risk of defeat. In the nuclear age, the impulse of waging total war would be even greater. A nation deliberately restraining itself from using its most powerful weapons will know that the other side, if not similarly restrained, would administer the first apocalyptic blow. This knowledge would place severe pressure upon military leaders on both sides to abandon war limitation and launch a total attack. As long as one side succumbs to the temptation, a nuclear war cannot be limited in the first place.[58]

Even were the two superpowers somehow able to avoid waging total nuclear war from the outset, by commencing their war in a limited fashion, the question of how the war would come to an end before escalating into total war is difficult to answer. By definition, in order for one side to win the war in a meaningful sense, the other must surrender without launching its invulnerable arsenal. In other words, for a nuclear war to remain limited — winnable — one side must accept defeat while *it still possesses the military capability to destroy its opponent easily.* In the grim realm of a major conventional or limited nuclear war between the Soviet Union and the United

---

58. Jervis, *The Illogic of American Nuclear Strategy*, (Cornell: Cornell University Press, 1984), pp. 19–46. The main critic of Jervis's argument that nuclear weapons had made great-power war unwinnable during the Cold War was Colin Gray — see especially his *Nuclear Strategy and National Style* (Lanham, MD: Hamilton Press, 1986). If there is a school of thought today which argues that a nuclear war between great powers is winnable in any politically meaningful sense, I am not aware of it.

States, one side would have to be able to discern that it was losing the war, order its armies, and/or its missile base commanders, to cease fire, and accept a major Cold War defeat at the hands of its rival: all the while being able to destroy the enemy totally with the turn of a few keys. It defies the imagination to see this occurring in the midst of World War Three — and it also seems unlikely that a winning side, in the tense business of negotiating a surrender of an enemy still capable of destroying you utterly, would find it easy to stop fighting as well.[59]

Unlike atomic weapons delivered by airplanes, thermonuclear missiles are very easy to hide and protect, very difficult to shoot down, and several dozen of them by themselves can obliterate all of the other side's major cities. Therefore, it is basically impossible for a major nuclear power to lose a war, in the Clausewitzean sense of being disarmed. Because of this, American nuclear strategists in the "golden age" were forced to advocate either surrendering during a limited war, if it came to that or escalation, or waging an offensive sort of general nuclear war, in the hope that the USSR might end up with several more million deaths than the United States. Neither alternative was appealing to American political leaders, and nuclear strategy fizzled out in the 1960s.[60]

The strategists' inability to solve the thermonuclear dilemma presents modern Realism with a basic paradox. Realist thinking has long stipulated that a nation must not only threaten, but actually wage, major war rather than allow an adversary to threaten its existence. Modern American Realism accepted this stipulation, and toughened it by appealing to the hard world-views of thinkers like Weber and Nietzsche, the memory of total warfare during the Second World War, and the totalitarian, global nature of the Soviet threat. In other words, American Realist thought at the outset of the Cold War embraced the *ultima ratio* of major war in an especially pure fashion.

To discover that nuclear technology was making *ultima ratio* absurd was for American Realists therefore a crisis of the first order. What follows is an account of that crisis, focusing on the three giants of American Cold War Realism: Reinhold Niebuhr, Hans Morgenthau, and Kenneth Waltz.

---

59. See Robert Jervis, "Deterrence Theory Revisited," *World Politics* 31 (January 1979), p. 300.
60. On this point, see Marc Trachtenberg, *History and Strategy* (Princeton: Princeton University Press, 1991), chapter 1.

2 Reinhold Niebuhr and the Emergence of American Realism

The last thing Americans cared about in 1932 was great-power politics. The Great Depression reached its nadir during this year, as a continuing string of bank failures, reports of malnutrition and starvation, and unemployment rates reaching 20 percent made a mockery of President Herbert Hoover's claim that "prosperity is just around the corner." Hoover was beaten badly in the 1932 presidential election by Franklin Delano Roosevelt, who promised Americans decisive government intervention in the domestic economy and, according to his campaign rhetoric at least, a total indifference to foreign policy. For Roosevelt, as for political commentators and thinkers around the nation, the burning question in American political life was whether the American capitalist system could survive the seemingly endless miseries of the economic downturn.

American political thought in the early 1930s was completely occupied with this question. The debate was reasonably straightforward. On one hand, such liberals as the educator John Dewey believed that the system could be saved. Dewey believed that social crises and injustice stemmed from irrational and ill-considered human behavior, and that therefore societies could become more stable and just if people could be educated to act more reasonably. By advancing the cause of reason in education and the mass media, American reformists could rid U.S. society of the greed, antagonism, and class resentment that had damaged American culture during the 1920s and threatened social breakdown in the early 1930s. By improving the rational faculties of all men and women this reform could usher in an era of social tranquility and justice while at the same time avoiding violence and class warfare.[1]

The other side of this debate was Marxian in orientation. Socialism had never gained much ground in American politics before the 1930s, largely because of the multi-ethnic makeup of the labor force and because the sheer size of the nation accommodated economic expansion, rapid capital mobility, and a steady stream of immigration. But the Depression's persistence and its spread to Europe emboldened many American thinkers to regard it as the final crisis of capitalism. Moderate social democrats, such as the historian Charles Beard, called for a government takeover of moribund industries and the development of a comprehensive welfare state. Further to the left, new radicals like Edmund Wilson called for working-class revolution and an emulation of the Soviet experiment.[2]

Moral Man and Immoral Society

Reinhold Niebuhr, a Lutheran minister, theologian, and occasional social commentator, strode into this debate in 1932 with his book *Moral Man and Immoral Society*. It was Niebuhr's mission to attack the optimism about human nature found in both the liberal and Marxian sides of the debate. Combining a traditional Christian belief in the immutably sinful nature of man with a political philosophy deeply influenced by Max Weber, Niebuhr articulated in his new book a pessimistic understanding of politics that constitutes the birth of modern American Realism.

Niebuhr believed that eternal human greediness and lust for power would always dash the liberal and Marxian dreams of a future without conflict. Writing in 1932, his more apparent objective in articulating this belief was to reject Deweyist liberalism as hopelessly idealistic in a world of self-interest and conflict, and to remind Marxists that the social revolution they sought could never be achieved without coercion and violence.[3] His aim was to

---

1. On this intellectual tradition, see Morton White, *Social Thought in America: the Revolt Against Formalism* (New York: Viking, 1949), esp. chapters 11–12.

2 See Christopher Lasch, *The New Radicalism in America,1889–1963: The Intellectual as a Social Type* (New York: Norton, 1965), chapter 9.

3. See Daniel F. Rice, *Reinhold Niebuhr and John Dewey: An American Odyssey* (Albany: SUNY Press, 1993).

contend with optimistic views on political economy. Yet in developing his thesis, Niebuhr put forth an analysis of international politics that established a foundation for future American Realist thinking.

Niebuhr maintained that politics derives from the essential human quest for survival. The human instinct toward self-preservation, he argued, is taken up by the group, which uses its mandate to protect the lives of its constituents in order to pursue power in its own right. But the group is more likely to act more aggressively and wantonly than the individual. "The proportion of reason to impulse, becomes increasingly negative when we proceed from the life of the individuals to that of social groups, among whom a common mind and purpose is always more or less inchoate and transitory, and who depend therefore upon a common impulse to bind them together."[4]

The inchoate and selfish characteristics of group politics thus transform the natural human "will-to-live" into a group's "will-to-power." Departing from Nietzsche, Niebuhr emphasized that the will to power is derivative, not essential: "the impulses for self-preservation," he wrote, "are transmuted very easily into desires for aggrandizement."[5] If the quest for economic sub-sistence transmutes easily into a drive for unlimited material wealth, so then does the desire for physical security evolve into aggression and expansion: in obtaining subsistence and security the groups who represent a given class of man will always want more. Niebuhr, however, describes the outcome of this transformation in modern terms: "The beast of prey ceases from its conquests when its maw is crammed," he stated, "but man's lusts are fed by his imagination, and he will not be satisfied until the universal objectives which the imagination envisages are obtained."[6]

This insight has two applications. On one level, Niebuhr argued that the gradual amelioration of the American economy that liberals and moderate socialists sought is impossible, because the collective in question here — the "privileged class" in America — was unlikely to cede its power and control by appeals to reason and morality. This is not because all members of this class were themselves necessarily evil, but because the class, acting as a group, would be unable to transcend its own basic material interests for the

---

4. *Moral Man and Immoral Society* (New York: Scribner's, 1932), p. 35.
5. Ibid., pp. 18, 41.
6. Ibid., p. 44. The imagery of insatiable human appetite comes from Rousseau's *Discourse on Inequality*.

sake of the general welfare, even if many influential members of this class were ethically predisposed to do so. Once groups come into a mature existence they take an egotistical and paranoid shape, stemming from the basest wants of their members, upon which post-facto individual altruisms can exert little influence. That is why, Niebuhr believed, relations between groups were so often more violent, apparently irrational, and uncompromising than were relations between individuals. Appeals to reason and morality would not solve the current crisis; only coercion, backed by the possibility of violent force, would.[7]

In this respect Niebuhr was siding with the revolutionaries. American capitalism could not evolve peacefully into a more egalitarian and just order. To change the American political system in a serious way, working-class movements would have to seize economic power by using violence. But, he continued, it was folly to believe that after the revolution a new government would emerge that was any more interested in equality and justice. Collective egoism pays no attention to ideology; all collectives become equally corrupt and self-serving. The communists, Niebuhr argued, could not destroy economic power without creating strong new centers of political power. "Societies risk the welfare of millions," he wrote, "when they gamble for the attainment of the absolute."[8] Perhaps the crisis at hand in 1932 justified revolution, but there would be no utopia on the other side. This stance signified Niebuhr's break from the Enlightenment tradition, and indeed from the tradition of American social thought. He did not assume that social problems could eventually be solved.

A second implication of the political philosophy Niebuhr was advancing in *Moral Man and Immoral Society* bore upon the nature of inter-group conflict. Here the application of his ideas to international politics became explicit. The inability of groups to transcend their own interests, Niebuhr maintained, makes interactions between them intrinsically contentious and actual empathy among them impossible. Because groups are bound to regard even their most aggressive demands and actions as defensive and understandable, they are likely to regard objections and resistance from other groups as hostile. National groups identify their own interests with the general good, and so are likely to regard alternative ideologies and demands as

---

7. Ibid., p. 83.
8. Ibid., pp. 192, 199.

destructive and evil. "Nations will always find it more difficult than individuals to behold the beam that is in their own eye while they observe the mote
that is in their brother's eye; and individuals find it difficult enough. A perennial weakness in the moral life of individuals," Niebuhr maintained, "is
simply raised to the nth degree in national life."[9]

The conflict that therefore raged among nations, however, was not simply
more common or violent than that among individuals: it was, in all likelihood, immutable. This was so because no supranational force existed "capable of bringing effective social restraint upon the self-will of nations, at
least not upon the powerful nations."[10] Liberal attempts to develop such a
force had failed miserably, as Niebuhr noted in a discussion of the League
of Nations; moreover, a world of socialist nations would probably prove no
less conflictual, as communist governments, he accurately foresaw, would
appeal to parochial identities and patriotisms, not economic solidarity, for
the purposes of their own aggrandizement.[11] In *Moral Man and Immoral
Society* Niebuhr discerned, rather than theorized, a fundamental distinction
between domestic and international politics. "The whole history of mankind," Niebuhr wrote, "bears testimony to the fact that the power which
prevents anarchy in intra-group relations encourages anarchy in intergroup
relations."[12] Advancement beyond this anarchy was unlikely, because neither
liberal nor socialist powerful nations were likely to forsake their wills-to-
power. A world beyond nations, moreover, seemed too distant to be worth
discussing. "What lies beyond the nation, the community of mankind, is too
vague to inspire devotion."[13]

In his final chapter Niebuhr retreated from this bleak view of international politics with the intention of incorporating a moral and religious dimension back into the amoral scene he had presented.[14] The responsible
political actor — the "rational moralist" — can recognize the irreducible egotism of the collective, and thus the necessity of using coercion to achieve
serious political goals, without transforming the means of coercion and
power into ends in themselves. In the field of international relations, the

9. Ibid., p. 107.
10. Ibid., p. 111
11. Ibid., pp. 90, 96.
12. Ibid., p. 16.
13. Ibid., p. 91.
14. This became a regular feature of Niebuhr's writing.

"wise statesman" — the rational moralist statesman — can recognize when the demands of his nation for more power and wealth were becoming ends in themselves, and as such destructive and dangerous in a world of competing sovereignties. Such a leader, Niebuhr claimed, "is hardly justified in insisting on the interests of his group when they are obviously in unjust relation to the total interests of the community of mankind."[15]

There are two problems with this assertion. As Niebuhr had argued emphatically earlier in the book, the tendency of national leaders to identify their own parochial interests with those of civilization and mankind make it difficult, if not impossible, for any statesman, no matter how wise, to assess the "total interests of the community of mankind" in any kind of objective fashion. With no supranational authority available to evaluate such claims, one leader's definition of the interests of mankind might be another's strategy for national aggrandizement. Niebuhr had already noted that this leads to an inevitable "hypocrisy of nations."[16] Furthermore, Niebuhr's emphasis on the irremediable sinfulness of human nature and hence the contingent, relative morality of human action and political ideology make his own claim that there exist a general set of interests for mankind dubious, to say the least. How could a set of interests for mankind be defined, without referring or connecting those interests to a particular position on international relations expressed in the parochial and contingent arena of human affairs? To identify the interests of humanity, something he had said is "too vague to inspire devotion," one would either have to transcend one's own interests completely, taking a Godlike view of mankind's destiny — a notion that was anathema to the Niebuhr of 1932 — or one would have to decide that a particular set of social interests were indeed the best for all humanity.

Weber had nicely solved this problem, by axiomatically supporting the power of the German nation over that of rival national cultures. This was precisely the way in which Weber avoided having to define and favor something as vague as a universal "interest." As long as Niebuhr remained unwilling to favor one force in world affairs over another — as long, in other words, as he was determined to maintain an objective, critical stance on the question of international relations — he would be caught within this universalist paradox. He could not have it both ways.

---

15. Ibid., p. 267.
16. Ibid., p. 99.

The Crisis

Along with many other American leftist intellectuals, and indeed the nation as a whole, Niebuhr moved away from radical politics in the latter part of the 1930s. *Moral Man and Immoral Society* catapulted him into academic stardom; he secured a professorship at the Union Theological Seminary in New York, and in 1939 was invited to deliver the prestigious Gifford Lectures in Great Britain. Moreover, Roosevelt's New Deal policies had, regardless of Niebuhr's doubts, ameliorated the economic crisis, making the question of reform or revolution less burning for comfortable intellectuals as the decade progressed.

The primary cause of Niebuhr's move away from left-wing domestic politics in the latter part of the 1930s, however, was the emerging global crisis. The advent of militarist governments in Germany and Italy — of regimes whose egoism knew no bounds — represented a problem to which his pessimistic view of power politics might now have real relevance. Any doubts Niebuhr may have had about whether the rise of European fascism constituted a serious problem were quashed during his time in Britain, where he was able to experience the Nazi threat firsthand, to appreciate the feeling of national insecurity, and to regard the descent of British politics into basic camps of appeasement and confrontation.[17] In letters home to his mother and sister Niebuhr articulated his new feelings. "Now either Hitler has to back down or there will be war," he wrote in April; the Nazi-Soviet pact, he continued later that year, "seals the doom of Europe." The Balance of Power was failing: Britain was "tired and lacking in resolution and too full of moralistic illusions" to reassert its global power. Living in a nation threatened by a messianic neighbor and yet apparently too jaded to do anything about it gave Niebuhr a different perspective upon international politics. "One gets accustomed," he wrote, "to the international tension."[18]

Niebuhr returned to an America still diffident about the burgeoning World War. As late as 1940 the majority of Americans hoped to stay out of the conflicts raging in Europe and Asia. This was so for a number of reasons.

---

17. See Richard Wightman Fox, *Reinhold Niebuhr: A Biography* (New York: Pantheon, 1985), pp. 187–92.
18. Letters to his mother and sister, April 1, 1939, May 7, 1939, August 1939 (no exact date), from Reinhold Niebuhr Papers, addition IV, Box 58, Library of Congress.

At the mass level, hostility toward Britain, especially among Irish-Americans and segments of the American Left, a quiet support for the Axis powers, especially among German- and Italian-Americans and the fringes of the far right, and nativistic isolationism, the kind found throughout the midwest, all contributed to popular opposition to American participation in the war.

But isolationism was hardly restricted to the masses. Many of Niebuhr's fellow Protestant churchmen, especially those writing for the liberal weekly *The Christian Century*, had not forsaken the disgust for modern warfare that so many liberal thinkers — including Niebuhr himself — had embraced after the slaughter of 1914–18. Not necessarily absolute pacifists, these intellectuals nonetheless regarded modern war as a barbaric monstrosity that no civilized person could support. Many of Niebuhr's fellow leftists, particularly in the wake of the Nazi-Soviet treaty, clung to the line that the war was nothing more than another imperialist struggle. To support Britain in the European war, they argued, was to support the enemy: better to let the capitalist tyrannies kill one another off.[19]

Throughout 1940 and 1941 Reinhold Niebuhr waged an intellectual crusade against Americans opposed to intervention in the European war, destroying in the process many friendships and almost single-handedly overhauling the political culture of liberal American Protestantism.[20] In making his case, Niebuhr targeted the same two groups he had criticized in *Moral Man and Immoral Society*: liberal, antiwar idealists, and the pro-Soviet left. Just as before, Niebuhr was on less sure ground when it came to the issue of American national interest, a problem that impaired his crusade until Pearl Harbor solved it for him.

Niebuhr had courted with the idea of pacifism after the First World War, putting him in the company of liberal and left thinkers throughout the West who viewed trench warfare as the death throe of Western civilization.[21] Writ-

---

19. For a recent study of antiwar politics before Pearl Harbor, see Justus Doenecke, *Storm on the Horizon: The Challenge to American Intervention, 1939–41* (New York: Rowman and Littlefield, 2001).

20. Fox provides a compelling story of Niebuhr's battle with his antiwar friends in *Reinhold Niebuhr*, pp. 193–209.

21. In 1923 Niebuhr wrote that "this is as good a time as any to make up my mind that I am done with this war business. . . . I am done with this business. I hope I can make this resolution stick." *Leaves from the Notebook of a Tamed Cynic* (Louisville: John Knox Press, 1980 [1929]), pp. 42–43.

ing during a time when international war was on no American's horizon, he repudiated pacifism in *Moral Man and Immoral Society*, but only because he was unwilling to condemn violence as a recourse to social injustice. If international relations also led to conflict and war that was a fact to be recognized rather than a policy to be justified.

Now, the stakes of international violence were on a different level. In the inaugural issue of *Christianity and Crisis*, the journal he and other interventionist Protestants established in early 1941 to compete with the antiwar *Christian Century*, Niebuhr revived the arguments of the Just War. The pacifists who opposed confronting Hitler had forgotten the Just War doctrine of defending innocent parties under attack: it was crucial to distinguish between "individual self-abnegation and a political policy of submission to injustice, whereby lives and interests other than our own are defrauded or destroyed." Reviving the language of Saint Augustine, Niebuhr charged the pacifists with caring more for love than for justice, for disregarding the injunction that "life should be prevented from exploiting, enslaving, or taking advantage of other life."[22]

If it was a "Christian" belief that "one cannot oppose tyranny without becoming transmuted into a tyranny," Niebuhr continued in June 1941, then "Christianity dooms us to slavery," just as "to say that democracy cannot resist tyranny without becoming totalitarian is to seal the doom of democracy." Furthermore, pacifists who took from the Sermon on the Mount the idea that all war is un-Christian failed to see that this is a stance of "genuine" political perfection suitable for an individual martyr but not for an isolationist group like America First. Idealists were blind to the necessities of survival in a dangerous world; the soft pacifists, unlike authentic religious perfectionists such as the Quakers, were guilty of using purist theology to justify a secular political position.[23]

The Augustinian distinction between antiwar idealism and pure pacifism was central to Niebuhr's critique. True pacifists are always willing to accept the political consequences of their beliefs, one of which is to be excluded from positions of political leadership. A pacifist may choose to turn the other

---

22. "The Christian Faith and the World Crisis," *Christianity and Crisis* 1 (February 10, 1941), pp. 4–5. On the influence of St. Augustine upon Niebuhr's political thought, see William R. Stevenson, *Christian Love And Just War: Moral Paradox And Political Life In St. Augustine And His Modern Interpreters* (Macon: Mercer University Press, 1987).
23. "Pacifism and America First," *Christianity and Crisis* 1 (June 16, 1941), pp. 3–4.

cheek in a situation of personal danger; what he or she must not do, as Niebuhr emphasized in *Moral Man and Immoral Society*, is make that decision on behalf of an entire group.[24] That is one reason why individuals are capable of acting more morally than groups. Now it was time for Protestant liberals and their spokesmen at the *Christian Century* to make up their minds. If their opposition to American intervention was to be on purely pacifist grounds, then they should avoid political argumentation and simply adopt a stance of personal conscientious objection. If, instead, they rejected the war for reasons of idealistic, antiwar sentiment, than admit as much and advocate an isolationist position along the lines of "America First." To put it another way, if the religious idealists Niebuhr was attacking believed that the Just War was still valid, then surely they had to admit that the Nazi conquest of Western Europe fell under its dictates. If it was not valid to them, he demanded that they either embrace pure pacifism or abandon the religious justification for their antiwar position. It was a strong argument, one which Niebuhr pounded home relentlessly in 1941.

Niebuhr's criticism of the Marxian left was more complicated, since it had to shift ground after the Nazi invasion of Russia in June. Before the invasion, Niebuhr attacked the anti-imperialists who celebrated their "sensitive conscience by enlarging upon all the well-known evils of our western world and equating them with the evils of the totalitarian systems." Adopting a line that would become familiar after the war, Niebuhr urged his fellow leftists to think seriously about whether they really saw no difference between the imperialism of the European powers and the modern oppression of states like Nazi Germany. Following the Nazi invasion, Niebuhr no longer had need to convince the left of the cause of intervention, and was content to mock the sudden pro-war sloganeering of the new popular front, recounting in the July 19 *Nation* "the tortuous logic by which the comrades and fellow-travellers transmute the imperialist war of yesterday into the holy crusade of today."[25]

Though Niebuhr's attacks on antiwar Protestantism and the "fellow-travelers" of the popular front were the most dramatic features of his interventionist crusade of 1941, costing him many friendships and affiliations, his most difficult argument was with the third branch of American antiwar

---

24. *Moral Man and Immoral Society*, p. 172.
25. "New Allies, Old Issues," *Nation* 153 (July 19, 1941), p. 50.

sentiment, the "strategic isolationists." Hitler's shocking conquest of western Europe in 1940, along with the invasion of Russia in 1941, had weakened, respectively, the soft pacifist and Marxian arguments against the war, making them fairly easy to shoot down. Less of a straw man was the position that the United States could survive a Nazi victory in Europe; that the oceans could allow America to maintain its civilization whatever happened to the Old World. Niebuhr had a difficult time with this argument because it was based upon the strict notion of *American* national interest, a concept he had shown in *Moral Man and Immoral Society* he was not ready to accept, and because it dealt with questions of military technology and geopolitics, issues in which Niebuhr was not a specialist.

Who exactly were the "isolationists"? Niebuhr took stock in the second issue of *Christianity and Crisis*. There were the nationalistic isolationists, who cared only for U.S. national interest, i.e., the physical preservation of the nation. These isolationists believed that events in Europe posed no threat to American survival. Nationalistic interventionists disagreed with interventionists like Niebuhr about the nature of the danger to the United States: but, Niebuhr stressed, there was no "moral issue" between the two sides. "The issue between them is purely strategic," he concluded, as if the strategic debate regarding waging war against Nazi Germany in 1941 could be divorced from morality.[26]

Exploring the problem further, Niebuhr tried to distinguish these strategic isolationists from "democratic isolationists," those, like Charles Beard, who wanted the United States to avoid militarization and war, in the hopes of preserving its own democracy as an island in "a possible ocean of anarchy and tyranny." Drawing a false dichotomy, Niebuhr demurred. "We might conceivably preserve the power and the prestige of our nation in a Nazi world. It is hardly conceivable that we could preserve our democratic values if the victory of the Nazis had been brought about partly by our indifference to the democratic cause. The idea of an island of democracy in a tyrannical world is a snare and delusion." Niebuhr reiterated this point in the March 22 *Nation*, suggesting that "we are not immune to the disaster which emerges from European anarchy."[27]

---

26. "Whosoever Will Save His Life . . ." *Christianity and Crisis* 1 (February 24, 1941), p. 1.
27. "Fighting Chance for a Sick Society," *Nation* 152 (March 22, 1941) p. 359.

These were assertions. Niebuhr had not demonstrated that a Nazi victory in Europe in 1941 would result in the kind of disaster which would make American democracy impossible — as opposed, say, to a German victory in the First World War. Were the "nationalist isolationists" really indifferent to the idea of preserving American democracy, and only concerned with maintaining "prestige and power"? Beard was calling for a continental social democracy uncorrupted by Old World wars and intrigues; he was urging the Europeans to defend themselves. How could Niebuhr contend with that?

In his June 1941 *Christianity and Crisis* article "Pacifism and America First" Niebuhr first dismissed the issue, arguing that whether the United States could stand alone and preserve its civilization in a totalitarian world "belongs in the category of military and political strategy. We know of no religion which throws any light upon such strategic questions." Then, oddly, Niebuhr added to his article a section titled "Geography, Christianity and Politics," apparently in order to throw religious light on this strategic question. Here Niebuhr bogs down again. Unsure how to prove that democratic civilization could not survive in a Nazi world, Niebuhr resorted to the curious stance of insisting that modern man "must venture out and mix with his fellows in the marts of commerce." American economic "vitalities," he insisted, would be stifled in a world of Nazi autarky. Commerce between nations is not merely the instrument of greed," the old leftist asserted; perhaps uncomfortable with that line of argument, Niebuhr went further and declared that "to equate peace with security against a physical invasion of our country is to reduce life to a primitive level. . . . Only vegetables are completely rooted to their own soil."[28] This rude metaphorical rejoinder to Beard's call for Americans to "cultivate their own garden" nevertheless left the question begging. Did the sustenance of American civilization really depend upon maximum global trade with non-fascist regimes? This was a weak reed, particularly for Niebuhr.

In the six months between the Nazi invasion of Russia and American entry into the war Niebuhr drifted toward a more forthright engagement with this question. The argument about trade and commerce was jettisoned. He flirted with (almost) pure geopolitics, brashly declaring in his July *Nation* piece that "if Hitler can gain the grain of the Ukraine and the oil of the Caucasus, he will be able to eliminate the Western world in a few years if

---

28. "Pacifism and America First," *Christianity and Crisis* 1 (June 16, 1941), pp. 5–6.

that world remains confused." Along these lines, in November Niebuhr warned of Hitler's upcoming "third Punic War."[29]

Niebuhr edged toward another argument, which would remain ill-formed when the Japanese attack over Hawaii saved him from having to hash it out. In distinguishing between strategic and moral analysis of the interventionist cause, Niebuhr, and other writers for *Christianity and Crisis*, had tended to give rather short shrift to the moral benefits of American survival, per se. That is, in making a moral argument for intervention Niebuhr stressed the importance of sustaining "democratic civilization" in general, and in particular helping Great Britain, the fount of that civilization, as he saw it, fend off the Nazis. Niebuhr wrote about American survival more when trying to contend with the "strategists" — the United States needed to worry about Nazi aggression not so much because American society was precious and was to be defended at all costs but because American interests might be threatened by Nazi victories.

"It cannot be denied that a nation which is in ultimate, but not immediate, peril will not act as if the peril were immediate," Niebuhr wrote in September.[30] The unlikelihood of any imminent attack and conquest of the United States persuaded Niebuhr to contrive a "strategic" argument for intervention that strayed from the ethical lines of inquiry he knew best. What Niebuhr failed to perceive in 1941 was the possibility that an ostensibly "strategic" rationale for ensuring American survival in a manifestly dangerous world might itself have an ethical basis. Like some other liberal American internationalists, Niebuhr really believed that the nation that must be saved if civilization, the "open society," were to continue was not safe and philistine America, but Britain. Britain was the last world power on the European scene; Britain embodied an advanced culture and politics. "The British," as the lead editorial of the first issue insisted, "are fighting for the kind of civilization which has made Protestantism possible."[31] By clinging to a cosmopolitan notion of Realist interest, Niebuhr left himself vulnerable to the same paradox that he had introduced in *Moral Man and Immoral Society*: how can a Realist who emphasizes the clash of parochial, collective

---

29. "New Allies, Old Issues," p. 52; "Armistice Day 1941" lead editorial in ibid., 1 (November 17, 1941), p. 1.
30. "American Doldrums," lead editorial in *Christianity and Crisis*, September 22, 1941, p. 2.
31. Lead editorial, "The Crisis," *Christianity and Crisis* 1 (February 10, 1941), p. 1.

egotisms possibly regard something like "democratic civilization" as a factor in international politics?

The Japanese attack on the American naval base at Pearl Harbor provided Niebuhr with two means of escape from this quandary. The shocking destruction of American forces, in American waters, fused democratic civilization and American national interest in the dramatic fashion only a military attack can accomplish. The enemy of democratic civilization and the United States was now one and the same, even if Niebuhr had not concerned himself too much with the Japanese threat before December. Moreover, the attack itself destroyed American strategic isolationism, in the sense that the ability of Japan to strike Pearl Harbor demonstrated that the technology of war had overcome natural American defenses. The demise of free security, in other words, provided Niebuhr with the geopolitical logic his argument had previously lacked.

A Nascent Theory of American Realism

During the war Niebuhr refined his thinking about international politics. His most conspicuous wartime publication was the two-volume opus *The Nature and Destiny of Man*, published in 1941 and 1943, which derived from his 1939 Gifford lectures. This was the grand work Niebuhr had been working toward since graduate school, a study which explicitly aimed to fuse his pessimistic political philosophy with Protestant Christian theology. *The Nature and Destiny of Man* remained relatively unconcerned with contemporary politics and international relations, however; it was addressed much more toward the American and European theologians — above all, the Swiss Karl Barth, but also Niebuhr's brother, H. Richard, a Yale theologian — who had attacked Niebuhr's preoccupation with temporal matters and political ethics.[32] Niebuhr was torn throughout his early career between the demands of public political philosophy and those of academic theology. After 1943, Niebuhr wrote mainly about politics.

As the war began to turn against Nazi Germany in 1942, Niebuhr began to focus more upon the nature of the postwar international order, and this led him to think about international relations in a more theoretical fashion.

---

32. See Fox, *Reinhold Niebuhr*, p. 214.

As had been the case before the war, he tested his new ideas out on the pages of *Christianity and Crisis*. In March of 1942 Niebuhr argued that Americans faced "a crisis of unparalleled proportions in world history," justifying a total war against the Nazi regime. If "the opponent is resolute and will not yield without using every available resource to execute his will," he continued in August, "either we must yield or use all our resources."[33]

The idea of America contending with an unyielding opponent using every resource to "execute his will" raised questions about international politics after the war, and it was on this matter that Niebuhr really began to articulate a new way of thinking. The Russians, he insisted in June 1942, subscribed to "a kind of religion which has sought to achieve its ends in opposition to the western Christian culture and civilization." The tyrannical nature of the Soviet government meant that "we will have to learn that there is little possibility of building a world order upon an absolutely common culture."[34] However, he continued,

> Russia is not imperialistic by presupposition. She may be as imperialistic as the rest of us are, in the sense that she cannot view the international scene from an impartial perspective. But she has no creed which commits her to a predatory relationship with other nations.[35]

Relations between the United States and the Soviet Union, Niebuhr was concluding, would define the postwar international order. As serious as the resolution of the war against Nazi Germany was, he wrote in October of 1943, it "must be subordinated to the even graver fact that a conflict of policy which will prevent a basic accord between Russia and the West will be fatal to prospects of a lasting peace."[36]

Such pessimism belied the widespread belief throughout the United States that the defeat of the Axis powers would finally usher in a real international government that would have learned from the mistakes made by the founders of the League of Nations. Here again Niebuhr demurred. The

---

33. Lead editorials, *Christianity and Crisis* 2, March 9, 1942, p. 2; August 10, 1942, p. 1.
34. "The Anglo-Russian Pact," ibid., June 29, 1942, p. 3.
35. Ibid.
36. "We are in Peril," *Christianity and Crisis* 3, October 18, 1943, p. 3.

"problem of avoiding international anarchy," he argued in January 1943, "is actually more difficult than the democratic liberalism of the past decades has realized. A mere balance of power between the nations is potential anarchy. A mere federation," he continued, "may be almost as near to the abyss of a new anarchy. A world organization must be controlled by power." Sustained peace would not be attained by constructing a transnational government wielding only a legal power above the nations: such a government would be toothless, and hence incapable of preventing a return to pure international anarchy. "Where the disproportion of power is too great and where an equilibrium of social forces is lacking," he argued, "no mere rational or moral demands can achieve justice." Rather, international order, he insisted in November, "lies in a global alliance of victors holding together long enough to furnish the inner core of power and order for a world community. History moves like that."[37]

The great question was thus posed: could the West, led apparently by the United States, cooperate with a regime opposed to its civilization and culture, in order to establish an authentic international order that might end the miseries of international anarchy? Drawing freely on the thinking of Max Weber, and introducing his own conception of American national interest, Niebuhr addressed this question in his 1944 book *The Children of Light and the Children of Darkness*, which may be regarded as the first expression of modern American Cold War Realism.[38]

The most conspicuous theme in Niebuhr's new work was its pessimism in the glow of (probable) wartime success. Niebuhr knew that an Allied victory over Japan and Nazi Germany would encourage his old adversaries, idealistic American liberals, to seek a new world order after the war, a form of world government that could make the Second World War, after all, the "war to end all wars." American liberals keen to achieve a permanent peace

---

37. "Plans for World Reorganization," ibid., 2, October 19, 1942, p. 3; Lead editorial, ibid., October 4, 1943, p. 1; "Politics and the Children of Light," ibid., November 29, 1943, p. 2.

38. Though see Nicholsas J. Spykman, *America's Strategy in World Politics* (New York: Harcourt, Brace, and Co., 1942). I regard Niebuhr's emphasis upon political and moral philosophy to have been fundamentally more influential upon American Cold War Realism than was Spykman's much more geopolitical work. Nevertheless, Spykman's work was in many ways prescient and constitutes an early American expression of traditional *Realpolitik*.

would combine with leftists eager to cooperate with the Soviet Union to create a formidable political faction in 1944 American politics. In fashioning an argument to quash such idealism, Niebuhr combined his earlier philosophical views with a new understanding of international politics revealed to him by the Second World War. In so doing, he developed a kind of model of international relations, within which he made a case for a Realist American foreign policy for the postwar order.

World War Two, in Niebuhr's view, was not a battle between good and evil; it was a battle between evil and somewhat less evil. The Children of Light, by which Niebuhr meant political actors who sought normative ends, rather then cynically accepting conditions as they were, had invited Nazi success not simply by failing to confront Hitler early on but also by failing to see self-interest in their own imperial dreams. Their secular, "boundless social optimism" had blinded them to the eternal truth of original sin: that "there is no level of human moral or social achievement in which there is not some corruption of inordinate self-love."[39] The Children of Light believed that they were free of cynicism, something the whole world could easily see, when in fact they were only less cynical than the Children of Darkness, and more blinded by their own self-love.

Niebuhr was not saying that the war was then simply a struggle between morally equivalent empires, with one side deluding itself about its higher motivations and the other with a clearer view of cynical reality. As his 1941 crusade had stressed, the one great stake in the war was the preservation of democracy: not the bourgeois institution of western capitalism, but democracy in itself, which Niebuhr believed to be a "potentially permanently valid form of social and political organization," a social good that transcended particular economic systems. The greatest virtue of democracy lay in its arming the common individual with the power to resist tyranny, "the inordinate ambition of rulers," while at the same time checking "the tendency of the community to achieve order at the price of liberty." Democracy was a tool, in other words, to achieve a Madisonian balance of power: it stopped the accumulation of power by the tyrannical few, on one hand, while at the

---

39. *The Children of Light and the Children of Darkness* (New York: Scribners, 1944), pp. 16–17.

same time preventing the mob, or a leader claiming to represent the popular will, from crushing dissent and difference.[40]

Why, then, could not the United States and its allies use their postwar power and goodwill to establish democracy across the globe, securing a second international victory after its defeat of Germany and Japan? Niebuhr's book offered a Realist answer to this question.

In the opening chapter of *The Children of Light and the Children of Darkness* Niebuhr set forth the basic political philosophy he had introduced in *Moral Man and Immoral Society*.[41] The will-to-survive, he argues, is the origin of all politics, but as society develops this will transforms into the will to self-realization, and then to power and glory. "There is of course always a natural survival impulse at the core of all human ambition," he states, but human conflicts "are never simple conflicts between competing survival instincts." As states develop their own egoisms, they clash with one another over issues of prestige and power, which are expressed "even more cruelly in collective than in individual terms."[42] Wars are "conflicts of rival lusts and ambitions," in which both sides often believe themselves to be on the side of justice and virtue.[43] This explained the continuing existence of "international chaos," which was only "slightly qualified by minimal forms of international cooperation."[44]

Could international anarchy be overcome? This, Niebuhr acknowledged, "has become the most urgent of all the issues to face our epoch."[45] American idealists were confident that world government could be easily achieved. Summarizing their case, Niebuhr notes that conceptions of universal human interest had been frustrated, so far, by particularist loyalties and rivalries, but universalism now was buttressed by global technologies, which linked people beyond national borders and at the same time posed the threat of global military destruction. National particularity, the idealists now claimed, was under pressure from technology, emerging from below, along with universalism, from above. This convergence had persuaded the Children of Light,

---

40. Ibid., pp. 46–47.
41. Niebuhr develops this argument at much greater length in his major theological treatise, *The Nature and Destiny of Man* 2 vols. (New York: Scribner's, 1941, 1943).
42. *Children of Light*, pp. 19–20.
43. Ibid., pp. 27–28.
44. Ibid., p. 153.
45. Ibid.

Niebuhr argued, that the development of a world community following the war is "a practically inevitable achievement."[46]

Developing a view that would come to underlie American Realism, Niebuhr shows at length why such a community would be difficult, if not impossible, to achieve. Idealists who foresaw some kind of effortless transition from national to international loyalties were beneath Niebuhr's scope: but he also rejected, if more respectfully, constitutionalists who foresaw the deliberate construction of a serious world government. This would prove much harder to realize than the constitutionalists believed, because they had forgotten that communities do not emerge from the top down, formed simply by the intellectual construction of a political order: rather, communities come into existence as a consequence of their unifying resistance to a challenge, a common foe. This was why the transition from smaller to larger collectives was "different in kind" from the transition from nations to an international community. "It is in fact so completely different," Niebuhr contended, that we cannot be certain that it is a step within the possibilities of history. If it is within the possibilities, only desperate necessity makes it so."[47]

Furthermore, the pressure from "below" of technology was insufficient to achieve immediate universalism. Technology, as Pearl Harbor had brought home to Americans, provided as never before cynical nations with the means of disruption, destruction, and conquest. Niebuhr understood that the advancements of war's destructiveness made international anarchy in the end unacceptable; it was just that the world had not reached the end, yet:

> [The] same technical situation which makes a universal community ultimately imperative, also arms particular nations, empires and centers of power with the instruments which make the unification of the world through imperialistic domination seem plausible, if not actually possible. The Nazi effort to unify the world under the dominion of a master race came close enough to success to prove how easily universal forces in history may be appropriated and corrupted for egoistic ends.[48]

---

46. Ibid., pp. 154–59.
47. Ibid., p. 168.
48. Ibid., p. 160.

The difficulties in transferring human loyalties beyond the state, together with the destructive, but insufficiently global, potential of modern military technologies led Niebuhr to predict an anarchical postwar order. Transcending anarchy required a "coalescence of power and the development of a core of international community among the great powers," but that was unlikely to occur, "since the fear of anarchy is less potent than the fear of a concrete foe."[49] Anarchy could be moderated to an extent by the willingness of the great powers to allow self-determination and constitutional rights among smaller nations — this was a wise policy as an unjust order "invites resentment and rebellion which leads to its undoing."[50] Anarchy could be moderated, for the self-interested purposes of the great powers; it could not now be eliminated.

The oncoming anarchy of the postwar order made the primary objective of the democratic powers simply one of preserving democratic civilization. To attain such an objective, the democratic powers had to realize that democracy could not be sustained by international organizations or cosmopolitan interest groups. In the anarchical world Niebuhr foresees, such groups could wield no significant power: they would quickly be crushed by cynical nations on all sides. Rather, democracy could be maintained only by "the preponderant power of the great nations" exerting their will in the postwar realm.[51] The democratic postwar powers, particularly the United States, must project their national power in traditional ways in order to contend with anti-democratic states projecting their own power. The United States could no longer divorce itself from international politics if it wanted to win the peace of the Second World War and maintain its culture.

The anti-democratic state Niebuhr had in mind, of course, was the Soviet Union. He regarded the emerging conflict between these two nations as ironic, as both subscribed initially to idealistic, Children of Light ideologies. It was true that Americans had become corrupted by "bourgeois illusions" of the moral superiority of capitalism, and failed to recognize "the perennial and persistent human egotism" in their own society.[52] To regard the existing state of Western life as "the end of human existence" is only "a less vicious

---

49. Ibid., pp. 161, 171–72.
50. Ibid., p. 181.
51. Ibid., p. 177.
52. Ibid., pp. 105, 111.

version of the Nazi creed."[53] Yet the capitalist nations, or at least the United States and Great Britain, had preserved democratic government despite these bourgeois illusions and self-satisfactions; this was the victory to be celebrated after the defeat of Nazism.

The Soviet Union, on the other hand, had forsaken the idealism of its founders. Its creed, Niebuhr declared, had "become the vehicle and instrument of the children of darkness."[54] The liberal creed, by using democracy, had withstood the threats of plutocracy and tyranny; the Marxian creed, by abandoning democracy, had been co-opted by the purely cynical Stalinists. If the democratic nations were to preserve their creed, conflict between the democratic powers and the Soviet Union — between the Children of Light and the Children of Darkness — could not be avoided. Anarchy would always prevail until all of the great powers subscribed to the less cynical creed of democracy. "Mankind must go through a period," Niebuhr argued, "in which corrupt forms of universalism must be defeated."[55]

In *The Children of Light and the Children of Darkness*, Niebuhr had made his pessimistic understanding of international relations more concrete. Democratic civilization remained the normative end, but now it depended upon the willingness of the "great nations," rather than its advocates in a vague sense, to wield their preponderant power against the regime that threatened this civilization, the Soviet Union. The great nations that could wield such power after the war were two: Great Britain, and the United States. In 1944 one could not be sure that Britain would emerge from the war with its great-power position intact. That the United States would emerge as one of the world's "preponderant" powers, however, was a virtual certainty.

Weber proceeded from the presupposition that the German nation was a good in itself, one that had to prevail over competing nations. He did not deny that this presupposition in the end had to be based upon a kind of irrational faith. Niebuhr took a different route. For him, democratic civilization initially connoted an abstract, cosmopolitan political order, to be preserved as a tangible entity. This kind of thinking contradicted his political argument that international conflict stems from the egoistic survivalist de-

53. Ibid., p. 133.
54. Ibid., pp. 32–3.
55. Ibid., p. 160.

sires of nation-states. The experience of World War Two, however, led Niebuhr toward a Weberian conclusion. If the British were in decline, then American survival was a good in itself — if only to defend a democratic civilization that could not be maintained, he now perceived, by any other means.

As befitted his Christian theology of human tragedy and original sin, the Realist approach to international politics that Niebuhr developed from 1932 to 1944 was a distinctly defensive one. It derived from a view of human nature that made the basic will to survive the source of political existence — not the primal will-to-power, as Nietzsche had held. Aggression occurred because states had transformed this will-to-survive into national wills-to-power, as a consequence of the egotistical logic of collectives.

Niebuhr regarded his nation in a similar fashion. The ideal foreign policy, in his view, was defensive: he was uninterested in national aggrandizement, and regarded expansion at best as an inevitable cost of involvement in power politics. In clear contrast with Weber, his nationalism with respect to the United States was extremely reluctant, forced upon him by the logic of Realism and his desire to protect democratic civilization, and tempered heavily by his continuing suspicions of American capitalism and empire.

The defensive nature of his Realism led Niebuhr to adopt a thorough-going pessimism about the future of international relations. There would be no triumphant victory: rather, the unavoidable anarchy of the postwar world, together with the impure motivations of the Children of Light would almost certainly make the collision between democratic civilization and its enemies violent and tragic. "We may live," Niebuhr wrote,

> for quite a long time in a period of history in which a potential world community, failing to become actual, will give rise to global, rather than limited, conditions of international anarchy and in which the technics of civilization will be used to aggravate the fury of conflict.[56]

This was not a rosy view of the future, particularly as the "technics of civilization" were about to unleash a fury even Niebuhr could not have foreseen.

---

56. Ibid., p. 162.

3 Hans Morgenthau's Cold War

Hans Morgenthau arrived in the United States in 1937, one of the many Jewish émigrés from Hitler's Europe who together transformed American arts and sciences in the middle of the twentieth century. Trained in political philosophy and international law, Morgenthau searched during his first few years in America for a permanent academic position and a niche in the American study of politics. He succeeded, landing a job at the University of Chicago in 1943.[1] By the end of the 1940s, Morgenthau had made himself the country's leading scholar of international politics.

Morgenthau was irreligious, and so regarded politics and international relations in a more secular, less redemptive way than did Reinhold Niebuhr.[2] Initially, Morgenthau expressed an even more grim view of human nature as it applied to international relations than did Niebuhr. Gradually, however, he abandoned this view, choosing in his 1948 and 1951 writings to empha-

---

1. See Christoph Frei, *Hans J. Morgenthau: An Intellectual Biography* (Baton Rouge: Louisiana State University Press, 2001), for a gripping account of Morgenthau's personal and intellectual formation in Europe.
2. Michael Joseph Smith, *Realist Thought from Weber to Kissinger* (Baton Rouge: Louisiana State University Press, 1986), p. 134.

size the nature of contemporary international politics rather than its philosophical underpinnings.[3]

Rationalism vs. the Lust for Power

In 1946 Morgenthau published his first U.S. book, titled *Scientific Man vs. Power Politics*. As the title implied, his thesis departed from Niebuhr's 1932 work in its emphasis upon the distinction between individual ration-ality and collective irrationality, rather than upon individual morality and collective immorality. Nevertheless, their targets were similar. Morgenthau, like Niebuhr, wanted to attack liberal and Marxian optimism, and he wanted to show how such optimism failed at the level of intergroup relations. Morgenthau's account for this failure, however, was even darker than Niebuhr's.

One strain of Morgenthau's critique of the liberal and Marxian faith in an ideal political future is identical to Niebuhr's, and recalls Weber's rejec-tion of the "economic way of looking at things." Morgenthau noted that the liberal belief in political progress stems from the ascension of the bourgeoisie to political power. Having overcome the ancien régime and its overt reliance on suppression and war, the bourgeoisie failed to see that it pursued power just as aggressively. Using the "invisible chains of economic dependence," Morgenthau argued, the new middle class dominates its foes while at the same time claiming to reject power politics.[4]

Niebuhr believed that the modern faith in human nature misjudged the egotism inherent in collective interests and politics. For Niebuhr, liberals and Marxists — "Children of Light" — underestimate the role sin and selfish-

---

3. As Christoph Frei writes, "a highly sophisticated young German jurist had turned into a pragmatic fighter." *Morgenthau*, p. 201. For a different view of Nietzsche's role in Morgenthau's intellectual evolution, see Ulrik Enemark Petersen, "Breathing Nietzsche's Air: New Reflections on Morgenthau's Concepts of Power and Human Nature," *Alter-natives* 24 (1999), pp. 83–118. Petersen, oddly, directs most of his attention to Morgen-thau's 1962 *Commentary* essay, "Love and Power," which, as this chapter and chapter five show, must be regarded in a very different light than his 1946 writing.
4. *Scientific Man vs. Power Politics*, pp. 45, 49. Carr, in *Twenty Years' Crisis*, p. 79, suggests that "theories of international morality are . . . the product of dominant nations or groups of nations."

ness play in their own programs, a naive idealism that handicaps them in their struggle with more cynical forces. For Morgenthau, there are no Children of Light. Politics is a contest between indistinguishably cynical actors, all driven by one force: "the lust for power which is common to all men."[5] The desire to dominate others, the *animus dominandi*, is, Morgenthau contends, the "essence of politics":

> For while man's vital needs are capable of satisfaction, his lust for power would be satisfied only if the last man became an object of his domination, there being nobody above him or beside him, that is, if he became like God. . . . For here the *animus dominandi* is not merely blended with dominant aims of a different kind but is the very essence of the intention, the very life-blood of the action, the constitutive principle of politics as a distinct sphere of human activity.[6]

It is important to underline the distinction between this line of thinking, taken straight from Nietzsche, from the political philosophy Niebuhr was setting forth. For Niebuhr, human beings were intrinsically sinful, but some — the Children of Light — managed partially to overcome this sin, to advance political life beyond purely cynical self-interest. The key to maintaining this achievement, he believed, was for the Children of Light to shed illusions of perfectibility about themselves and about their relations with other collectives. For Morgenthau, there appears to be no such dualism: all men are equally lustful for power, and therefore all politics are equally dominated by irrational power drives. This unequivocal view of human nature disinclines Morgenthau to regard a particular form of politics as superior, as does Niebuhr regard "democratic civilization": little is said in *Scientific Man vs. Power Politics* about the merits of democracy, or indeed any particular political system.

Like Niebuhr, Morgenthau applied his view of human nature to the even more violent and evil realm of international relations. The "outstanding and most consequential manifestation of the lust for power" in international politics is, of course, war. With the rise of domestic state authority, the *animus dominandi* of the individual is limited, prompting him to look upon

---

5. Ibid., p. 16.
6. Ibid., pp. 165, 167.

the state as a vehicle for his power lust in the international arena. Unable to exert power satisfactorily in his stultified industrial existence, modern man glories in the exploits of his nation. Such vicarious desires are even more destructive than struggles for power among individuals, as the absence of centralized authority in the international realm places no natural limits to expansionistic state policies. Power politics embodies the competing lusts for power among such states, a process that culminates in modern war, memorably defined by Morgenthau as a "murderous conflagration of human collectivities through which the individual egotisms and aggressive instincts find vicarious and morally expedient satisfaction."[7]

Because the simple and universal lust for power, rather than economic inequality or the existence of undemocratic civilizations, drove international conflict, war would persist in the international realm indefinitely. Democratic regimes, Morgenthau contended, are just as warlike as autocracies; free trade no more peaceful than autarky. The undying lust for power makes any political solution to war impossible: even in a perfect Wilsonian world of liberal free trade and democracy, there "would still be nations that would covet the territory, the colonies, the markets, the economic resources of their neighbours."[8]

What is the duty of a state, then, in a world of such mayhem? It is to engage in political action. The liberal West had become enamored with scientific, rationalistic means of ameliorating power politics both at home and abroad. Such trusting in reason, Morgenthau wrote, "is to leave the field to the stronger irrational forces which reason will serve."[9] This "decadent liberalism" came within a hair's breadth of allowing those stronger irrational forces, by which Morgenthau meant Nazi Germany, to realize its power lusts on a global scale. The only way to contend with such forces is to act, to pursue power, knowing fully that such action will inevitably bring about injustice and conflict.[10] Morgenthau's assessment of international political action in *Scientific Man and Power Politics* is dichotomous. A modern nation can do two things: seize power, or eschew that power in favor of a rationalistic plan to change the world. Choosing the latter always

7. Ibid., pp. 171, 184.
8. Ibid., pp. 46, 82.
9. Ibid., p. 134.
10. Ibid., pp. 65, 159–62.

means defeat, no matter the intentions, political system, or moral stature of the nation in question.

In the final sections of *Scientific Man vs. Power Politics* Morgenthau further distinguishes his philosophy of international politics from Niebuhr's. Whereas Niebuhr struggled to find a moral cause in national war, finally justifying it in terms of the defense of democratic civilization, Morgenthau perceives a justification immediately. Moral behavior is to engage in power politics, of apparently any sort, because political action, in a world governed by national interests defined in terms of power, is the only means of survival. Where Niebuhr justified war strictly in defensive terms, as a tragic necessity to rescue civilization from the Children of Darkness, Morgenthau castigates defensiveness, seeing it as a manifestation of the decadent liberalism responsible for the tragedies of the late 1930s.[11] The "tragedy of scientific man," as Morgenthau argues in his emotional final chapter, is not only to embrace a rationalistic view towards politics that assures the triumph of irrationality; it is to regard such defeatism as "moral."[12]

Morgenthau's passionate philosophical argument in *Scientific Man vs. Power Politics* doubtless stemmed from the visceral attitude toward Nazi Germany that Morgenthau, as an escapee from Hitler's inferno, would always possess, and thus as well from his anger toward an Anglo-American world that had initially sought to deal with Hitler in a rationalistic fashion. As Joel Rosenthal has suggested, Morgenthau was seeking above all in his early writing to alert Americans to the stark nature of international politics, to shock them into recognizing that power politics at that level could not be smoothed over by political bargaining and deal-making.[13] Ironically, however, it also stemmed from the political ideas Morgenthau had embraced as a German scholar, and in particular Friedrich Nietzsche's idea that politics is animated only by the lust for power.[14] Soon after the book's publication, however, Morgenthau turned away from this ironic political philosophy.

11. Ibid., pp. 64–65.
12. See Smith, *Realist Thought from Weber to Kissinger*, p. 137.
13. Joel Rosenthal, *Righteous Realists: Political Realism, Responsible Power, and American Culture in the Nuclear Age* (Baton Rouge: Louisiana State University Press, 1991), pp. 2–3.
14. See Frei, *Morgenthau*, p. 189, and James P. Speer II, "Hans Morgenthau and the World State," *World Politics* 20 (June 1968), p. 218.

From Philosophy to Policy

Two years after writing *Scientific Man vs. Power Politics*, Morgenthau published *Politics Among Nations*. In this work, Morgenthau abandoned the angry manifesto of political philosophy and human nature he had put forth earlier, in favor of a comprehensive analysis of international relations in the postwar period and a series of recommendations aimed at guiding American foreign policy in the new international era.[15] Certainly, Morgenthau's objective in writing this different kind of book was to shape American Cold War policy, an objective that he realized like perhaps no other American intellectual of his day.[16] To accomplish that, he had to discuss the immediate problems facing U.S. foreign policy, a task which in itself did not necessarily compel a retreat from his philosophical views. Yet there was another reason for Morgenthau to move away from the stark philosophy of *Scientific Man vs. Power Politics*. The Nietzschean worldview which underlay that book collided head on with American political culture, not only because of its profoundly illiberal and even brutal portrayal of human nature, but also because of its refusal to distinguish between American policies and those of other nations. If all power politics derived from primal lusts for power, then the emerging struggle with the Soviet Union was simply an amoral contest for world domination — not an attempt by the United States to defend itself and western Europe from Soviet totalitarianism. As it turned out, Morgenthau was unwilling to sustain such a position.

Politics Among Nations is, in effect, two books intertwined in one volume. Sections of it deal with the art of diplomacy: drawing examples from European diplomatic history, Morgenthau offers a series of rules about diplomatic practice that are obviously designed to guide American policymakers. While these recommendations stem from his Realist understanding of international

---

15. Later editions of *Politics Among Nations* became more analytical; David Fromkin describes the first edition as "written as a polemic, without full regard to niceties." Fromkin, "Hans Morgenthau: A Memoir," unpublished paper presented to conference on American Realism, Bard College, February 1991, p. 7. *Politics Among Nations* remains in print, and is still widely assigned in international relations courses.
16. See Robert Jervis, "Hans Morgenthau, Realism, and the Scientific Study of International Relations," *Social Research* 61 (Winter, 1994), pp. 853–54.

relations, and indeed are meant to apply within such a framework, the more substantial parts of the book deal with the realities, as he sees them, of contemporary power politics.

In his forceful introduction, Morgenthau posited two such realities. The United States, he asserted, has become in the postwar period one of two superpowers, whose preponderance over previous great powers is so great as to have created a bipolar world. The locus of international power politics has shifted away from Europe. Nations that had survived the game of power politics during the previous centuries had been destroyed by the World Wars, physically demolished in the cases of Germany and Japan, economically and morally weakened, in the cases of Britain and France. As a result, the latent power possessed by the United States and the Soviet Union had become so great that no single other nation could shift the balance of power by allying itself with one or another side — even those nations which only a few years earlier had been among the world's mightiest powers. Furthermore, the dimensions of this bipolar rivalry are now, as a consequence of intercontinental military technology, global: whereas the European system, he argued, was centered within the continent, expanding gradually to East Asia and certain important colonies, the limits of military technology prevented the European great powers from regarding the entire planet as the arena for their conflict.[17] Now, the extra-European location of the two superpowers, together with their technological capability to attack any target on the planet, had brought the entire world within the scope of power politics.

The United States, therefore, was powerful, yet vulnerable. It possessed tremendous power capabilities and dominated huge swaths of the planet, but the power of its new rival and its vulnerability to intercontinental attack made it insecure. These two facts led Morgenthau to offer the main recommendation of the book. To survive in this new climate, and to avoid a third world war that portended global destruction, the United States had two choices. It could seek a "normative transformation" of international relations, by which Morgenthau meant a deliberate policy to move beyond traditional power politics and establish a new regime of global cooperation and government; or it could pursue a traditional balance of power between itself and the USSR. Morgenthau's overarching contention in *Politics Among*

---

17. *Politics Among Nations* first edition, (Chicago: University of Chicago Press, 1948) pp. 7–8.

Nations was to show that the first choice would lead to disaster, leaving the second as the only sane option.

In his first chapter Morgenthau reiterated the position taken in *Scientific Man vs. Power Politics*, but in a much briefer and less harsh form. The lust for power drives politics, though not as exclusively as he had previously argued. The "aspiration" for power is "the distinguishing element of international politics, as of all politics," he wrote, yet it is not the only force in human nature: "the drives to live, to propagate, and to dominate are common to all men." Furthermore, the lusts for power within societies are tempered. "Most societies condemn killing as a means of attaining power within the society," he pointed out, "but all societies encourage the killing of enemies in that struggle for power which is called war."[18] By acknowledging this distinction Morgenthau seems to be arguing that the lust for power no longer exists, at least in its pure form, within society; this signifies a retreat from his 1946 book.[19]

The drive for power manifests itself at the international level in three forms. Nations seek to maintain, increase, or demonstrate their power. The first course is taken by content, status-quo–oriented powers, such as Great Britain; the second is taken by dissatisfied or messianic powers, such as Napoleonic France, Imperial Japan, Hitler's Germany, and — Morgenthau suggested — contemporary Russia.[20] Retreating again from his 1946 writing, Morgenthau is stating here that the quest for power at the international level can again be distinguished; power politics is not the contest of undifferentiated insatiable hegemons, but rather of satisfied and less-satisfied powers. This raises the possibility of a world dominated by defensive, status-quo powers, which would presumably be less warlike than the world described by Morgenthau in his earlier writing.[21]

In his introductory section, then, Morgenthau establishes the elements of international politics. Human nature, now defined less categorically,

---

18. Ibid., p. 17.

19. See Petersen, "Breathing Nietzsche's Air."

20. The demonstration of power, "prestige," is a third goal, though Morgenthau claims that (p. 50) it is rarely "an end in itself." Consequently, he does not deal with this sort of power much in the book.

21. This possibility animates contemporary debate among Realists. See Stephen Van Evera, "Offense, Defense, and the Causes of War," in Michael E. Brown, et al, eds., *Theories of War and Peace* (Cambridge: MIT Press, 1998).

causes states to pursue power, though not always with equal aggressiveness. The states capable of pursuing such power are now two, the United States and the Soviet Union. How will this new conflict play out? How can the United States survive this conflict without unleashing total war?

A balance of power maintained the state system of Europe from its beginnings in the seventeenth century until the First World War. The great nations of Europe avoided total war among themselves by forming and re-forming alliances so as to prevent one side from attaining predominant power. They were able to do so by engaging in skillful diplomacy designed precisely to preserve the balance, and by keeping to a tacit agreement, an "international morality," as Morgenthau calls it, to refrain from campaigns of hegemonic conquest.[22] The rise of Napoleonic France was the exception that proved the rule: the French conqueror defied the system, forcing the other nations of Europe finally to wage a great war against him to restore the balance. At the center of this diplomatic system was Great Britain, a prosperous maritime power whose unvarying strategy was to preserve the balance on the continent, by allying against whatever power seemed to be on the ascent. By acting as Europe's "balancer," Britain was free to embark upon its global empire without having to worry about an invasion from a European superstate.

In Morgenthau's view, the postwar balance of power had become dangerously precarious. The "limitations upon the struggle for power on the international scene are weaker today," he argued, "than they have been at any time in the history of the modern state system."[23] This is so for two reasons. First, the "international morality" of previous centuries had disappeared, replaced in the twentieth century by a "nationalistic universalism," with which great powers seek, as did Napoleon, total victory over their adversaries and the triumph of a particular national ideology. Nations no longer felt bound to the notion of European, or Western civilization: the morality — something not mentioned by him in 1946 — that kept "the aspirations for power of the individual states within certain bounds," Morgenthau maintained, "has, except for certain fragmentary restraints, given way to the ethics of individual nations."[24] The survival of the system, in other words, had

---

22. *Politics Among Nations*, p. 267.
23. Ibid.
24. Ibid.

become less important to the great powers than their own nationalistic quests.

Second, the "absolute bipolarity" that characterized the Cold War discourages skillful diplomacy. In the days of several great powers, adept balancing and deal-making could shift a volatile situation back toward equilibrium. Now, Morgenthau wrote, all nations, including those with the most diplomatic experience, are in the "orbit of one or the other of the two giants whose political, military, and economic preponderance can hold them there even against their will." No longer could Great Britain, or any other nation, deftly balance one side against the other; diplomacy takes a back seat to straightforward military confrontation, since the overweening power of the two superpowers means that little can be gained by diplomatic maneuvering.[25]

Not only had the system become more precarious; the stakes of its collapse, i.e., great power war, had become far worse than in the multipolar era. Before the twentieth century, nations waged limited wars — again, excepting the Napoleonic anomaly — for limited objectives. European nations in the eighteenth and nineteenth centuries took to arms against one another regularly, and often, but apart from Napoleon their aims had been restrained. The advent of nationalistic universalism, combined with modern military technologies, had put an end to the tradition of limited, purposeful warfare. Great-power war was now total. It had become embraced by modern societies, eager for absolute, nationalistic victory, and willing to dedicate their massive industrial might to achieve this aim. Worse still, the absolute stakes of total war and the weaponry churned out by industrial nations prompted military leaders to wage war against their adversary's civilian populations. Where war once had been the province of small armies and decisive battles, it now manifested itself in the terror bombing of large industrial cities. What is more, technology not only allowed modern nations to kill vast numbers of their enemies; it also allowed them to parlay their military victories into the kind of permanent political domination Napoleon could never have achieved. By using advanced forms of social control, propaganda, and force, conquering nations could impose tyrannical rule over their new dominion that popular uprisings could not hope to overcome. The technics of civilization (as Niebuhr would have put it) "make the conquest of the world

---

25. Ibid., pp. 273–74.

technically possible, and they make it technically possible to keep the world in that conquered state."[26]

The stakes of international power politics, in other words, had become absolute. Conquest at the hands of another nation now meant permanent subjugation and national death, rather than the adjustment of boundaries and payment of tribute. Therefore, a nation had to devote everything it could to protecting its national security; it had to be prepared to wage major war.[27] The challenge facing the United States was to find a way to maintain its existence in such grave conditions without unleashing World War Three.

As Morgenthau stated in his introduction, there were two possible ways to meet this challenge. The United States could seek a normative transformation of international politics by attempting to establish some form of world government. If successful, such an entity could suppress international anarchy and thereby eliminate the causes of total war. Alternatively, the U.S. could accept the existing system, and seek to establish a balance of power against the Soviet Union. Niebuhr had argued in *The Children of Light and the Children of Darkness* that an attempt to perfect international relations would result in disaster, because egotism always prevails over ideals in an anarchical order. Yet he did not explain specifically why a serious international order could not be attained in the existing context of international politics; it was a general, philosophical claim. Morgenthau specified very clearly why a normative transformation of international relations is, for the moment, impossible, and in so doing he laid out ideas that become central to the modern Realist argument.

For a normative transformation of international relations to occur, Morgenthau explained, something must come into being that reliably prevents great-power nations from going to war. This new entity must have the real and permanent authority to impose its will on the world's most powerful nations; otherwise, its power will be fictitious, and thus can be used malevolently by powerful nations to lull others into letting down their defenses. In that sense, a weak global entity would be worse, much worse, than no entity at all. Serious advocates of world government, recognizing this danger,

---

26. Ibid., pp. 294, 296–97.

27. Writing in 1948, Morgenthau guesses that germ weaponry might in the end become more destructive than atomic bombs. Of course, he changed this view in later editions. See chapter five, below.

call for the establishment of a powerful international body, the United Nations. Others go further and demand the creation of an actual world state. Morgenthau shows why neither will succeed.

The United Nations Security Council was designed to prevent global conflict. By giving five powerful nations permanent membership within the council, its framers hoped to provide some "teeth" to a collective security body that had notably lacked them in its previous incarnation within the League of Nations. However, and for Morgenthau predictably, the five permanent nations each possessed a veto over all Security Council decisions. Each, moreover, retained autonomous control over its own military forces. These two facts turned the Security Council into a powerless entity, at least for the purpose of preventing great-power conflict. That conflict, as Morgenthau wearily pointed out, would be a war between the United States and the Soviet Union, the two most powerful members of the council. Should either of the two superpowers wish to initiate war, it could either ignore the Security Council completely, or try to amend the veto stipulation. In the former case, the ineffectiveness of the United Nations would be apparent. Were the latter to occur,[28] it hardly needs to be stated that the isolated nation would simply drop out of the council and prepare its defenses. The chances of one of the two superpowers passively allowing the United Nations to wage war against it in the name of collective security were zero. As long as that were so, the Security Council was powerless, "constitutionally unable," to prevent great-power war.[29] It could prevent other kinds of wars, if all members of the council supported such prevention; as the Cold War was becoming global, even this was unlikely.[30]

A collective security entity cannot prevent great power war if that entity relies upon the sovereign military capabilities of those great powers. Its power is therefore chimerical, and so, as Morgenthau implied, worse than nothing. A more radical, and conceptually more serious, alternative, then, would be an actual world state — i.e., a sovereign entity possessing the world's military power. Facing the specter of total war and global destruction, could nations come together and create such an entity?

---

28. As was attempted by the U.S. in its proposal to transfer atomic energy technology in 1946.

29. *Politics Among Nations*, p. 387.

30. This was also demonstrated by the Soviet Union's declining to rejoin the Security Council in order to protest against the decision to intervene in the Korean War.

In addressing this question, Morgenthau discussed what a state's possession of power actually means. Why do citizens within a state avoid using violence to get what they want, while states routinely do so? Drawing upon traditional political philosophy, Morgenthau presented three reasons. First, a genuine state normally possesses far more armed force than any group within it. Thus it is able to prevent social groups from using organized violence for their own domestic purposes, forcing them instead toward nonviolent forms of social competition. The state, Morgenthau declares (without citing Weber), possesses a "monopoly of organized violence."[31] Second, citizens accept this inequality of power because they feel a stronger loyalty to the state — "to society as a whole" — than to any section of it. Whatever sectional loyalties they may possess are less important to them than their "suprasectional" loyalty to the nation. Therefore few citizens would side with a group intending to wage war on the state. Third, and in exchange for this loyalty, the citizen expects a degree of justice from the state. A tyrannical state that denies its citizens justice will foster sectional loyalties, and foment rebellion.[32]

A key argument in *Politics Among Nations* is Morgenthau's demonstration of why these very features of modern citizenship and state power are absent at the international level, and hence why a world state was, at the time of his writing, impossible. States emerge, he argues, from the demands of a society. They cannot be imposed from above, as the failed examples of international government had proven. Therefore, for a world state to emerge, a world society would have to form, with enough power and influence to: a) persuade majorities of the world's national populations to transfer their loyalties from their own state to a world entity; b) ensure somehow that the citizens of this world state can expect justice from it; and c) then compel all of the world's states to turn over their arms to the new world entity. To have even a chance at achieving this, a large percentage of the world's population would have to work energetically to develop such a society. Yet, as Morgenthau wrote:

> Under the present moral conditions of mankind, few men would act
> on behalf of a world government if the interests of their nation would

---

31. Ibid., p. 395.
32. Ibid., pp. 392–400.

require a different course of action. On the contrary, the overwhelming majority would put the welfare of their own nation above everything else, the interests of a world state included. . . . The odds are to such an extent in favor of the nation that men who might be willing and able to sacrifice and die that the world state be kept standing do not even have the opportunity to do so in the world as it is constituted today.[33]

Morgenthau's point here is crucial. In the age of modern military technology, revolutionary activity *within* a modern nation is difficult enough. In the past, revolutionary and transnational political action had actually been easier, because radicals had faced less rigid forms of nationalism and less effective technologies of nation-state social control. To create a world state, under "present moral conditions," world-state revolutionaries would have to seize control of all of the great powers simultaneously, they would have to find a way to eliminate national loyalties among the new world citizenry without resorting to tyranny, and they would have to come into possession of and maintain most of the world's military force. Writing in 1948, Morgenthau reasonably stated that such an event is not even remotely possible.

A world state, Morgenthau concluded, can occur only following the development of a postnational, global community. It would have to develop gradually, from the community upwards. That is to be lamented, because, as he argued, there "is no shirking the conclusion that international peace cannot be permanent without a world state, and that a world state cannot be established under the present moral, social, and political conditions of the world." What is worse, he added, is the fact that "in no period of modern history was civilization in more need of permanent peace and, hence, of a world state, and that in no period of modern history were the moral, social, and political conditions of the world less favorable for the establishment of a world state."[34] Here is the tragic dimension of *Politics Among Nations*: the factors that make a world state impossible are the same factors that make it more necessary than ever.

The "preservation of peace," Morgenthau states at the outset of the book, "has become the prime concern of all nations. It yields in importance only

33. Ibid., pp. 400–401.
34. Ibid., p. 402.

to the most elemental considerations of national existence and security."[35] Because the elemental and institutionalized desires of the great powers to maintain their national security outweighed humanity's nascent and ill-formed interest in the creation of a world state, an authentic transformation of international relations would be impossible. As a result, the world would have to rely upon a traditional balance of power to keep the peace. This was a pessimistic conclusion indeed, particularly in light of Morgenthau's low regard for the quality of American diplomacy; but it was well removed from the bleak picture Morgenthau painted in 1946.

A Normative National Interest?

Morgenthau published his third major work in 1951, a shorter work titled *In Defense of the National Interest*. This book signified his continuing movement away from the aggressive political philosophy he articulated in *Scientific Man vs. Power Politics*, in which international relations comprises a struggle for maximum power among morally indistinguishable states, toward the Niebuhrian idea of defending an imperfect American civilization from the threat of an even worse Soviet one.

In Defense of the National Interest is in large part a summary of the main themes of *Politics Among Nations*. Morgenthau reiterated his attack on universalism — with an eye, certainly, on the increasingly Manichean tone of American Cold War anti-communism — and his defense of the traditional balance of power system. What distinguished his new book from his previous writings was his sustained treatment of Soviet aggressiveness. America's national interest is not, as he wrote earlier, to project its power as all great powers must, but rather to defend itself from the threat of the USSR.

What threatens American security? Allying himself with diplomat and author George Kennan, Morgenthau answers: not communism as such, but a Russian imperialism intensified by the imperative of Marxist revolution. Presaging his later criticisms of American involvement in Vietnam, Morgenthau distinguished between authentic communist, or anti-colonial, revolutions in Asia and the cynical Marxism-Leninism of the Soviet Union. Soviet attempts to spread communism throughout Europe was simple Rus-

---

35. Ibid., p. 8. Also see Speer, "Hans Morgenthau and the World State," p. 209.

sian imperialism — the desire of a nation to increase, rather than maintain, its power, as he defined it in 1948.[36] Just as Napoleon rationalized his conquest of Europe under the tricolors of Republican France, the Russians were cynically using the slogan of working-class revolution to seize control of the continent. This was the real threat to the United States — not grass-roots rebellion in China or Southeast Asia.

It was the purpose — "the sole purpose" — of the United States to respond to Soviet aggressiveness in the same manner as another status quo power, Great Britain, responded to Napoleon: by using massive military force to stop it in its tracks. Its interest in doing so was not to rid the world of communism, or prevail in some final contest between good and evil, but rather to preserve its security against — as Morgenthau quotes William Pitt on Napoleon — "the greatest danger that ever threatened the world."[37] By overreacting to the spread of communism in impoverished colonial lands, the United States was running the risk of becoming distracted from this primary purpose. The United States needed to defend itself from Russian imperialism, not communism; an American obsession with the latter would only strengthen the former.

Any questions about the seriousness of the Soviet threat had come to an end with the Soviet test of an atomic bomb in 1949. Morgenthau regarded this as a grave setback to American security. In fact, he wrote, "in comparison with it, all the great issues of the postwar period fade into insignificance."[38] The balance of power established in Europe after the war had been based upon a kind of military equilibrium, as the immense Soviet military presence in Eastern Europe had been offset by the American monopoly over the bomb. In the event of a war between the two superpowers over Europe, the United States would have been able to drop atomic bombs upon Russian industrial and military targets, giving America the time it needed to mobilize a serious expeditionary army that could defeat the Russians in Europe. This premise was now "shattered." Russian imperialism, which had been ignored by Morgenthau in 1946, and not stressed by him in 1948, now stood as an immediate and dire threat.[39]

36. *In Defense of the National Interest*, pp. 77–78.
37. Ibid., p. 88.
38. Ibid., p. 174.
39. See Smith, *Realist Thought from Weber to Kissinger*, p. 150.

In 1948, before the Soviet atomic test, Morgenthau regarded skillful diplomacy and cultivation of a balance of power as the key to peace in a world not ready for a transformation of international politics. Indeed, in *Politics Among Nations* he was highly critical of militaristic Cold War policies, seeing them as signs of excessive nationalism and highly dangerous in a world of total war. In *Defense of the National Interest*, he abandoned this critique. "Now," he declared, "we need a new foreign policy, based upon new assumptions to be formulated in the light of a new balance of power."[40] By this he meant simply massive American rearmament. France and Britain were too weak to provide large armies. The rearmament of Germany would alarm the French but enrage the Soviet Union, making a "Third World war almost inevitable."[41] The only nation politically able to defend Europe from a Soviet Union armed with atomic bombs is the United States. America must embark "with frantic speed" upon a large military buildup, to restore equilibrium in Europe and thus prevent Russia from seizing Europe.[42]

As Michael J. Smith has perceived, Morgenthau failed to see that the Soviet development of an atomic bomb might create a more, not less, stable equilibrium in Europe.[43] The possession of large arsenals of atomic bombs by both sides might deter either nation from launching a war in Europe, irrespective of an imbalance in conventional forces. However, this became a moot point soon enough. The U.S. government agreed wholeheartedly with Morgenthau's views on the Soviet bomb, but its preferred means to restore the military balance was to embark upon a rush program to build an arsenal of thermonuclear weapons.[44]

Two Discrepancies Emerge

In 1952 Morgenthau sought to assess the emerging field of postwar international relations, a field which he himself had largely created.[45] The

---

40. *In Defense of the National Interest*, p. 178.

41. Ibid., p. 188.

42. Ibid., p. 179.

43. Smith, *Realist Thought from Weber to Kissinger*, pp. 153, 159.

44. *In Defense of the National Interest*, p. 193.

45. See Richard Wolin, "Reasons of State, States of Reason," *New Republic* (June 4, 2001), pp. 51ff.

politics of international relations derived, he maintained, from human nature, a "universality, transcending any particular area and common to all," which manifested itself at the international level in the form of an anarchy states could not overcome. Yet the role of human nature in Morgenthau's philosophical conception of international politics was no longer evident. In 1946 he had put forward a bleak vision of power politics based upon an even bleaker view of human nature. The ubiquitous lust for power, "common to all men," forced states into a perennial struggle based not in the end on defensive survivalism but rather the desire to dominate all others. Americans could either accept this fact and play the game of power politics or seek a rationalist solution to international conflict that could only spell their doom.

Morgenthau altered his position fundamentally after 1946. His Nietzschean philosophy was too extreme for American sensibilities, not only because its extreme pessimism, bordering on nihilism, collided so directly with the traditions of American liberal optimism, but also because its moral relativism with respect to the United States and the Soviet Union was simply unacceptable to a nation — perhaps any nation — searching for meaning in its new and active role in foreign affairs. Keen to introduce his European writing on power politics to an American audience, Morgenthau toned down his grim philosophical understanding of that tradition, emphasizing instead how modern political and technological realities defined the emerging Cold War.

In adopting this new tack, however, he introduced a serious inconsistency into his conception of international politics, one that is revealed conclusively in his 1951 book. When he argues, in *Defense of the National Interest*, that the United States needed to defend itself from Russian imperialism by rearming in Europe — a step which Morgenthau clearly characterizes as *not* motivated by the lust for power — he implies inescapably that the Soviet Union and the United States were motivated by different political urges. In *Politics Among Nations* he had already acknowledged that domestic politics is governed by other forces than power lust; by 1951, he has extended this acknowledgement to the international arena. The American interest, as he was now defining it, is security from an aggressive Russian imperialism, not the attainment of more and more power.[46]

---

46. An excellent discussion of Morgenthau's inconsistency here can be found in Speer, "Hans Morgenthau and the World State," pp. 223–25.

This was a fundamental retreat, because it invalidated his claim that power politics originates from an essential quality of human nature — his claim that international politics can be explained by means of traditional political philosophy. He wrote in his 1952 article that a "universality" in human nature governed international politics, but he no longer — in contrast to his assuredness in 1946 — could assert clearly what that universality actually is. Was power lust the universal quality that defined power politics? If it was, then he would have to stick to the difficult premise that the motivations of the United States, the Soviet Union, and even Hitler's Germany were in the end the same. If he was no longer willing to go that far, then he would have to abandon universality, and find another means of justifying his pessimistic view of international politics.

A second inconsistency, deriving from the first, concerns the increasingly destructive prospect of great war, a prospect bad enough during the first few years of the Cold War but then suddenly magnified tremendously following the Soviet atomic test of 1949. In *Politics Among Nations* Morgenthau called upon Cold War statesmen to heed the lessons of traditional European power politics.[47] To avoid the holocaust of total war, leaders must, against increasing odds, try to restore the traditions of balancing diplomacy, limited objectives, and, above all, the use of compromise and political negotiation rather than the blunt object of military force in securing policy objectives.

Yet Morgenthau made the centerpiece of his 1951 book a demand for massive American rearmament. Why? Having characterized the American national interest as security in the face of aggressive Russian imperialism — having defined it as *defensive* — rearmament was his only answer to the devastating news of the Russian atomic bomb. To contain the Soviets — itself a highly un-Nietzschean objective — the United States would have to counter the Soviet technological breakthrough with its own military response. The nature of that response was obvious. In a 1950 article in the *Bulletin of the Atomic Scientists*, Morgenthau asserted that the "question of the moral justification" of the American program to build the H-Bomb "cannot fail to be answered in the affirmative." The "modern state," he wrote, "can no more afford to be without all the weapons which modern technology puts at its disposal than could the medieval knight afford to be without a sword since

---

47. See in particular Stefano Guzzini, *Realism in International Relations and International Political Economy* (London: Routledge, 1998), pp. 28–30,

his potential adversary was thus armed." Recalling the American decision to bombard cities during the Second World War, Morgenthau noted that nations will always use their most destructive technologies rather than risk defeat. The wreckage of Dresden and Hiroshima give "eloquent testimony to the impotence of moral scruples" in the face of modern military technologies.[48] Morgenthau concluded the article by explaining why the international political order will not permit disarmament; the "calamity of a war fought with H-bombs" can only be forestalled by the day-to-day war avoidance of the great powers.

In developing his formidable blueprint of international affairs at the outset of the Cold War, Morgenthau gained fame as a philosopher of international politics and an advocate of an anti-militaristic, balance-of-power diplomacy regulated by the threat of limited warfare. Yet in dealing with Cold War politics and the atomic bomb, he retreated decisively from these two positions. In justifying the American position in the Cold War Morgenthau abandoned his essential, human nature explanation of power politics, characterizing American and Russian motivations in qualitatively different terms. In calling for a successful campaign to stop Russian imperialism in Europe, he ended up supporting the development of a weapon that defied the very idea of cool-headed, limited war. These inconsistencies left his conception of international politics anomalous in two crucial respects. He would revisit each problem soon enough, as the specter of thermonuclear war caused him to rethink everything.

---

48. The H-Bomb and After," reprinted in *Politics in the 20th Century* vol. 3 (Chicago: University of Chicago Press, 1962), pp. 119–20.

4 Niebuhr and the Thermonuclear Dilemma

Niebuhr and Morgenthau were both Cold War Realists, determined to persuade their fellow Americans that power governed international politics, and that the USSR must be confronted with this maxim in mind, but their intellectual experiences during the early Cold War period were quite dissimilar. Aiming to apply ideas he had articulated in pre-war Europe more systematically to the postwar world, Morgenthau formulated his understanding of modern international politics *during* this period: he incorporated the specific features of the emerging Cold War — bipolarity, the end of the European system, the specter of total war — into his new framework of international relations. In other words, he was able to take the basic facts of the Cold War as given as he announced an American vision of modern power politics. Niebuhr, on the other hand, had developed the elements of his philosophical understanding of international politics gradually over the period 1932–44. For him, the Cold War *fit in* to a pre-existing view; it did not facilitate a new way of thinking.

Furthermore, Niebuhr occupied a very different intellectual position than did Morgenthau. While Morgenthau, at the outset of the Cold War, was an unknown émigré hoping to make a name for himself, ensconced in the hermetic world of Chicago's Hyde Park, Niebuhr was a national figure, perhaps the most influential public intellectual in New York and a leading personality in east coast liberal politics. His well-remembered campaign for American intervention had, with the successful resolution of the war, given him a prophetic reputation. He was a leader of New York's Liberal Party, a columnist for *The Nation*, the main force behind *Christianity and Crisis*, a founder of Americans for Democratic Action, and a member of countless editorial boards and political action groups. In 1948, he was widely touted as a possible candidate for the presidency.[1]

Niebuhr's embrace of the Cold War, therefore, was a political stance based upon a previously articulated concept of international politics. His intellectual mission was not to develop a new means of understanding that topic, but rather to attack American leftists, in the style of his 1940–41 campaign, who called for a more conciliatory policy toward the Soviet Union. In so doing, Niebuhr did nothing more than solidify the position he had expressed in *The Children of Light and the Children of Darkness*: a pessimistic view of power politics in which the defensive aims of democratic civilization have no defined limits.

Niebuhr's Cold War Realism

In *The Children of Light and the Children of Darkness* Niebuhr developed a coherent interpretation of international politics. International anarchy derives from sinful human nature, as the human desire to survive is transformed by the state into egotistical and aggressive foreign policies. Yet his interpretation never approached the positivism of Morgenthau's early writing. Niebuhr constantly seeks to justify American involvement in international politics by postulating a positive moral good: the preservation of democratic civilization. The American role in the world is to confront the Children of Darkness, which it cannot do effectively — and this is perhaps the point Niebuhr repeats most often — if it adopts an idealistic view of international relations. Niebuhr does come to recognize, following Weber, that the objective of defending civilization must be folded within a policy of national security — that a transnational political aim cannot exist independently in a world governed by nation states. But Niebuhr stops short of articulating a "national interest," as Morgenthau, and other Realists, had done.[2] Niebuhr's Christianity, together with his Augustinian bent, prevented him from making the American nation — or any nation — the final end of

---

1. Richard Wightman Fox, *Reinhold Niebuhr, A Biography* (New York: Pantheon, 1985), p. 233.
2. See Michael Joseph Smith, *Realist Thought from Weber to Kissinger* (Baton Rouge: LSU Press, 1986), pp. 120–21. Smith's chapter on Niebuhr in this book provides an excellent treatment of Niebuhr's Cold War policies.

politics. The preservation of "the whole civilization of which we are a part" is always preeminent.[3]

For these reasons, Niebuhr turned against the Soviet Union quickly following the end of the war. While it took Morgenthau until 1951 to identify, at least openly, Russian imperialism as the aggressive force in international politics, Niebuhr began attacking the Soviet Union almost immediately. In late 1945 he clung to the notion of Soviet defensiveness, arguing in October that "Russian mistrust and fear" is the cause of its "drive for unilateral security." In 1946, however, he shifted ground. That summer he visited Germany, where he discovered strong anti-Soviet sentiment among fellow liberal clergymen. Soon after Niebuhr returned to the United States, Secretary of Commerce Henry Wallace gave a celebrated speech at Madison Square Garden, where he denounced American militarism, the revival of British imperialism, and the emerging anti-Soviet mentality in the Democratic Party.[4] Here was a provocation reminiscent of the battles of 1940–41, and Niebuhr was not slow to react.

In the October 21, 1946, issue of *Life* magazine, Niebuhr presented a hard line on Soviet expansionism in Europe that well preceded mainstream opinion and, arguably, Truman administration policy. With the demise of the traditional European powers, he stated, the United States is the only nation able to provide a "real guarantee of security against Soviet expansion and the only final security against war." Soviet aims, to Niebuhr, were clear: to "conquer the whole of Europe strategically and ideologically." If American liberals — always Niebuhr's target audience — wished to avoid war, they would have to support American confrontation of the USSR. For once the Russians threatened true domination of Europe, "the instincts of survival in the West would prompt decisive action and a joining of the issue."[5]

Anticipating a likely liberal objection, Niebuhr added a decisive point, one which Morgenthau, two years later, would make a central theme. The anarchical nature of international relations still exists, even after the trauma of the Second World War. "Significant decisions of policy," he argued,

are obviously not being made through the United Nations. Nothing must be done, of course, to destroy this organ. It must continue to

---

3. Lead editorial, "The Crisis," *Christianity and Crisis* 1 (February 10, 1941), p. 1.
4. See Fox, *Reinhold Niebuhr*, pp. 228–34. On the "Wallace affair," see Alonzo Hamby, *Man of the People* (New York: Oxford, 1995), pp. 356–68.
5. "The Fight for Germany," *Life* (October 21, 1946), pp. 65, 67.

function, so far as it may, as a minimal bridge over a wide chasm. It will have its uses, but it obviously does not have the power to prevent war, since all of its functions presuppose a unanimity among the great powers, the lack of which is the very crux of the present situation.[6]

Two years later, with the United States waging Cold War in Europe along the lines he had proposed, Niebuhr went further. In a second *Life* article, published at the height of the Berlin blockade crisis, he reminded his liberal readers that political and economic containment was, in the end, insufficient. The United States must run the risk of war if it were to maintain its position in Europe. The Soviet Union was unlikely to push matters too far, because the United States held a "preponderance of power" (read: atomic monopoly) that was "preserving the peace." But that did not mean Americans could rest easy. "No nation," Niebuhr intoned, has ever played for bigger stakes than our powerful nation is playing now."[7]

Niebuhr's Cold War activism was, in terms of its political effects, of the highest historical importance.[8] His reputation as a clear-eyed and brilliant leader of the American left gave his anti-Sovietism a credibility that could not be easily dismissed. With these feature pieces in *Life*, together with hundreds of other articles and essays, Niebuhr used this reputation to rend the American left in the late 1940s into a small, and increasingly isolated camp of pacifists and hard leftists, and a large mainstream that supported the Cold War while maintaining liberal views on domestic issues.[9] Had intellectuals like Niebuhr, Walter Lippmann, Joseph Rauh, Arthur Schlesinger, Jr., and others on the anti-Soviet left not beaten the drums for Cold War during the immediate postwar period, the Democratic party rank and file would likely have remained, as it was during the war, vaguely pro-

---

6. Ibid., p. 70.

7. "For Peace, We Must Risk War," *Life* (September 20, 1948), pp. 38–39.

8. The relative influence of Morgenthau and Niebuhr upon public American attitudes toward international relations is still debated. As far as the Cold War is concerned, I think the distinction is clear: Niebuhr was far more important in rallying liberals to the anti-Soviet position during the early Cold War years — 1946 and 1947 — while Morgenthau played a much larger role in introducing a entire generation to the idea of Realist foreign policy in the late 1940s and 1950s. In this respect I would say that Niebuhr was more politically influential, in that if one removed him from the scene in the immediate postwar period, American foreign policy might have proceeded in a different manner. By the time Morgenthau attained national prominence, the Cold War was already on.

9. See Smith, *Realist Thought from Weber to Kissinger*, pp. 118–21.

Soviet, keen to return to a peacetime footing, and willing to turn international relations over to the United Nations. In that event, an American decision to wage the Cold War might well have led to a serious political crisis.[10]

As for his philosophical understanding of international politics, however, Niebuhr made no advancement during the late 1940s. His critique of the pro-Soviet line was based upon his growing conviction that the USSR was a simple tyranny, and a threat to democratic civilization, not upon any new insight into the working of international politics. His attacks upon pacifists and United Nations utopians reiterated the arguments he used before and during the war. While Morgenthau was developing a formal conception of international politics, culminating in the epic *Politics Among Nations*, Niebuhr was writing editorials, speaking at dinners, and doing organizational work for the Americans for Democratic Action.[11]

In fact, in his Cold War campaign of the late 1940s Niebuhr began to edge away from the political philosophy he had advanced in *The Children of Light and the Children of Darkness* in a manner similar to that of Morgenthau. His conception of human nature, as applied to international politics, became inconsistent, if not tautological. He had originally argued that the human quest for survival manifests itself on the international plane in conflict between egotistical states, a conflict in which cynical Children of Darkness possessed an inherent advantage over liberal Children of Light. Now, he was moving toward the view that the current state of power politics comprised simply a struggle between defensive liberals and aggressive cynics. Not only did this revision conflict with his earlier understanding of international history, and in particular his critique of liberal capitalist imperialism, it also raised the question of the universality of human nature, as it had with Morgenthau. Were the Children of Light inherently defensive, and Children of Darkness expansionistic? If so, then all were perhaps not born equally corrupted by sin. Take that presumption away, and Niebuhr's conception of international politics, like Morgenthau's, loses its philosophical basis in human nature.

Niebuhr's willingness to justify American actions also became stretched to the point of apologetics. If international politics had moved from a struggle

---

10. For a personal account, see Arthur Schlesinger, Jr., *A Life in the 20th Century: Innocent Beginnings, 1917–1950* (New York: Houghton Mifflin, 2000), chapter 20. Also see John Fousek, *To Lead the Free World: American Nationalism and the Cultural Roots of the Cold War* (Chapel Hill: University of North Carolina Press, 2000).
11. See Fox, *Reinhold Niebuhr*, pp. 228–37.

between evil and slightly less evil egotistical states to a battle between defensive democracy and aggressive totalitarianism, a battle in which the Children of Light would "have to play hardball" if they were to survive, then it becomes difficult to see how Niebuhr could plausibly oppose *anything* the United States might do to prevail over the Soviet Union. Evil action in the international realm invariably is for Niebuhr "tragic," something he must "reluctantly" accept at a time of maximum danger.

The politics of the early Cold War led Niebuhr and Morgenthau to dilute their political philosophies. Their respective conceptions of international politics as derived from universal human nature could not withstand the moral distinctions each of them felt compelled to draw between the United States and the Soviet Union; their portrayal of scientific man out of control, channeling the "technics of civilization" away from human betterment and toward humanity's destruction, could not withstand their conclusion that the United States was justified in building larger and more destructive forces to wield against its adversary. Like many prominent scholars, Niebuhr and Morgenthau faced a choice between ongoing policy relevance and scholarly consistency. That was an easy choice for them to make in the early Cold war years, but their inconsistencies would come to catch up with them.

Justifying Atomic War[12]

Niebuhr, as has been shown, reluctantly supported the American and British bombardment of German and Japanese cities in the latter years of the Second World War. The bombing of Hiroshima and Nagasaki did not appear to be a shock to him; he wrote in September 1945 that atomic warfare signaled a logical "climax" of saturation bombing, and in a letter to Harvard's James Conant in March 1946 he asserted that "no absolute distinction could be drawn from the new level of destructiveness and the levels which a technical civilization had previously reached."[13] Niebuhr did admit that the development of the bomb has confronted the world with "the threat of mutual

---

12. The following sections of this chapter are adapted from Campbell Craig, "The New Meaning of Modern War in the Thought of Reinhold Niebuhr" *Journal of the History of Ideas* 53 (October–December 1992), pp. 687–701.

13. Niebuhr, "Our Relations to Japan," *Christianity and Crisis* 5 (September 17, 1945), p. 5; Niebuhr to Conant, March 12, 1946, Reinhold Niebuhr Papers, Library of Congress (hereafter RNP).

annihilation," which "proves that the atomic bomb heralds the end of one age and the beginning of another in more than one sense."[14] But the atomic issue did not overwhelm him as it did many others. Indeed, in the first few years after World War Two Niebuhr seemed almost to welcome the existence of atomic weaponry, as it so vividly affirmed the tragic elements of the American role in international politics. "The fear of mutual annihilation," he declared two months after Nagasaki, "ought indeed to persuade us that a very radical step is necessary to secure the survival of civilization. But unfortunately ultimate perils, however great, have a less lively influence upon the human imagination than immediate resentments and friction, however small by comparison."[15]

If the Soviet atomic test "shattered" Morgenthau's vision of the Cold War, it only appeared to deepen Niebuhr's resolve. He supported, without much overt anguish, the decision taken by the Truman administration in early 1950 to react to the Soviet success by building a thermonuclear bomb. In a February 1950 editorial he acknowledged the new levels of "moral perplexity" facing those who struggled between pacifism and the sort of war that the new H-bomb portended. Without a fundamental change in international politics, however, Niebuhr saw the United States as having no choice but to go ahead.[16] What is more, he argued that America must be willing not simply to build, but actually to use, such a weapon if necessary. In his contribution to the Federal Council of Churches report of 1950, a document to which he was the most prominent signatory, Niebuhr accepted the possibility of a just nuclear war.[17] Not only should nations consider atomic war against a sufficiently evil aggressor, he wrote in the report's preface, but the conduct of such a war could be carried out justly as well. Niebuhr noted that the report rejected an "absolute line of distinction between [atomic] destruction" and other "modern weapons," and warned of the dangers in drawing such a distinction:

The heart of the moral perplexity, which is illumined in this discussion, is that all measures, designed to prevent the spread of Commu-

14. Niebuhr, "The Atomic Issue," *Christianity and Crisis* 5 (October 15, 1945), p. 6.
15. Ibid., p. 7.
16. Niebuhr to Bennett, no date (1950), RNP. "Editorial Notes," *Christianity and Crisis* 10 (February 6, 1950), p. 2.
17. This was an updated version of a similar report issued in 1946.

nism and the outbreak of war, contain an unavoidable risk of war, including the risk of atomic war. Christians burk [sic] at this risk, their cause is imperiled.[18]

Niebuhr tempered this hard-line exposition by condemning preventive atomic war; he had always rejected the latter as a violation of the Just War tradition of *Jus ad Bellum*. But he emphasized that timidity on atomic matters could lead to appeasement. "Our report will be a shock to the churches," Niebuhr wrote to his close friend Will Scarlett, "for it shows that no absolute line can be drawn on any weapon."[19]

Niebuhr believed in the early 1950s that to draw an "absolute line" between conventional and atomic war indicated weakness in the face of the Soviet threat. In his book *The Irony of American History* (1952) he launched his most angry polemic against those who would appease Stalin, or even question American intentions in the Korean War. Reconciliation, even in an atomic age, was impossible. International politics was no longer the contest between sinful collectives impelled to conflict by a common human nature. "We are dealing," he wrote, "with a conflict between contending forces which have no common presuppositions."[20] Niebuhr also rejected the fatalistic (and thus secular) view that the "almost unmanageable destructiveness" of atomic weapons meant an end to the possibility of redemption, the creation of the City of God. Such "a purely tragic view of life," he wrote, "is not finally viable. It is, at any rate, not the Christian view."[21] Nevertheless, he feared that a (perhaps necessary) policy of countering Soviet expansionism "everywhere in the world" would "make the final conflict inevitable."[22]

Niebuhr's argument here signifies the furthest departure from his pre-1945 understanding of international politics. His unwillingness to make unqualified moral distinctions between states, given the commonality of human nature and the impossibility of supranational objectivity, is abandoned

---

18. Niebuhr, "The Christian Conscience and Atomic War," *Christianity and Crisis* 10 (December 11, 1950), p. 161. This is his introduction to the reprinting of the Federal Council report; "burk" here probably means "balk."

19. Niebuhr to Scarlett, no date (1950), RNP.

20. Niebuhr, *The Irony of American History* (New York, 1952), pp. 66–7, 128, 173.

21. Ibid., p. 157.

22. Niebuhr, "The Two Dimensions of the Struggle," *Christianity and Crisis* 11 (May 28, 1951), p. 66.

in favor of a demonization of the USSR. His resistance to the ideology of total war, and his suspicion of the crusade, is abandoned in favor of the suggestion that an all-out atomic war against the Soviet Union could be a just war, and that such a war might be "inevitable." Combining these nationalistic conclusions with his continuing belief in international anarchy, Niebuhr foresees a justifiable, and perhaps unavoidable, total nuclear war.

In February of 1952 (after *Irony* had been sent to the publishers) Niebuhr suffered from a serious stroke that debilitated him for the remainder of that year and much of 1953 as well. By the time he returned to discussing atomic affairs at length, the intensity of the Cold War had abated: Stalin was dead, the Korean War was over, McCarthy was discredited. Also, the Soviets now had the "super" bomb, making a just war to defend democracy something even more apocalyptic.

President Eisenhower's declaratory policy of threatening massive atomic retaliation all levels of conflict provided Niebuhr with a made-to-order topic, to which he began to devote extensive attention. Coexistence for Niebuhr represented the proper application of Christian realism to the atomic dilemma: in a letter to Will Scarlett he declared simply "for it is either that or oblivion."[23] In a *New Leader* article he stressed that coexistence with the Soviets was not to be confused with "toleration of any of the evils of Communism." Rather, "it implies only one moral preference, and that is that survival is preferable to annihilation." But in the same paragraph Niebuhr added that we "must seek to repel Communist political and military expansion at every point." Coexistence, Niebuhr made clear, should by no means be confused with appeasement.[24]

Massive Retaliation, however, was a reckless strategy that not only entailed great danger, but also damaged the "moral and political prestige" that Americans needed if they were to lead the western alliance. Brinksmanship signaled to the world that "we are heedless in measuring, or in failing to measure, the risks of global war."[25] Here was a precise fit. Niebuhr could point to the universalist Left as carelessly trusting, and the crusading right as dangerously "hard-headed," even to the point of needlessly risking atomic war. The doctrine of coexistence could then be placed in the rational center.[26]

---

23. See Fox, *Reinhold Niebuhr*, pp. 248–50.
24. Niebuhr to Scarlett, July 14, 1954, RNP.
25. Niebuhr, "The Case for Coexistence," p. 6.
26. Michael J. Smith notes Niebuhr's formula of placing himself between utopian naivete and dangerous militarism in *Realist Thought from Weber to Kissinger*, p. 114.

Niebuhr's endorsement of coexistence revealed a certain unfamiliarity with the emerging field of nuclear strategy. Relatively few could disagree with coexistence were the alternatives either all-out nuclear war or rolling over for the Soviets. The harder question to answer was whether a just nuclear war was still possible. Coexistence was fine, but in an anarchic realm of international politics the United States and the Soviet Union could easily find themselves in a confrontation in which retreat or nuclear war seemed the only two choices. Niebuhr confronted this question. In 1955, he and the Episcopal Bishop Angus Dun responded to a pacifist statement issued by a Protestant committee, "Peace is the Will of God," with their own "God Wills Both Justice and Peace." Their rebuttal was a traditional Just War refutation of pacifism, which included an essay on "The New Dimension of War." Niebuhr and Dun wrote: "The notion that the excessive violence of atomic warfare has ended the possibility of a just war does not stand up." They went on to reject proposals for preventive atomic war, and warned that the "claims of justice" in an atomic age needed to be examined more closely than ever before. But a just war could exist, theoretically. "Because the ultimate consequences of atomic warfare cannot be measured," they concluded, "only the most imperative demands of justice have a clear sanction."[27] Niebuhr, along with Bishop Dun, still accepted the premise of a just atomic war.

The Unfolding Unambiguity of Thermonuclear War

In 1955 and 1956 Niebuhr continued to call for confrontation against the Soviets — he wrote Norman Thomas after the Hungarian and Suez crises that President Eisenhower "is becoming the Chamberlain of our day"[28] — while at the same time warning of the perils of modern warfare. Against these extremes he continued to set the amorphous idea of coexistence. In a July 1955 letter to John Bennett, Niebuhr was optimistic about Khrushchev and the international climate. "How interesting that the dread of atomic conflict which preoccupied us only five years ago should now have receded so far into the background," he added, "perhaps too far."[29] This last remark,

27. Niebuhr and Bishop Angus Dun, "God Wills Both Justice and Peace," *Christianity and Crisis* 15 (June 13, 1955), p. 78.
28. Quoted in Fox, *Reinhold Niebuhr*, p. 265.
29. Niebuhr to Bennett, July 15, 1955, RNP.

which pointed to the moral dilemma of deterrence *per se*, accurately characterizes Niebuhr's forthcoming approach to the bomb.

In September of 1957, Niebuhr despaired of the apparent Soviet acquisition of intercontinental missile capability. In a gloomy article entitled "The Dismal Prospects for Disarmament," Niebuhr predicted little success for the bilateral talks then being held, and wondered how this "stalemate" would remain peaceful in a time of political struggle for Europe.[30] The answer seemed to arrive suddenly in the form of Henry Kissinger's new work *Nuclear Weapons and Foreign Policy*. Niebuhr gave this book a glowing review in the November 11 *Christianity and Crisis*, because Kissinger's argument, that a reliance upon ultimate weapons was stagnant and dangerous foreign policy, appealed to Niebuhr's desire to overcome the dilemma that he had perceived in his difficult justification of nuclear war. Kissinger's strategy of limited nuclear options, Niebuhr reasoned, clearly outshone the current state of inertia, under which we were "incapable either of conceiving limited wars or of winning them." At the end of the review, Niebuhr concluded that "we must be ready to fight limited wars in terms of our objectives and to win them with the appropriate weapons." Such an approach, he added, "makes more sense" than the fatalism of ultimate deterrence, or the recklessness of massive retaliation[31]

Soon after this new revelation, Niebuhr recanted. To his apparent dismay, he discovered that the "tactical" (his quotes) weapons touted by Kissinger were of the same magnitude of those dropped on Japan.[32] And a "dozen Nagasaki bombs in Europe and Asia would mean the destruction of any moral claim for our civilization." Did Kissinger, or the Council on Foreign Relations (which sponsored his book) understand this? Niebuhr demanded to know: was it because George Kennan already "knew this truth" that he recommended that Europeans disdain nuclear weapons?[33] Retreating at full

---

30. Niebuhr, "The Dismal Prospects for Disarmament," *Christianity and Crisis* 17 (September 16, 1957), pp. 113–14.
31. Niebuhr, "Editorial Notes," *Christianity and Crisis* 17 (November 11, 1957), p. 147.
32. Niebuhr, "The Moral Insecurity of Our Security," *Christianity and Crisis* 17 (January 6, 1958), p. 177. He is somewhat disingenuous in this article, I think: it is doubtful that he was as unaware of the destructive potential of tactical weapons as he suggests. Moreover, Niebuhr slyly injected "we" (meaning the editorial board) rather than "I" when referring to the author of the earlier review. It seems that he was embarrassed by his previous position and was trying to cover it up.
33. Niebuhr is referring here to George Kennan's famous Reith Lectures, which he de-

speed, Niebuhr averred, "There is obviously no security in the armaments which our realists so insistently commend, nor in the disarmament proposals which intrigue our idealists."[34] Following his formula, Niebuhr placed himself in the center, this time between the ethically unacceptable doctrine of limited nuclear war, and the politically naive hopes of nuclear disarmament.

This hasty disavowal of Kissinger's thesis signified a crucial shift in Niebuhr's approach to nuclear war. The official estimates of Soviet nuclear parity, the emergence of limited war theory, and the revelation of the destructiveness of tactical weapons forced Niebuhr to rethink American interests. The above developments, he believed, made it imperative to avoid general war rather than try to restrain one.[35] Justifying tactical nuclear war as somehow less than catastrophic, Niebuhr wrote Bennett, was simply using sophistry to "quiet the conscience of the nations. . . . I think this is monstrous and I am saying so." International politics had changed. "The only issue is how the ultimate war can be avoided," Niebuhr declared, and ". . . if war breaks out at all it will be a suicidal one for both victors and vanquished."[36] This categorical rhetoric was a decisive break with what Niebuhr had argued only two years earlier, in the article co-written with Bishop Dun. The "excessive violence of atomic warfare" now meant mutual suicide; nuclear war was unwinnable. In this spirit of contrition Niebuhr also revised the 1950 Federal Council study, admitting that "the development of the hydrogen bomb, of guided missiles and of tactical atomic weapons has made many of our conclusions otiose."[37]

The implications of Niebuhr's emerging view of thermonuclear war were fundamental. Departing from his early political philosophy, Niebuhr had come to advocate during the first decade of the Cold War a hard line toward

---

livered in Great Britain and to a worldwide radio audience in the autumn of 1957. Kennan was widely attacked in the U.S. for suggesting that the Europeans refuse to accept nuclear weapons. See Kennan, *Russia, the Atom and the West* (New York: Harper, 1957). For a recent treatment of Kissinger and nuclear weapons, see Campbell Craig, "The (Il)logic of Henry Kissinger's Nuclear Strategy," *Armed Forces and Society* 30 (2003), forthcoming.

34. Niebuhr, "The Moral Insecurity of Our Security," pp. 177–178.

35. Niebuhr, unpublished essay, "The Problem of Nuclear Warfare" (1957), RNP.

36. Niebuhr to Bennett, December 16, 1957, RNP. "The Problem of Nuclear Warfare," pp. 5, 9.

37. Niebuhr, "The Problem of Nuclear Warfare," p. 1. See also Bennett, "Niebuhr's Ethic: The Later Years," *Christianity and Crisis* 42 (April 12, 1982), pp. 93–94.

the Soviet Union, justified by a clear moral distinction he was now drawing between the two superpowers and backed up by his willingness to accept any means the United States might use to prevent a Soviet victory. In an anarchical international order major war is the final means to prevent the other side's victory, which was precisely why Niebuhr went to such lengths to defend the idea of just nuclear war and lament that such a war might be inevitable.

The premise that great-power war is unwinnable and suicidal brings down the entire edifice. Not only did it invalidate Niebuhr's Cold War realism: it also undermined the philosophical basis of Realism as he had originally conceived it. Even in a world of similarly immoral, defensive-minded states, the anarchy of international politics made war likely, and the core national instinct of self-preservation ensured that states would, and indeed must, wage war rather than surrender.

Few thinkers of any stripe or of any time are able to recognize the invalidation of their core ideas, accept it as their due, and recommence their intellectual career afresh. It may be easy to see the logic from the future; Niebuhr, however, was wrestling with emerging technologies, unfamiliar new strategies, and the ceaseless pressure of Cold War crises during the period 1957–62. To give up immediately on Realism, moreover, was to abandon a worldview that had brought him fame and political influence, in favor of a vague notion of nuclear pacifism that was unlikely to cap off a spectacular intellectual career. Here was the crisis facing American Realism, of which Reinhold Niebuhr was the first, and most intellectually honest, casualty.

Philosophically Afloat

In the late 1950s Niebuhr moved to distinguish his new thinking about nuclear war from the views he had put forth earlier in the decade. Whereas previous articles had not pointed out the inconsistencies between coexistence and *Jus ad Bellum*, in 1958 Niebuhr simply decided that "nuclear war is impossible." He repeated this point in his vast book *The Structure of Nations and Empires*: the advent of nuclear weapons and advanced delivery systems made "large-scale war as calculated policy for either side impossible." Nuclear war would not be the potentially just conflict envisioned earlier, but instead an "ultimate and suicidal holocaust." Moreover, the "line" between tactical and general nuclear war was so "symbolic and psychological" in the light of modern armaments that "there is no chance of avoiding the ultimate conflict if this line is obscured."[38] Here was a truculent rejection of even the most careful of limited-nuclear-war strategies.

Niebuhr was at his most vehement in a September 1959 *Christianity and Crisis* article "Coexistence under a Nuclear Stalemate." The piece began not with his usual equanimity, with reference to recent events or discussion of Christian affairs, but rather:

> The most obvious condition of our existence is the nuclear balance of terror. Each side has enough of the dreaded weapons to make the difference between victory and defeat irrelevant and to make it imperative for the whole world that a nuclear war be prevented. There is little prospect of reducing any general war to non-nuclear proportions.[39]

What did this dramatic rhetoric entail? Niebuhr was unsure. While he now rejected the idea of just nuclear war, doing so even in desperate terms, he continued to dismiss universalist solutions as utopian and careless. Nuclear war was to be avoided, and this was now the global "imperative." But the eternal lawlessness of international relations, a verity even more lamentable in a nuclear age, could not be wished away. If "the most obvious condition" of contemporary history was the balance of terror, the "second condition," Niebuhr was sure to add, was that "the inevitable rivalries that have existed since the beginning of time continue." The job was to "cool off the animosities of the cold war" rather than yearn for "nuclear disarmament or the total abolition of nuclear weapons."[40]

Niebuhr was at a loss to find a solution. He followed his "Nuclear Stalemate" piece with a somewhat less strident essay in which he described a "cloud of uncertainty" that the balance of terror cast over the world. For this moral perplexity — and here Niebuhr plainly repudiated his earlier argument in *The Irony of American History* — "there are no Christian solutions if we mean by that purely moral ones." The familiar dilemma of nuclear deterrence — neither disarmament nor the status quo ethically suffice — merely

---

38. Niebuhr, "Editorial Notes," *Christianity and Crisis* 18 (April 28, 1958), p. 55; *The Structures of Nations and Empires* (New York, 1959), pp. 11, 280.

39. Niebuhr, "Coexistence Under a Nuclear Stalemate," *Christianity and Crisis* 19 (September 21, 1959), p. 121.

40. Ibid.

"raised the moral ambiguity of the political order to the nth degree."[41] There were no means of solving the nuclear dilemma by moral action — by even the most heroic action undertaken by the Children of Light. Yet somehow, even the specter of thermonuclear war could not be regarded in absolute terms — it merely raised the moral ambiguity of international politics to a new level. Approaching a complete break with Realism, Niebuhr pulls back.

In late 1960 and 1961 Niebuhr returned to a more dramatic interpretation. In an interview in *Harper's*, he wondered whether we could find "some residual imagination" to bridge the common fate of the nuclear dilemma. "Our ability to do this is, I think, the price of our survival." He reiterated this idea in *Christianity and Crisis*, pointing to the "terrible chasm of mutual fear" that confronted both Cold War powers.[42] The confrontation in Berlin in the summer of 1961 predictably led Niebuhr to an even more dramatic position. The showdown in the old German capital meant that "we are wrestling with a resolute and resourceful foe on the very rim of the abyss of disaster." And then: "Thus modern history has moved into the eschatological dimension in which all our judgments are made under the shadow of the final judgment. May the Lord have mercy on our souls."[43]

A few weeks later, Niebuhr wrote to June Bingham about his fear that we could have "start[ed] the nuclear catastrophe for the sake of Berlin, even before we have seriously negotiated. There must be some limits to moral ambiguity. I dont [sic] know where they are but this may be the limit." At the same time, he blasted those fence-sitters who were unwilling to recognize the gravity of the nuclear dilemma, "a problem greater than mankind has ever faced before."[44]

Faced with an unsolvable problem, Niebuhr questioned whether the moral ambiguity that underlay his pessimistic political philosophy could be maintained. Niebuhr's comment about the limits of moral ambiguity are

---

41. Niebuhr, "The Long Haul of Coexistence," *Christianity and Crisis* 19 (November 30, 1959), pp. 172–73.

42. "A Christian View of the Future: A Conversation with Reinhold Niebuhr," *Harper's* 221 (December, 1960), p. 77; "Rising Hopes for Arms Control," *Christianity and Crisis* 21 (March 6, 1961), p. 22.

43. Niebuhr, "The Resumption of Nuclear Testing," *Christianity and Crisis* 21 (October 2, 1961), p. 162.

44. Niebuhr to Bingham, October 29, 1961, RNP; "Nuclear Dilemma," *Union Seminary Quarterly Review* 17 (March, 1962), p. 242.

revealing, because in his postwar writing he had clearly suggested that the preservation of democratic civilization was not morally ambiguous, even though the idea of moral ambiguity was central to the political philosophy he had developed earlier. This was not quite consistent, as he had seemed to define the destruction of democratic civilization as an unambiguous evil. The problem for Niebuhr, as it would be for Morgenthau, was that his philosophical inconsistency did not require fixing before the onset of the thermonuclear dilemma. Niebuhr had regarded the Cold War as, effectively, a morally unambiguous struggle, worthy of winning at any cost. And why not: the preservation of democratic civilization in the face of totalitarianism justified it, as it had the war against Nazi Germany. The forces of technology, forces that Niebuhr had urged on in the name of preserving democracy, now made him confront this inconsistency. Was the destruction of democratic civilization an unambiguous evil? Or, had the specter of thermonuclear war transcended his original political understanding, moving the question of ultimate political justice back into the "ambiguous" category? Philosophically speaking, Niebuhr could no longer have it both ways.

The Cuban Missile Crisis of 1962, during which the world was forced to confront the dilemma Niebuhr had been considering for five years, forced him to make up his mind. Immediately after the crisis he celebrated "our escape" from a war that would "make irrelevant the difference between victors and vanquished." Perhaps the crisis would provide the superpowers with the "common sense" they needed to "avoid a nuclear holocaust"; both sides would have to understand that "even a very unpeaceful coexistence is preferable to mutual annihilation."[45]

These sentiments were uncontroversial. Many now understood that a nuclear war would have no victor; few would argue with the proposition that even an "unpeaceful" coexistence was better than total nuclear war. Waiting to be answered was the question of what, in the Realist scheme of international politics, would allow the superpowers to avoid such a war with certainty. Niebuhr understood that this had become an unavoidable question, and in 1963 he addressed it.[46] In an unpublished article, "International Poli-

---

45. Editorial Notes, *Christianity and Crisis* 22 (November 26, 1962), p. 205; "The Cuban Crisis in Retrospect," *New Leader* 45 (December 10, 1962), p. 9.

46. The three pieces in which he deals with this question are "History's Limitations in the Nuclear Age, *New Leader* 46 (February 4, 1963), p. 19; "Preventive War," and "International Politics Under the Sword of Damocles," both unpublished papers found in

tics Under the Sword of Damocles," he described the thermonuclear dilemma as a "common peril" that had befallen mankind, like a disease. The
key, Niebuhr argued, was to endure the peril, to outlast it, rather than act
against it futilely by trying to eliminate the "survival impulse" of sovereign
states.[47] But Niebuhr was no longer content to let the dilemma go unanswered. Yes, the future of democracy required resistance to the "the evils of
communist tyranny." But as awful as the communist system was, "the evils
of a general war with modern means of mass destruction are so terrible and
so incalculable that it is *immoral* to prefer them to the present evils."[48] In
this article, which remained unpublished for obvious reasons, Niebuhr was
choosing between the two absolutes.

To avoid that momentous choice, the United States had to abandon any
plans to take the offensive in the Cold War with the aim of defeating the
Soviet Union. Coexistence, even for an indefinite future, would be preferable to the post-nuclear end of civilization. There could be no City of God,
at least not for now, and those who sought one were now enemies of peace.
"A world which had escaped a nuclear catastrophe would not be the ideal
world of messianic and utopian dreams," Niebuhr argued. "But it is certainly
not too speculative to assert that it would be superior to a world which had
survived a nuclear catastrophe."[49]

Niebuhr was aware that a war could occur without anyone seeking to
fulfill a messianic dream, and he thought therefore as well about how nuclear war could be avoided in the secular realm of international politics.
Morgenthau had suggested that a world state could only come about as a
consequence of global community, an argument with which Niebuhr concurred in *The Children of Light and the Children of Darkness*. Anarchy could
not be overcome by government imposed from the top down. Yet if thermonuclear war were to be prevented over the long term, a global state was
necessary. Thus Niebuhr cautiously advanced a notion "of mankind's real-
izing for the first time a sense of the unity of the human race in a nuclear
age." This utopian vision would not be based on a grand political scheme
but upon a "stoic universalism" and the Pauline doctrine of human solidar-

---

the RNP, written probably in 1963 or shortly thereafter. In this discussion, they will be
taken together as a single argument.

47. Niebuhr, "Sword of Damocles," pp. 8, 27.
48. Ibid., pp. 1–2, "Preventive War," p. 4. Emphasis added.
49. Niebuhr, "Sword of Damocles," p. 31.

ity. Perhaps the fear of nuclear war would engender a "common responsibility for avoiding disaster," leading to the kind of mass society necessary to achieve a genuine world state.

Always the critic more than the visionary, Niebuhr defended this idea as a way to rebuff those who predicted the inevitability of a great-power (i.e., nuclear) war. For to accept an eternity of international anarchy in an age of thermonuclear weapons was, apparently, to accept the inevitability of nuclear holocaust, and this was an outcome no philosophy could condone. In the face of such an absurdity, the true philosopher must recognize that he has a greater duty to humanity than to the preservation of his erstwhile worldview. To accept an indefinite future of thermonuclear anarchy simply because it is, rather than ought to be, is an abnegation of responsibility, an ideological clinging to a pessimism that can lead only to disaster. "Such defeatism," Niebuhr wrote, "is morally wrong because it obscures our paramount moral duties."[50]

A Dissolving Realism

Niebuhr recognized that the advent of thermonuclear weaponry had invalidated the main aspects of his philosophical understanding of international politics. His pessimistic belief in the continuing anarchy of the international realm could no longer be morally justified, as it seemed to portend an inevitable nuclear holocaust in a world in which technology cannot be uninvented. His view that the preservation of democratic civilization justified the American policy of waging major war rather than putting that civilization at risk collapsed as well. Most salient of all, perhaps, was his conclusion that the "paramount moral duties" of individual people were to find a way to prevent a thermonuclear war. This was precisely the line of thinking that Niebuhr pilloried mercilessly in his attacks upon antiwar liberals before World War Two and during the early years of the Cold War. It was why he went to such lengths to distinguish between the idealistic desires of moral man and the realities of collective conflict. Yet now he seemed to believe that the fate of mankind depended upon world citizens recognizing their

---

50. Niebuhr, "Sword of Damocles," pp. 15, 31–32, "Preventive War," p. 4, "History's Limitations," p. 19.

duty and putting an end to international politics. All of the certainties had crumbled.

It was one thing to recognize this new condition; another to act upon it. Niebuhr did nothing to transform his insight into a political manifesto, much less a new scholarly argument, and it is easy to understand why. By the early 1960s Niebuhr was an aging scholar, a veteran of too many ideological struggles, and in ill health. His reputation as a hard-nosed Realist had been carved in stone during the visceral battles of the 1940s; to come out suddenly in favor of a moral crusade to rid the world of international politics would have made him appear ridiculous, an elderly crank. Indeed, Niebuhr's awareness of this likely outcome can explain why he never published the more radical of his 1963 writings.

As it happened, furthermore, Cuba was the last of the shattering Cold War crises. As the possibility of thermonuclear war receded during the 1960s, Niebuhr, like other Americans, naturally turned his attention away from the nuclear threat and toward the new foreign policy problem of that decade: Vietnam. Along with Morgenthau, Niebuhr publicly criticized the American war, denouncing it, in classical Realist terms, as a disaster for U.S. Cold War interests.[51]

Even had Niebuhr managed to maintain his interest in avoiding nuclear war, however, it is unlikely that he would have found much of an audience. A generation of new students of international politics was appearing on the scene, and they were not going to be interested in the ill-formed nuclear fears of the aging theologian Niebuhr, however basic the intellectual debt they owed to him.

---

51. Further discussion on Niebuhr's and Morgenthau's opposition to the Vietnam War can be found in chapter 5.

5 Morgenthau and the Thermonuclear Dilemma

In attempting to provide a realist framework for the American Cold War project, Morgenthau had altered his philosophical understanding of international politics, as it was expressed in his 1946 book *Scientific Man vs. Power Politics* and the first edition of *Politics Among Nations*, published in 1948. In his first book Morgenthau had explicitly argued that all political action, especially including action in the international arena, derives from the lust for power, the insatiable desire of man to dominate all around him. Yet in his 1951 book *In Defense of the National Interest*, and in future writings, as will be seen, Morgenthau dropped this argument, in favor of the more acceptable one that the American actions in the international arena were motivated by different urges than those found in the Soviet Union. In *Politics Among Nations* Morgenthau attacked twentieth-century foreign policies of nationalistic universalism, the trend among modern nations to replace the skillful diplomatic pursuit of limited objectives, backed up the threat of limited war, with highly militaristic policies of confrontation, backed up by the threat of total war. Yet in 1950 and 1951 Morgenthau supported the U.S. government's decision to build the hydrogen bomb, for the purposes of confronting Russian aggression in Europe by threatening total nuclear war.

Like Niebuhr, Morgenthau perceived the problems inherent in his Cold War position. But Morgenthau, more than Niebuhr, tried to get around the nuclear dilemma by clinging to the idea of limited nuclear war. In so doing, Morgenthau betrayed another of his earlier-expressed principles, his insistence that rational and scientific planning cannot ameliorate the anarchy and totality of international politics — that Scientific Man can never overcome Power Politics. This betrayal did not last long, however: after skirting the dilemma in his writings during the late 1950s, Morgenthau adopted a radical interpretation of the thermonuclear dilemma that resembled Niebuhr's in every important respect.

Morgenthau's Strategic Interlude

In 1953 and 1954 Morgenthau perceived the dilemma created by the American Cold War policies he had supported. In developing a thermonuclear arsenal to defend itself from Soviet imperialism, the United States had put itself in a situation where major war had become self-defeating. In a 1953 essay, he recognized that a war to defend Europe from the Russians would, if fought with the only arsenal the United States possessed that could stop the USSR, destroy the continent utterly. Such an outcome would demoralize the Europeans, making the whole notion of European containment questionable. "Why," he asked, "should men fight?"[1]

As the Soviet Union developed intercontinental bombers, the absurdity of a major nuclear war to defend Europe would extend to a war fought to protect the United States. Atomic war, he wrote in 1954, "is no longer, as was traditional war, an instrument of rational policy; rather, it is a means of universal destruction and, as such, a last resort of desperation." A nuclear war between the superpowers waged in the manner of World War Two would destroy the combatants beyond repair. Thus the "overwhelming military concern of the United States must be the prevention of an atomic war."[2]

Morgenthau recognized that the possession of atomic arsenals by both superpowers would deter either side from aggression, but he also knew that the anarchy and misunderstanding that characterized international politics made deterrence an imperfect business. The two nations might easily find themselves unwilling to back down from a confrontation sparked by some-

---

1. "The Unfinished Business of United States Foreign Policy," essay originally published in the *Wisconsin Idea* (Fall, 1953), reprinted in *Politics in the 20th Century* vol. 2 (Chicago: University of Chicago Press, 1962), p. 11.
2. "The Political and Military Strategy of the United States," originally published in the *Bulletin of Atomic Scientists* (October, 1954), reprinted in ibid., p. 18.

thing less than outright aggression undertaken directly by one of the two sides. "It is easy," he presciently wrote, earlier that year,

> to imagine situations where local aggression will not be deterred by
> the threat of atomic retaliation but will be regarded by the aggressor
> nation of such vital importance to itself that it must be undertaken in
> spite of the risk of an atomic war. One can well imagine a situation
> arising in Central Europe which will induce the Soviet Union to take
> military measures which come under the heading of local aggression.[3]

Moreover, a daring aggressor, such as the Soviet Union, might guess that the United States would not be certain to respond to aggression with atomic war, for fear of the devastating consequences of a total war. This will "invite that kind of miscalculation that has so often in the past led to the outbreak of a general war which nobody wanted"; rather than deterring general war, an atomic stalemate might actually make one more likely.[4]

Within the space of about a year, then, Morgenthau managed to identify the central features of the thermonuclear dilemma. Well before Niebuhr had given serious consideration to the novelties of nuclear war, Morgenthau had perceived the revolutionary aspects of the new technology and the major problems that would beset nuclear strategists later in the decade. But as Morgenthau understood, it was one thing to identify the problem of total nuclear war, and quite another — the "overwhelming concern" — to see how one could be averted. As an analyst of international politics, Morgenthau might have been content simply to identify the problem, to warn of its dangers. After all, the total threat of Russian imperialism and the dimensions and stakes of total war — the very aspects of the Cold War he had spent his American career highlighting — might well have persuaded him that the nuclear dilemma was a tragic inevitability, about which nothing, short of indefinite coexistence, could be done.

To take such a sanguine position, however, would be to eschew the power and prestige that would come to the scholar who found an escape from the dilemma. In the past, Morgenthau had preferred to modify his political philosophy in order to make his policy recommendations attractive to the

3. "Will it Deter Aggression?" *New Republic* 137 (March 29, 1954), p. 12.
4. Ibid.

American government. Not immune himself to *animus dominandi*, Morgenthau wanted his ideas to dominate American Cold War discourse — an objective he had realized to a startling degree already.[5] He could perceive that the issue which would dominate such discourse over the next several years was the problem of total nuclear war. How could the United States confront Soviet aggression without unleashing general thermonuclear war? He who found an answer to this question would become the philosopher king of international relations. That, at least, was how an increasing number of ambitious American strategists saw it, and the odd redirection of his writing in 1955 and 1956 suggests that Morgenthau was not going to back down from that competition.

Morgenthau's first attempt to solve the dilemma harkened, naturally enough, to the legacy of nineteenth-century diplomacy. Encouraged by the apparent successes of the 1955 Geneva summit conference, Morgenthau claimed to perceive a return to the traditions of balance of power and limited war — which, if true, might painlessly solve the nuclear dilemma. In a forceful piece in the January 1956 *Bulletin of Atomic Scientists*, titled "Has Atomic War Really Become Impossible?" Morgenthau went as far as to assert that Geneva signified a "new era" in international relations. Before 1955, the two superpowers had been stuck in a bipolar stalemate. Now, Cold War diplomacy "is likely to be characterized by greater flexibility within the power blocs, tending toward a loosening of their inner coherence if not their dissolution, and consequently, by greater flexibility between the two power blocs as well."[6] In a 1956 essay he repeated this argument, though in a less declaratory, more wishful tone. "As the conditions of the Cold War led necessarily to the disuse and misuse of the practices of [traditional European] diplomacy," he argues, "so the new era of international relations with equal necessity calls for the restoration of these practices."[7]

He added to this unusual argument an increasingly critical stance regarding American inaction in Europe and the Middle East. If Morgenthau believed the United States needed to exhibit a "greater flexibility" in its Cold War policies, this did not prevent him from adopting a militaristic Cold War

5. See Frei, *Hans J. Morgenthau*, pp. 74–79.
6. "Has Atomic War Really Become Impossible?" *Bulletin of the Atomic Scientists* 11 (January 1956), pp. 7, 9.
7. "Diplomacy," originally published in *The State of the Social Sciences*, reprinted in *Politics of the 20th century*, vol. 2, p. 207.

line. In late 1956, following the Hungarian and Suez crises, he denounced American passivity in the face of Soviet challenges. Echoing Niebuhr's comment about Eisenhower becoming the Neville Chamberlain of the Cold War, Morgenthau wondered, in a letter to the *New York Times*, whether we are "not well on the road to surrender on the installment plan."[8] In a *Commentary* piece the following February, he attacked Eisenhower again for his inaction in Hungary and Suez, critically concluding that the United States "refused to use, or threaten the use of any kind of force for fear that the threat or use of force might provoke an all-out atomic war."[9] Morgenthau demanded in June that the United States embark upon a massive buildup of American conventional forces, in order to overcome this passivity; following the Sputnik debacle in October, Morgenthau wrote an alarmist piece in *The New Republic*, comparing Sputnik to Pearl Harbor, assuring his readers that the Soviet Union was sure to acquire intercontinental ballistic missiles "long before the United States," and calling for a massive American remilitarization program before the USSR attained total superiority.[10]

Finally, Morgenthau moved decisively after 1955 to embrace the idea of limited nuclear war. If the Cold War were to be characterized by a greater flexibility, and if, at the same time, Americans were to become more willing to confront Soviet aggression in key Cold War theatres, then the United States would have to find a way to wage and win limited war. In his 1956 essay in the *Bulletin of Atomic Scientists*, Morgenthau suggested that the United States and the Soviet Union must adapt to the "new diplomatic era" by developing military policies of maneuver and limited warfare. Both superpowers, "committed as they are to foregoing the deliberate resort to all-out atomic war," must "limit themselves to the use of conventional forces

---

8. November 13, 1956 letter to *The New York Times*, reprinted in *Politics of the 20th Century*, vol. 2, p. 25. An alert colleague, Frank Altschul, reminded Morgenthau of this phrase in 1961, after Morgenthau had embraced more radical views of international politics in light of the nuclear threat. Would not the policy implied by your new views, Altschul asked, "merely serve as a prelude to handing the world over to the Soviet Union on the installment plan?" September 19, 1961, letter to Morgenthau from Frank Altschul, Hans Morgenthau papers, Library of Congress, Box 100.
9. "The Revolution in United States Foreign Policy," originally published in *Commentary* (February 1957), reprinted in ibid., p. 44.
10. "Atomic Force and Foreign Policy," *Commentary* 23 (June 1957), pp. 501–5; "Decline of American Power," originally published in *The New Republic* (December 9, 1957), reprinted in *Politics in the 20th century.*, vol. 2, pp. 48–51.

and tactical atomic weapons." The latter kind of force was particularly suited to American needs: the U.S. must counter Soviet conventional superiority "with tactical atomic weapons, sufficient for this purpose but falling short of all-out atomic retaliation."[11]

Morgenthau's recommendations in this piece anticipate the macabre nuclear strategies put forth later in the decade. The "United States," he argued, "must prepare for, and fight if necessary, a limited atomic war, with the atomic ingredient carefully adapted to the challenge to be met — strong enough, at the very least, to avoid defeat, but not so strong as to provoke all-out atomic retaliation." By administering "just the right atomic dosage," he added, the United States could win a limited war in Europe rather than unleashing the absolute war implied by the Eisenhower and Dulles strategy of massive retaliation.[12] To deny that this clinical kind of war was possible was to give the Soviet Union a decisive advantage. Thus in a December 1956 article in *The New Republic*, he stated that the claim that the use of force was no longer acceptable in the thermonuclear era "has no merit," and went further to say that such a concern "actually increases the risk of atomic war, for it is tantamount to impotence before the threat of force."[13]

Morgenthau's simultaneous call for a diplomatic revolution, a more confrontational stance against the Soviet Union, and a policy of limited nuclear war during the years 1955–57 constituted the most inconsistent, even muddled, thinking of his intellectual career. His logic was faulty on several grounds. His claim — for it was no more than that — that a new diplomatic age had arrived after Geneva was simply wishful thinking, as shown indeed by the fact that Morgenthau identified the "revolution" as a reality in his 1955 article, and advocates one for the purposes of international stability in 1956. On pure methodological grounds, Morgenthau was in error here — like many scholars of international politics, he oscillated between description and prescription, between identifying a reality and calling for it to be.[14]

---

11. "Has Atomic War Really Become Impossible?" p. 9.

12. Ibid.

13. "The Decline and Fall of American Foreign Policy," *New Republic* 139 (December 10, 1956), p. 13.

14. As Robert Jervis points out, "It is a bit anomalous to be telling statesmen that they must follow the inevitable laws of international politics." Jervis, "Hans Morgenthau, Realism, and the Scientific Study of International Politics," *Social Research* 61 (Winter

Furthermore, he did not attempt to show how it was that the great powers could somehow preside over a shift in international relations to the routines of the nineteenth century. Indeed, the thrust of his writing in the late 1940s and early 1950s had posited a decisive transformation of international relations away from traditional diplomacy and toward "universalistic nationalism" and total war. This shift had occurred, he argued, in large part because technology allowed nations to wage total war and pursue total victory. Would the great powers of the world — would the Soviet Union — voluntarily reject these realities and agree to return to the days of Metternich and Castlereagh? That was the kind of idealism Morgenthau liked mercilessly to ridicule.

Morgenthau's inconsistency on this question became even more apparent in his hard-line writing about U.S. policy in Hungary and Suez. Having called for a greater "flexibility" in American-Soviet relations, for a return to the less Manichean traditions of the nineteenth century, one might have expected Morgenthau to applaud, not condemn, the U.S. decision to refrain from intervening in the Soviet repression in Hungary, not to mention its temporary siding with the Soviet Union against its usual allies Britain, France, and Israel during the Suez affair. Were not both of these actions a clear sign of American flexibility, a moving away from the absolutist Cold War mentality Morgenthau had just condemned? Morgenthau's clear contradictions on this question illustrate the shallowness of his "diplomatic revolution" argument, and it is noteworthy that he would abandon this line of thinking after 1956.

Far more inconsistent than his odd revision of trends in international relations, though, was his embrace of the idea of limited nuclear war. The implication of his writing in 1955 and 1956 was that limited nuclear war was possible — that it could be waged between the two superpowers in a limited, nineteenth-century manner. This was the thrust especially of his 1955 article in the *Bulletin of Atomic Scientists*: by combining traditional diplomacy with the careful, almost clinical use of atomic weaponry, American leaders could wage limited wars for limited objectives.

This kind of thinking departed totally from Morgenthau's earlier writing. He had argued quite forcefully in the early 1950s that modern war between the great powers had become total war, waged in an absolute manner both

---

1994), p. 859. On this point also see Stanley Hoffman, *The State of War: Essays on the Theory and Practice of International Relations* (New York: Praeger, 1965), p. 12.

COLORADO COLLEGE LIBRARY
COLORADO SPRINGS
COLORADO

by and against societies, for the total stakes of permanent victory or permanent defeat. For a modern great power like the United States to overcome this reality, to adopt purposefully the limited diplomacy and warfare of the old world, it would not only have to overthrow its own mentality of total war; far more important, it would have to verify with absolute assurance that its adversary was committed to doing the same. As Morgenthau normally would have been the first to point out, in an age of thermonuclear bombs and intercontinental airplanes, a nation that unilaterally adopted a limited and moderate military policy would be at some disadvantage, to say the least, to a nation that did not. He had described the Soviet Union as an aggressive regime, bent upon expanding its universalist ideology for the purposes of Russian imperialism, and hence an unlikely candidate to go along with the American quest to limit modern war. Even a trusting government would see clearly the extreme risks in adopting a policy of limited war without being able to compel the other side to do the same; even an idealistic one would see clearly the extreme advantages in going to war against a nation determined to moderate its attacks. These were all obvious implications of Morgenthau's own writing.

It was one thing to advocate using "limited atomic doses" in a war between the two superpowers, as he put it in 1955, and quite another to show why the Soviet Union would be likely to accept defeat, after the administering of such a "dosage" by its superpower rival, when it retained hundreds or thousands of nuclear bombs. That was the crucial question of the day, yet Morgenthau was hesitant to face it forthrightly. In his 1954 article on Massive Retaliation," he had implied that atomic war was intrinsically total: advocating a continued U.S. conventional presence in Cold War theatres, he argued that "a Korean war, even one fought in perpetuity, is cheaper in every respect than an atomic war."[15] This demonstrated that Morgenthau, at least as late as 1954, regarded the difference between atomic and conventional war as qualitative — the worst kind of conventional war is better than any atomic one. But thenceforth Morgenthau skirted the question, announcing a revolution in diplomacy, calling for a hard line, embracing the idea of limited atomic warfare — all without explaining how it was that the world he had described in the late 1940s and early 1950s could possibly allow such radical changes.

---

15. "Will it Deter Aggression?", p. 14.

As the Cold War descended into the crisis era Morgenthau had little difficulty abandoning many of the ideas he expressed during the 1955–57 period. The post-Geneva "revolution" disappeared from his writing without a trace, and he eased away from the Strangelovian atomic strategizing as well. But he was much more reluctant to accept the premise that limited war was impossible, even though this premise was inherent in his most prominent writings. It is not difficult to see why: to abandon the idea of limited — winnable — nuclear war was to acknowledge that the *ultima ratio* of Realism had become untenable. For an analyst of international politics committed to the Realist worldview, that is not an easy conclusion to draw; nor was it for a public intellectual whose international fame was based upon his forceful articulation and justification of American Cold War toughness.

But the question of limited war in the nuclear age raised an even more profound dilemma for Hans Morgenthau. As this question became the dominant topic among American scholars of international politics during the late 1950s, Morgenthau was forced to confront the very basis of his political philosophy. For it became clear to him that the only way to arrive at a solution to the intractable problem of limited war was to insist that scientific man could overcome power politics. In the end, that Morgenthau could not accept.

Scientific Man vs. the Thermonuclear Revolution

Morgenthau was not the only American scholar keen to find an escape route from the nuclear dilemma. In 1955 and 1956, strategic thinkers such as William Kaufmann, Bernard Brodie, Oskar Morgenstern, James King, and Henry Kissinger, along with many, many others, began to examine the problem of nuclear war closely, with the aim of finding a way to confront the Soviet Union and risk major war without unleashing a total nuclear holocaust. These scholars were less interested in analyzing the larger picture of international politics than in articulating a new form of strategic thinking that accommodated, and mastered, the unique problems of nuclear war. As such, their approach to policy was explicitly partisan: they wanted to influence the contemporary development of American military policy, and, ideally, to be invited to contribute to the actual making of that policy.

The common, and indeed necessary, assumption of all American nuclear strategy during the "golden age" of the late 1950s was that limited war be-

tween the two superpowers was possible. Some writers, such as King and
Paul Nitze, believed that the United States should attempt to keep a war
with the Soviet Union beneath the nuclear threshold; by waging conventional war, the United States could avoid crossing the nuclear line and risking all-out war. Other writers, such as Morgenstern and Herman Kahn, believed that nuclear war could be kept limited — in other words, that a nuclear
war could be won without blowing up the planet. Others still alternated
between these two views — sometimes, as in the case of Henry Kissinger,
within the same piece of writing. Yet all of these writers concurred that
limited war was indispensable to all strategy — to deny that war between the
nuclear powers could be limited was to deny the possibility of victory, and
hence to make strategy purposeless.[16]

Underlying the strategists' common argument that war between the great
powers could remain limited was a core belief that American and Russian
leaders could remain rational and level-headed during a nuclear war between the two sides. For nuclear strategy to work, leaders on both sides would
have to perceive that the costs of overreacting to the other's attack — say a
thermonuclear bombardment of two major cities — would be a total nuclear
war: an irrational outcome. Therefore, the rational leader, in recognizing
this, would be able to resist the urge to reply with a massive retaliation to
an initial bombardment — even though that leader could not be sure that
bombardment was not simply a prelude to an all-out attack. Because total
nuclear war is never rational, the strategists all believed, rational leaders
would be able to restrain themselves from excessive retaliation even during
such moments of maximum uncertainty and total stakes.

Russian and American politicians, in other words, would have to possess
almost superhuman reason and nerve, trusting in the scientific logic of the
strategists that this level of nuclear war does not signify an all-out attack while
that one does. Indeed, many of the strategists were quite clear that the success of their strategies depended upon the mutual rationality of the statesmen
on both sides, and indeed upon their willingness to communicate to one

---

16. Two excellent histories of U.S. nuclear strategy are Fred Kaplan, *The Wizards of
Armageddon* (Palo Alto: Stanford University Press, 1983), and Lawrence Freedman, *The
Evolution of Nuclear Strategy* (New York: St. Martin's Press, 1981). A pioneering article
that gets mentioned less than it ought to is James King, "Nuclear Plenty and Limited
War," *Foreign Affairs* 35 (January 1957). A discussion of the problems of limited war can
be found in my "The (Il)logic of Henry Kissinger's Strategy," cited in Fn 33 of chapter 4.

another the costs a given move would entail in a precise, almost robotic fashion. "The impossibility of war has to be of a technological character," wrote the game theorist Oskar Morgenstern.[17]

As we have seen, Morgenthau had stated clearly that the destructive potentialities of modern weaponry and the extreme nationalisms of contemporary states had made twentieth-century war total. With modern technologies of conquest and control, the stakes of defeat were total; with modern arsenals of genocidal weapons, the means of victory were also total. In particular, he argued, at least after 1951, that the Soviet Union epitomized the totality of modern war. That was why he argued for the development of the hydrogen bomb, and why he continually called for American military confrontation of the USSR, especially in Europe. But by embracing the logic of limited nuclear war strategy, Morgenthau was pinning his hopes upon the ability of Soviet leaders to react moderately to an American nuclear attack, to avoid total escalation once the bombs began to drop — and for the Americans to do the same. Such an assumption wholly contradicted his description of international politics and war in the postwar era.

More than that, the strategic presumption of rationality and scientific precision in the nuclear statesman could not have collided more directly with Morgenthau's core thesis in *Scientific Man vs. Power Politics*. If Morgenthau was saying anything in that book, it was that power politics, above all at the international level, is the realm of irrationality and power lust, a realm in the end impregnable to the thrusts of rationalist or scientific amelioration. The strategic writings of the late 1950s portrayed a leader coolly waging graduated nuclear war, not overreacting to the destruction of his nation's main cities, and ready to accept defeat if necessary, even though powerful bombs remained in his arsenal. But such a leader would get eaten alive in the world Morgenthau described in 1946, a world governed by the "elemental subordination of factual knowledge to interests and emotions."[18] The apocalyptic specter of absolute nuclear war, the instantaneous prospect of total victory or total defeat if one side errs on the side of moderation — these are the kind of problems that would inflame the power lusts and irrationality of international politics to a white heat. And if such irrationality

---

17. Morgenstern, *The Question of National Defense* (New York: Random House, 1959), p. 270.

18. *Scientific Man vs. Power Politics*, p. 180.

and power lust were to be found only on the Soviet side, as Morgenthau had implied in 1951, then it is the Russians who would be at advantage in a war with the American scientific man.

The quest of nuclear strategy was simple: it was to see Scientific Man triumph over Power Politics. Morgenthau's temporary flirtation with such a school of thought indicated a shocking abandonment of the core Realist philosophy he had developed in the late 1940s. After 1957, he began to retreat from this position, and to return to a Realism that could not accommodate nuclear weapons in its present form.

The Demise of the Nation-State

The germinal problem for Morgenthau, as it was for all would-be nuclear strategists, was the feasibility of limited war between two nuclear superpowers. In 1955 and 1956 Morgenthau, as we have seen, advocated the development of a limited nuclear war strategy, despite its apparent incompatibility with his understanding of international politics. By early 1958, he abandoned this position, at least rhetorically. In a lecture at Dartmouth College in February, he argued that the strategy of limited nuclear war faces the dilemma of "distinguishing between strategic and tactical weapons, a dilemma which has confused the writers of military doctrine since the time of Clausewitz." Limited nuclear war, he concluded, would too likely escalate into total war.[19] But his concurrent published writings contradicted this view. In a March 1958 article in *Current History* Morgenthau concluded that the United States needed a "capability to fight local wars with conventional weapons and without resort to all-out atomic weapons." He continued with this argument in December, lamenting that "we are unprepared to fight a limited war," and warning that "we are moving quickly into a zone of mortal danger created by the military superiority of the Soviet Union."[20] These warnings indicated that Morgenthau was maintaining his belief in a limited

19. "A Reassessment of United States Foreign Policy," lecture at Dartmouth College, February 10, 1958, in *Politics in the 20th Century*, vol. 2, pp. 63–4.
20. "Russian Technology and American Policy," *Current History* (March 1958), reprinted in *Politics in the 20th Century*, vol. 2, p. 149; "The Last Years of Our Greatness?" *New Republic* (December 29, 1958), pp. 12, 13–14.

war to defend Europe, in direct contrast to the opinions he expressed at Dartmouth.

Which was his true attitude? Since 1955 he had been trying to formulate a military strategy that could allow the United States to prevail over the Soviet Union in Europe without unleashing a total nuclear war, but at the same time was suggesting, if not in his published writings, that any such strategy was hopeless. Faced with this classic dilemma, Morgenthau, like Niebuhr, began to turn away from strategic writing altogether. Great-power war in the nuclear age, he was beginning to believe, was simply a problem his Realism could not solve. Instead, Morgenthau turned toward a more radical conception of international politics that departed from his original Realist worldview.[21]

Following classical political philosophy, Morgenthau had postulated in his early writings that a primary function of the nation-state, in terms of its utility to the citizen, is protection. The state may also serve as a vehicle for power lust, but its irreducible purpose is to defend its society from external attack and conquest. In the nuclear age, the state can no longer provide this function. The nuclear-age state "must rely upon its psychological ability to deter those who are physically able to destroy it," Morgenthau wrote in the June 1957 issue of the *Yale Review*, because no state can physically prevent such destruction. The collapse of this protective function signaled the end of the predominance of the nation-state. "Nationalism," he concluded, "has had its day."[22] In *The Purpose of American Politics*, a publication of a series of lectures given at Johns Hopkins in 1959, Morgenthau continued with this theme. The thermonuclear revolution had obviated "the elemental task of any political organization: to safeguard the biological survival of its members."[23]

---

21. Morgenthau's more radical writings on the nuclear dilemma after 1956 will be organized thematically, as Niebuhr's were in the previous chapter.

22. "The Paradoxes of Nationalism," *Yale Review* 46 (June 1957), pp. 490–91, 496. For a similar argument, expressed at the same time, see John Herz, "Rise and Demise of the Territorial State," *World Politics* 9 (July 1957), p. 489. Also see Deudney, "Nuclear Weapons and the Decline of the *Real*-State," pp. 212–16.

23. *The Purpose of American Politics* (New York: Knopf, 1960), p. 308. As John Herz was arguing at the same time: see *International Politics in the Atomic Age* (New York: Columbia University Press, 1959), esp. chapter 1. Also see Daniel Deudney, "Nuclear Weapons and the Waning of the *Real*-State," *Daedalus* 124 (Spring, 1995), pp. 213–16..

Any doubts about whether the nation could still protect its population from a general nuclear war disappeared from Morgenthau's writing after 1960. "Qualitatively speaking," Morgenthau wrote in a review of Niebuhr's *The Structures of Nations and Empires*, this vulnerability to total destruction "is the only structural change that has occurred in international relations since the beginning of history." All-out nuclear war, he informed the readers of the 1961 *Encyclopedia Britannica*, is "likely to destroy all belligerents and thus to eliminate the very distinction between victor and vanquished. No possible end can justify it; it is an instrument of mass murder and suicide."[24]

The question remained, however: was such a total nuclear war inevitable following the onset of armed hostilities between the two superpowers? Morgenthau continued to dance around this central problem. In a 1959 *Commentary* article he discusses the ongoing Berlin crisis at length without even attempting to elaborate on whether a war over that city was possible; he simply evaded the question. In *The Purpose of American Politics* he clings to the possibility of limited war, stating, in contradiction to his 1958 Dartmouth lecture, "the capability for limited war, atomic or conventional, might actually be used in support of the national interest, as the circumstances would require."[25] Yet in a March 1961 address at the University of Maryland he was not so evasive, bitterly attacking the "scientist" view that nations could be manipulated to strategic ends. Could the United States survive even a major nuclear war, as the writer Herman Kahn was arguing? It could, Morgenthau allowed, only if we accepted Kahn's vision of human society as "a primitive ant colony."[26]

This withering comment belied the fact that Morgenthau himself was remaining evasive about limited war in his published writing. Even as he was attacking the idea of winnable nuclear war in public addresses, he equivocated on the subject: in his 1959 *Commentary* piece, *The Purpose of American Politics*, and in the third edition of *Politics Among Nations*, which was also released in 1960, he steered clear of the question. While Niebuhr was

24. Review of Niebuhr originally published in *Christianity and Crisis*, February 8, 1960, reprinted in *Politics in the 20th Century*, p. 12; "International Relations," entry originally published in *Encyclopedia Britannica* (1961), reprinted in *Politics in the 20th Century*, vol. 3, p. 174.

25. Ibid., p. 168.

26. "Intellectual and Political Functions of a Theory of International Relations," address given at the University of Maryland, March 1961, published in ibid., vol. 1, p. 70.

denouncing Kissinger's limited nuclear theories, and stating by 1959 that nuclear war is simply "impossible," Morgenthau, in print, was declining to go that far. One can speculate on the reasons for this equivocation: most likely, Morgenthau was reluctant to put himself squarely against the idea of limited war in the charged political climate of the late 1950s. More politically careful at this time than was Niebuhr, Morgenthau may not have wanted to appear to take a controversial position on a question central to American military policy, and indeed fundamental to the Democratic party's critique of President Eisenhower. Following the election of John Kennedy, Morgenthau began to write more directly.

The New Leviathan

"If a nation cannot resort to nuclear weapons without risking its own destruction," Morgenthau asked in 1961, "how can it support its interests in a world of sovereign nations which is ruled by violence as the last resort?"[27] Here, pithily, was the big question, and one more genial to Morgenthau's way of thinking than the strategic issues he avoided confronting. In thinking about this problem, Morgenthau pushed — as did Niebuhr — toward a solution that derived from Realist principles. Morgenthau pushed considerably further, however, envisioning the sources of a Leviathan for the nuclear age.

In a September 20, 1959, piece in *The New York Times Magazine*, "What the Big Two Can, and Can't Negotiate," Morgenthau introduced an interesting proposition. The article's subject was negotiation between the two Cold War superpowers, and Morgenthau naturally identified conflicts between the two sides that were not negotiable, and ones to which they both would have a common interest in adhering. One common interest, Morgenthau notes almost in passing, is the "common fear of atomic destruction," which "ought to neutralize the United States' and Russia's fear of each other."[28] This of course was not an unimportant point, for if the United States and Russia no longer feared one another, the other questions of Cold

---

27. "International Relations." Also see James P. Speer II, "Hans Morgenthau and the World State," *World Politics* 20 (June 1968), p. 219.
28. "What the Big Two Can, and Can't Negotiate," originally published in the *New York Times Magazine*, September 20, 1959, reprinted in *Politics in the 20th Century*, vol. 3, p. 320.

War negotiation would fall by the wayside, not to mention the Realist pre-sumption that mutual fear between the two superpowers could not be elim-inated by concerns about war. What could Morgenthau have meant by this?

In his 1961 address at the University of Maryland, Morgenthau elabo-rated. Nuclear power, he said, "requires a principle of political organization transcending the nation state and commensurate with the potentialities for good or evil of nuclear power itself."[29] He continued:

> For all-out nuclear war is likely to obliterate the very distinction be-tween victor and vanquished and will certainly destroy the very objec-tive for which such a war would be fought. . . . It is at this point that the realistic and utopian approaches to politics in general and to in-ternational relations in particular merge.[30]

The utopian approach to international relations, as Morgenthau had spec-ified in the first edition of *Politics Among Nations*, separated into two cate-gories: the quest for international organization; and the quest for an actual world state. In another piece in *The New York Times Magazine*, published in October 1961, Morgenthau saw in the United Nations an "opportunity to point the world in the direction of replacing national sovereignty with supranational decisions and institutions, for the fundamental argument in favor of the United Nations is the incompatibility of national sovereignty with the destructive potentialities of the nuclear age." Yet, as he had sug-gested in his earlier writing, the United Nations could only provide direction; to attain true supranational control over nuclear war, a world state would be necessary.[31]

In his *Encyclopedia Britannica* essay, Morgenthau shows how such a state might emerge. His discussion is worth quoting at some length. The imme-diate dilemma of Cold War conflict suggests a higher principle of interna-tional organization, which might eliminate "local threats to peace" and cool off the Soviet-American rivalry. The larger dilemma of total nuclear war, he wrote,

---

29. University of Maryland address, pp. 75–76.
30. Ibid., p. 76.
31. "The threat to, and hope for, the United Nations," originally published in the *New York Times Magazine*, October 29, 1961, reprinted in *Politics in the 20th Century*, vol. 3, p. 284.

suggests the abolition of international relations itself through the merger of all national sovereignties into one world state which would have a monopoly of the most destructive instruments of violence. Both kinds of solutions are supported by the awareness of the unity of mankind underlying the inevitable fragmentation of international relations. However inarticulate and submerged, this awareness has never disappeared even in the heyday of nationalism, and it has been sharpened by the threat of nuclear destruction facing all mankind. These solutions are also supported by the longing to give that unity a viable political form . . . through theoretical schemes and practical measures to transform international relations into a supranational political order. This longing, in times past mainly a spiritual or humanitarian impulse, in the nuclear age has been greatly strengthened by the desire, innate in all men, for self-preservation.[32]

Morgenthau's suggestion here cannot be easily dismissed as an inconsequential detour from his Realist worldview, a lament that anyone might have made in the dark days of 1961. Because, unlike Niebuhr, Morgenthau tried systematically to integrate his new understanding of international politics into his old framework. He is not, in a weak moment, acknowledging that the utopian school was right all along; he is arguing, rather, that the prospect of thermonuclear war has caused the utopian and realistic approaches to merge. This argument, moreover, is not simply asserted, as was his claim about a "diplomatic revolution" in 1956; it is based upon his perception that humanity's instinct for self-preservation, central to all Realist explanations of world politics, can now regard the threat to its survival not the conquest of other states, as was the case before the atomic age, but the very prospect of great war. Here, in other words, is the social motivation, previously lacking, that can generate the political pressure necessary to create a genuine world state — a new leviathan that can protect its citizenry from external threat. Morgenthau recognized that a Realism which countenances great-power war in the thermonuclear age defies its core justification as an ideology of survival. For a time, he tried to make great-power war fit into his original conception; by 1961 he altered his Realism to account for a technology that made great-power war unjustifiable.

---

32. "International Relations," pp. 174–75.

Death in the Nuclear Age

In the second and subsequent editions of *Politics Among Nations*, Morgenthau put forward as his first chapter an essay titled "A Realist Theory of International Politics." The ideas in this essay did not really constitute a theory, in the scientific sense of the term, but rather, a kind of praxeology: a guide, informed by Realist political philosophy and a generalized reading of international history, to the practice of international politics.[33]

Writing at a time — as will be discussed in the ensuing chapters — when more rigorously theoretical conceptions of international relations were beginning to appear on the scene, Morgenthau sought to use his insight into the revolutionary implications of nuclear weapons as a means of developing a new theory. He first introduced the idea in a 1959 volume edited by William Fox, titled *Theoretical Aspects of International Relations*.[34] A theory of international politics is "not an easy thing" to write, Morgenthau notes, because the quest to look beyond the moral claims of nations and discover pure reality behind them makes the theoretician "suspect of being indifferent to all truth and all morality." Yet such a quest, he continues, "has become paramount in an age in which the nation, deeming itself intellectually and morally self-sufficient, threatens the human race itself with extinction." A great theory of international politics, he was suggesting, might prove to be the one way for reason to solve the nuclear dilemma, for "the mind of man" to master "that blind and potent monster which in the name of God or history is poised for universal destruction."[35]

Morgenthau was less optimistic by 1961. His address at the University of Maryland attacked the "pretense" of modern theory for creating "the illusion that a society of sovereign nations . . . can continue the business of foreign policy and military strategy in the traditional manner without risking its destruction." The collapse of Western civilization after a nuclear war, he said, signifies the point where "the theoretical understanding of international

---

33. On this point see Aron, *Peace and War*, p. 599, and Hoffmann, *The State of War*, pp. 7–8.

34. Fox, ed., *Theoretical Aspects of International Relations* (South Bend: University of Notre Dame Press, 1959). This is the only publication I have found in which Niebuhr, Morgenthau, and Waltz all appear.

35. Ibid., pp. 117–18.

relations reaches its limits." Any new theoretical understanding must begin with the problem of nuclear war, not only with its effect "upon the structure of international relations" but also the "intellectual, political, and institutional changes which this unprecedented revolutionary force is likely to require."[36]

Morgenthau never attempted to devise such a theory. Like Niebuhr, by the early 1960s he was getting near retirement, preoccupied with public affairs, and unfamiliar with contemporary theoretical methodology. In the end, though, his disinclination to pursue a serious theory of international politics was based upon core philosophical grounds. For Morgenthau, as for Niebuhr, international politics not only derived from basic elements of human nature that could be characterized in normative terms; it was also conducted *for* human objectives that could be so classified. To wit, both Niebuhr and Morgenthau, following Max Weber, regarded the objective of survival in a dangerous world as a normative good, as something all political entities ought to pursue. To be sure, they clarified this assumption throughout their career: Niebuhr defined the normative good as democratic civilization in the face of tyranny; Morgenthau, the United States in the face of Russian imperialism; both, humanity, or "civilization," in the face of thermonuclear war. But they always, if often unconsciously, sought to justify their conceptions of international politics by referring to the goal of human survival. Their Realism was based upon a certain conception of human nature, but equally based upon the assumption that Realism served a particular goal. Thus Morgenthau, in his 1961 address, could ingenuously propose that a new theory of international relations could derive from the political transformation the thermonuclear revolution "is likely to require." For him, theories are devised to serve normative ends.

Both Niebuhr and Morgenthau failed to develop a systematic or theoretical understanding of international politics because they could not accept the key demand of theoretical inquiry, which is explanation, not justification. Both of them came close to theory, Niebuhr particularly in *The Children of Light and the Children of Darkness*, Morgenthau in *Scientific Man vs. Power Politics* and the first edition of *Politics Among Nations*. But as the Cold War progressed they backed away from theoretical rigor, returning to their normative and philosophical approach to world politics. It is not dif-

---

36. University of Maryland address, pp. 66, 71, 76–77.

ficult to see why: by the late 1950s, both of them became acutely concerned with the novel moral problem of war in the nuclear age, a problem they could not resist addressing in normative terms, namely the supreme moral importance in avoiding one. Pure theory explains how a total nuclear war can occur. Neither man could abide that.

Facing conceptual breakdown, both returned to core ideas in the early 1960s. Niebuhr, as we have seen, went so far as to see in nuclear war an unambiguous evil that transcended the relative immoralities and proximate justice of collective politics. "May God," he wrote, "have mercy on our soul." As for Morgenthau, he returned to the pessimistic and ironic European political philosophy of his roots.[37] Such was the tone at least in his most brilliant treatise on nuclear war, a piece he published in the September 1961 issue of *Commentary* called "Death in the Nuclear Age."[38]

"It is obvious," Morgenthau began, "that the nuclear age has radically changed man's relation to nature and to his fellow men."[39] Nuclear power had made political revolution within industrial society impossible, and it had made great power war "an absurdity." By making two essential forms of political violence senseless, the thermonuclear revolution had transformed the meaning of international politics. There was to be no raising the possibility of limited nuclear war in this article: for Morgenthau, nuclear war now simply meant total destruction.

By total destruction, Morgenthau meant the permanent obliteration of any society involved in a nuclear war. A full-scale nuclear exchange would mean social death within all the belligerent nations, "by killing their members, destroying their visible achievements, and therefore reducing the survivors to barbarism."

Such a calamity would have a meaning beyond the physical and political destruction of nation-states and their peoples, because it would eliminate the transcendent meaning of death. Man overcomes his inevitable mortality by leaving monuments to himself, most nobly in the form of individual and

---

37. See Frei, Hans J. Morgenthau, pp. 225–26.

38. This essay seems patterned after Sigmund Freud's World War One essay, "Thoughts for the Times on War and Death," in Freud, *Civilization, War, and Death*, ed. John Rickman (London: Hogarth Press, 1939), esp. pp. 16–20.

39. "Morgenthau, "Death in the Nuclear Age," *Commentary* 32 (September 1961), p. 231. Cf. Niebuhr in September 1959: "The most obvious condition of our existence is the nuclear balance of terror." See chapter 4, above.

collective cultural achievements that are remembered by future societies forever. Knowing this, secular man and society understand that death is not meaningless. Indeed, the act of choosing death, by seeking danger in order to attain glory — to commit "suicide with a good conscience," as Morgenthau quotes Friedrich Nietzsche — constitutes the most heroic kind of action modern civilization knows.[40]

The death that results from nuclear war does not permit this kind of meaning. It is unheroic — hundreds of millions dying following the "turning of a key" — and it is not chosen by those who die. But there is far more to it than that. Not only will a total nuclear war destroy the societies that wage it, making it impossible for those societies to leave monuments to themselves, it will, by permanently putting an end to civilization, destroy the monuments left by peoples and societies since the dawn of history. "Man gives his life and death meaning by his ability to make himself and his works remembered after his death," Morgenthau writes. "Patroclus dies to be avenged by Achilles. Hector dies to be mourned by Priam. Yet if Patroclus, Hector, and all those who could remember them were killed simultaneously, what would become of the meaning of Patroclus' and Hector's deaths?" Heroism loses its meaning if no one exists to appreciate it:

> Thus we talk about defending the freedom of West Berlin as we used to talk about defending the freedom of the American colonies. Thus we talk about defending Western civilization against communism as the ancient Greeks used to talk about defending their civilization against the Persians. Thus we propose to die with honor rather than to live with shame.
>
> Yet the possibility of nuclear death, by destroying the meaning of life and death, has reduced to absurd clichés the noble words of yesterday. To defend freedom and civilization is absurd when to defend them amounts to destroying them. To die with honor is absurd if nobody is left to honor the dead. The very conception of honor and shame require a society that knows what honor and shame mean.[41]

"Death in the Nuclear Age" shows how the threat of nuclear war had changed Morgenthau's intellectual approach to international relations. As

---

40. Ibid., p. 232.
41. Ibid. See Schell, *The Fate of the Earth*, pp. 94–96.

we have seen, during the 1950s Morgenthau became a commentator on American foreign policy, shelving his more abstract philosophical views in favor of the public intellectual role as pundit and policy analyst. The severe inconsistencies that this role forced upon his philosophical understanding of international politics came to a head in the late 1950s, as he realized that his day-to-day criticism of American foreign policy had led him to support a Cold War hard line and the idea of limited nuclear war. The anguished, lyrical style of his 1961 writing, epitomized by this *Commentary* piece, reflects Morgenthau's repudiation of his previous ways. He looks for deep meaning rather than policy defect; and for the first time in his scholarly life, he cites Friedrich Nietzsche.

After 1961 Morgenthau persisted with the nuclear question more rigorously than Niebuhr did. In a 1962 *Commentary* piece he attacked the limited nuclear war position line by line, denouncing nuclear strategists like Herman Kahn and Henry Kissinger. If Morgenthau had flirted with the idea of limited nuclear war until 1960, he was positively contemptuous of it now. Ridiculing the supposed "rationality" of the strategists, he stated that "there is no way of overcoming the immensity of nuclear destruction, which is all out of proportion to the ends sought and, hence, is irrational."[42] He continued this argument in a more thorough fashion in 1964, in a detailed *American Political Science Review* article.[43]

Like Niebuhr, however, Morgenthau turned his primary attention after the Cuban Missile Crisis away from the problem of nuclear war and toward the problem of American military intervention in Vietnam. Morgenthau had written with amazing prescience since the early 1950s about the dangers of U.S. involvement in Asia, and of the risks of regarding communism there in Manichean Cold War terms. By the middle of the 1960s, Morgenthau established himself as perhaps the nation's most prominent critic of the war, attacking it not with idealist or pacifist language but with the language of Realist national interest. His withering criticism of the war, culminating, perhaps, in a televised debate with President Johnson's National Security Adviser McGeorge Bundy, gave an interesting boost to the American antiwar

---

42. Morgenthau, "Truth and Power," *Commentary* 32 (January 1962), p. 155.
43. "The Four Paradoxes of Nuclear Strategy," *American Political Science Review* (1964), pp. 23–35.

movement, for Morgenthau was able, unlike many other antiwar figures, to refute the government's position on its own terms.[44]

At the height of the Vietnam War Morgenthau and Niebuhr sat for a discussion with the editor of the short-lived journal *War/Peace Report*. The discussion, of course, centered on the war, but the two aging scholars, particularly Niebuhr, often redirected it toward the problem of nuclear war. Neither had anything new to say. Niebuhr reiterated his belief that nuclear war is an unambiguous evil — it is, he stated, "certainly out of proportion to any ends." Yet he had no solution to the dilemma, other than reminding American leaders of this fact. "I don't know whether we'll ever have perfect peace," he said. "What we've got to do now is avoid Hell and nuclear disaster." This could be accomplished not by a transformation of international politics, which he regarded as currently impossible, but by a muddling through. "I would say that the precarious nuclear balance makes it inevitable that coexistence," he concluded, "be the first order of values."[45]

Morgenthau was slightly more optimistic, but no more systematic. Perhaps, he noted, the two superpowers could "tell the world that for its own salvation it is necessary for the two of them to exercise a condominium over all the world. This action would give a new legitimacy to power that traditional power could not have." In the meantime, the United States and the Soviet Union would have to rely upon effective diplomacy to avoid war. "That," Morgenthau said, "is the immediate hope."[46]

Hans Morgenthau and Reinhold Niebuhr each developed a political philosophy that aimed to understand modern political nature and the depth of modern war. Taking their cues from the political thinking of Max Weber and Friedrich Nietzsche, they each constructed an ideology of Modern Realism which demanded that the United States engage in the violent world of international power politics. At the core of their Realism was the requirement that the United States be prepared to wage great war rather than acquiesce to its adversary, as this was the only sure means of survival in an environment of anarchy.

---

44. See Rosenthal, *Righteous Realists*, p. 15; Smith, *Realist thought from Weber to Kissinger*, pp. 157–58.
45. "The Ethics of War and Peace in the Nuclear Age," (interview with Niebuhr and Morgenthau), *War/Peace Report* (February, 1967), pp. 4, 5, 7.
46. Ibid., p. 7.

By the late 1950s, both men realized that their Realism now constituted a justification of total thermonuclear war. Their choice was to accept this or reject it. Both eventually chose the latter, a decision that led to philosophical agonizing and the collapse of their confident vision of international politics. They made this decision because they each concluded that a political philosophy that justified thermonuclear war in the name of human survival had become, by definition, absurd. Niebuhr and Morgenthau therefore presided over the expiration of their political philosophy of Modern Realism, lamenting its demise and offering no suggestions for its resurrection. All they could call for was the avoidance of war. In that sense, they committed a form of intellectual suicide, but it was a suicide with a good conscience.

6   The Waltzian Turn

The attention of young American thinkers and political leaders was turning rapidly toward the problem of nuclear war in the fall of 1957. Secretly, President Eisenhower had just rewritten, in the face of tremendous internal opposition, American military policy so as to treat any major war with the USSR as a general nuclear war.[1] Misunderstanding his purpose, Democratic leaders in Congress accused the administration of placing the United States in a position of having to choose between "holocaust and humiliation" in any Cold War showdown, a concern that escalated into panic following the Soviet Sputnik test in early October. Leading politicians and military figures alike warned that unless the United States acted quickly and massively, the next U.S.-Soviet crisis — be it in Korea, the Taiwan Straits, Berlin — would lead either to a thermonuclear war against a now-obviously superior Soviet Union or a devastating defeat. Senator Henry Jackson of Washington captured the political mood of the fall of 1957, when he called, following the Sputnik flight, for a "week of national shame and danger."[2]

As we have seen, the initial response to the thermonuclear dilemma

---

1. See Campbell Craig, *Destroying the Village: Eisenhower and Thermonuclear War* (New York: Columbia University Press, 1998), chapter 4.

2. Jackson quoted in John Newhouse, *War and Peace in the Nuclear Age* (New York: Knopf, 1989), p. 117. On reaction to Sputnik, see Peter Roman, *Eisenhower and the Missile Gap* (Ithaca: Cornell University Press, 1995), and Robert Divine, *The Sputnik Challenge* (New York: Oxford University Press, 1993).

among politicians and scholars critical of Eisenhower was to seek a nuclear strategy that could allow the United States to prevail in a war with the Soviet Union without triggering total apocalypse. While Niebuhr and Morgenthau were reaching the conclusion that nuclear war was simply "impossible," and that therefore the *ultima ratio* of great-power Realism was now an absurdity, the new strategists were trying to develop strategies of limited war that might give the U.S. an option between, as John F. Kennedy called it, "holocaust or humiliation."[3]

Yet limited-war strategy had its own dilemmas. Those who demanded that the United States attempt to wage a conventional war with the Soviet Union, resisting the temptation to cross the nuclear threshold, were forced to admit that the U.S. would have to allow the Soviet Union to prevail if a war came to that or nuclear escalation. At the height of the Cold War, a strategy which urged American surrender when megaton weaponry was still at hand was unappealing to American leaders. Those who believed that the United States could wage, and win, a limited nuclear war were forced to admit that, even if such a war remained limited, tens or perhaps hundreds of millions of Americans would perish in the process. This, too, was an unappealing scenario. The inadequacies of limited-war strategy were, as we have seen, beginning to shake the foundations of traditional Cold War Realism.

In September 1957, a young political scientist named Kenneth Waltz read a paper at the American Political Science Association conference that offered another way to look at the dilemma. Contemporary writing sought to advocate particular policies. The United States *must* avoid war at all costs; or, it *must* find a way to wage major war without triggering the apocalypse. This was not scholarship: it was normative policy recommendation. International politics had a logic all of its own that defied the policy wishes of anguished political leaders and intellectuals. It was time, Waltz said, to study this logic analytically.

The Structuralism of Kenneth Waltz

The study of international relations, in this young scholar's view, had been insufficiently philosophical and theoretical. "The pragmatic and fluctuating

---

3. John F. Kennedy, *The Strategy of Peace* (New York: Harper, 1960), p. 184.

character of work in the field" reflected the tendency of international relations scholars to react to changes in world politics, to describe problems and
devise solutions, all without attempting to understand and explain the larger
picture.[4]

What is the "larger picture"? Perhaps, Waltz suggested, it is the picture
of an international order which determines the actions of people and states,
rather than the other way around. This structural view of politics was nothing
new; it was an important theme in the works of Thomas Hobbes, Alexander
Hamilton, and above all Jean-Jacques Rousseau.[5] The classical tradition of
political philosophy, Waltz wrote, took a more detached view of international
relations, analyzing the process, or the structure, of relations among large
nations rather than the immediate problems facing them.[6]

Contemporary writing on international politics, Waltz continued, had
forsaken this classic method in favor of a preoccupation with human nature
and a predilection for day-to-day punditry. Who was responsible for this
trend? Waltz had certain thinkers in mind. In a review of Hans Morgenthau's

---

4. Political Philosophy and the Study of International Relations," in William T. R. Fox,
ed., *Theoretical Aspects of International Relations* (South Bend: University of Notre Dame
Press, 1959), p. 53. This is a "slightly revised" version of the APSA paper.
5. Ibid., p. 66.
6. It is important to mention that Waltz, like most political scientists in the postwar era,
had incorporated the basic methodology of *behavioralism* into his systemic understanding
of international politics. Behavioralism (which as far as I can tell is sometimes, and sometimes not, distinguished from the term *behaviorism*) seeks to derive systemic generalizations from empirically observed data — measureable behavior — rather than from unmea-
surable phenomena such as intentions or natures. It often stipulates that behavior is shaped
or conditioned by the external environment, or system, rather than deriving from some
internal aspect of the behaving unit.
I am inclined to agree with K. J. Holsti, who writes in *The Dividing Discipline:
Hegemony and Diversity in International Theory* (London: Allen and Unwin, 1985), p.
34, that the distinction between behavioralism and classic social science is overdrawn, at
least with respect to the study of international politics. Waltz's departure from the classic
political philosophy of Niebuhr and Morgenthau is fundamental, and certainly centers
in an important sense upon method. But Waltz's embrace of a structural interpretation
of international politics stemmed, in my view, much more from a leap of philosophical
insight than from an application of new methodology. And as Holsti writes, and as we
shall see, the normative problematic — the causes of war — had not changed. Disagreeing
with Holsti are Barry Buzan, Richard Little, and Charles Jones, *The Logic of Anarchy:
Neorealism to Structural Realism* (New York: Columbia University Press, 1993), p. 14.

book *Dilemmas of Politics* he had criticized Morgenthau for failing to provide a theory of international politics. The "materials" for one are there,
"with 'power' as the organizing principle and 'sin' and 'interest' as companion concepts," but the question of whether interest and sin determine the
nature of power or vice-versa went unanswered by Morgenthau. Causes and
effects remain "in uneasy juxtaposition." Reinhold Niebuhr came in for
similar criticism in another Waltz review: Niebuhr's *The Structure of Nations
and Empires* leaves "the relation between ideological pretension and political power as an elliptically illustrated assertion," Waltz charged. To understand the meaning of nations and empires across time, he stated, "requires
a more careful and thorough examination of economic and social, military
and political conditions than is here given; in short, more concern with the
structure of nations and empires."[7]

Not playing for small stakes, Waltz appeared on the scene in the late
1950s with the explicit aim of supplanting the inconsistent and unsystematic
scholarship of Niebuhr and Morgenthau with a structural, theoretical explanation of war and peace. He was introducing this new form of thinking
just as traditional Cold War Realism was unraveling under the pressure of
the thermonuclear dilemma. The treatise which would pioneer a new theory
of American Realism was Waltz's book *Man, the State and War*, published
by Columbia University Press in 1959.

Waltz's thesis in *Man, the State and War* springs from a simple question.
Why does war among great powers recur? Scholars and diplomats have since
the beginning of recorded history sought an answer to this question, many
of them with the overt aim of identifying great war's essential causes in order
to prevent future great wars. This search only intensified in the twentieth
century, as the increasing levels of destruction associated with modern war
led politicians and writers to intensify their efforts to find a solution. Yet
despite such efforts, wars continued to happen. No one believed that the
European powers would throw themselves at one another again after the
slaughter of 1914–18, but they did; few foresaw after 1945 that the two main
allies in the war against Nazi Germany would find themselves perched on

---

7. Review of Morgenthau's *Dilemmas of Politics* in the *American Political Science Review*
53 (June, 1959), pp. 529, 531; review of Niebuhr's *The Structure of Nations and Empires*
in *International Journal* (1959), p. 260. I am grateful to Ken Waltz for bringing my attention to, and giving me his copy of, the latter review.

the seemingly permanent brink of war, but they were. Inevitably, the world's major powers formed alliances, established a balance of power, and eventually went to war.[8]

Recurrence of a phenomenon throughout time and space suggests a potential for generalization. Rather than looking to the specific historical antecedents of a particular war, a scholar interested in explaining why great war recurs in general can try to uncover something essential in the nature of politics that inexorably causes large states to fight. Traditionally, Waltz proposed, scholars have found the causes of war in one of two political realms, or "images." Some see war as deriving from human nature. Something violent within man leads him to fight. Others see war as deriving from the political nature of certain states. States with malign ideologies commit aggression, forcing other states to fight back. In *Man, the State and War*, Waltz shows why these two images fail to account for the recurrence of war, and how a third image, deriving from the anarchical nature of relations among states, can.[9]

Political philosophers since the Classical period, Waltz began, traced the source of war to the "fixed nature of man."[10] Waltz pointed in particular to the ideas of Spinoza, in the seventeenth century, and to those of Niebuhr and Morgenthau, in the twentieth, as representative of the political philosophy that attributes the occurrence and recurrence of war to human nature. Spinoza, Niebuhr, and Morgenthau all regard man as essentially warlike. For Spinoza, man's all-encompassing quest for survival makes him intrinsically suspicious of his fellows. This suspicion often overcomes the benign side of human nature, leading men to take up arms at the first hint of a threat.[11] Niebuhr and Morgenthau believed that a more general human evil — be it original sin, or the *animus dominandi* — is the source of all human conflict, including, at its highest level, war.[12]

---

8. *Man, the State and War* (New York: Columbia University Press, 1959), pp. 1–2, 8–13.

9. On Waltz's desire to adopt a less empirical, more deductive methodology, see Richard Little, "International Relations and the Methodological Turn," *Political Studies* 39 (1991), pp. 471–73.

10. *Man, the State and War*, pp. 20–21.

11. Ibid., pp. 22–23. Also see Torbjorn Knutsen, *A History of International Relations Theory* 2nd ed. (Manchester: Manchester University Press, 1997), pp. 95–97.

12. *Man, the State, and War*, pp. 25–26, 39–41.

Following the social scientific method of the anthropologist Emile Durkheim, Waltz argued that the human nature explanation, by attempting to account for all political phenomena with a single cause, becomes in the end unable to explain anything.[13] The "importance of human nature as a factor in a causal analysis of social events is reduced by the fact," Waltz stated, "that the same nature, however defined, has to explain an infinite variety of social events." By pointing to an unchanging, essential cause, the advocate of the human nature explanation is unable to distinguish among the variety of human experience. This explanation cannot show why, for example, certain periods in international history are more violent, and others less; by classifying all war as an outcome of human nature, the important differences between, say, the period 1550–1650 and 1815–1914 can be attributed only to randomness. "Historical development," as Durkheim put it, "would be purely teleological."[14] Waltz perceived how Durkheim's insight applies to international politics. "Human nature," he continues, "may in some sense have been the cause of war in 1914, but by the same token it was the cause of peace in 1910." Like any reductionist explanation, the human-nature argument is unfalsifiable: by accounting for all phenomena it satisfactorily accounts for none.[15]

In a single stroke, Waltz provided not a historical, but a theoretical explanation for Niebuhr's and, especially, Morgenthau's abandonment of their purer views on human nature. Both originally sought to attribute all conflict and war to a single, universal factor: the original sin, or the *animus dominandi*, of the political human. Each might have stuck to this argument through thick and thin, but that would have forced them to draw unsatisfactory conclusions about the political world they were trying to describe. Both of them were unwilling to adhere to the idea of universal human nature when that meant morally equating the United States with Nazi Germany or the Soviet Union. If human nature drives all politics, then the actions of Germany or Russia were indistinguishable from those of America. Neither Niebuhr nor Morgenthau could maintain this position, and hence, as we

---

13. See Emile Durkheim, *Rules of Sociological Method* (London: Macmillan, 1982), pp. 125–35. A critical treatment of Waltz's use of Durkheim is John Barkdull, "Waltz, Durkheim and international relations: The international system as an abnormal form," *American Political Science Review* 89 (September 1995), pp. 669-84.

14. Durkheim, p. 133.

15. *Man, the State and War*, pp. 27–28.

will examine further, they turned toward the second image, whereby states are distinguished as warlike or peaceful.

Relying upon Durkheim, Waltz had emphasized the methodological problems inherent in the human nature position. Its reductionist mode of analysis cannot account for variance in history, and hence must resort to contingency or to other factors if it is to explain why sometimes there is peace and sometimes war. Yet Waltz's critique of Niebuhr and Morgenthau subtly, and perhaps inadvertently, exposes a second defect of their reliance upon human nature explanation.

This is the fact that normative understanding cannot be divorced from an interpretation of politics based upon human nature. For Niebuhr and Morgenthau, as for their predecessors, such as Spinoza or Saint Augustine, human nature is not a neutral factor that mechanically causes war, in the way boiling water produces steam; it is the lustful, sinful, weakness of human beings that causes the *evil* of war. If war is presumed to be a scourge, as Niebuhr and Morgenthau do presume, then the thing in human nature that causes it is malevolent. Even if they agree that this malevolence is permanent, not to be wished away, their interpretation of politics remains intrinsically moral, normatively judgmental. As William T. R. Fox, speaking for the normative wing of Realism, put it, "War, particularly two-way thermonuclear war, is for us what cancer is for medical research." To acknowledge that the cure for cancer is difficult to find is not to diminish one's moral consideration of it.[16]

Having made this concession, human-nature Realists find it impossible, as Waltz interestingly implied, to stop themselves from applying their judgments to the realm above the individual human being. Accustomed to thinking in terms of moral distinction, nothing philosophical prevented Niebuhr and Morgenthau from regarding the behavior or the great powers in moral terms. And as we have seen, looking at their experience from a historical point of view, that was precisely what happened. Waltz's critique of the "first-image" human-nature argument actually predicted Niebuhr's and Morgenthau's gravitation to the "second image" in the 1940s and 1950s. And, as we have also seen, this gravitation merely served to undermine the explanatory power of their first-image argument.

---

16. Fox, *The American Study of International Relations* (Columbia: University of South Carolina Press, 1968), p. 100.

Waltz turned next to a critique of the second image, the explanation of war that points to malign regimes rather than evil human nature. His primary targets here were the same as those aimed at by Niebuhr and Morgenthau: the liberals and Marxists of the late nineteenth and early twentieth centuries. His argument, however, was again subtly different. The earlier Realists attacked the liberals and Marxists on two grounds. On one hand, they rejected the idea, explicit in Marxism, implicit in the liberal capitalism of Woodrow Wilson and other capitalist ideologues, that economic materialism underlies all politics.[17] Following Max Weber, both Niebuhr and Morgenthau (together with all Realists) were in agreement: economic wants do not satisfy the desires of human beings and their states. On the other hand, they rejected the idealism explicit in both the liberal and Marxist visions. The liberal idea that it was possible for all states to pursue their interests peacefully and reasonably struck them as a utopian dream; this was especially so for Niebuhr and Morgenthau, who looked around and saw Hitler and Stalin. And while both thinkers were in some ways respectful of Marxism — particularly Niebuhr, as we have seen — they each found laughable the idea that a proletariat revolution would automatically usher in an eternity of selfless brotherhood. The struggle for power that animated all men would never disappear.[18]

Waltz, of course, cannot make a similar case, because he rejects the human-nature argument that liberal and Marxist ideologies overestimate the idealistic capabilities of man. Having just completed a critique of human-nature argumentation, he cannot turn around and denounce second-image ideologies as overly idealistic. Instead, he must show how these ideologies fail to explain actual behavior. He did this brilliantly, by pointing to the tendencies of liberals and Marxists to cling to the state in defiance of their expressed ideologies. Liberals, of course, wish to maintain the (liberal) state. It is the protector of liberal domestic objectives, such as liberty and justice. Thus they face an insurmountable dilemma. If the liberal seeks an idealist foreign policy, in a world in which illiberal states exist, she clearly runs the risk of putting her own state in severe danger — as world leaders discovered

---

17. On Wilson's latent materialism, see N. Gordon Levin, *Woodrow Wilson and World Politics* (New York: Oxford University Press, 1967).
18. This is one of Niebuhr's main points in *Moral Man and Immoral Society*; see chapter 2, above.

in the 1930s.[19] By insisting upon a peace-seeking approach to foreign relations, the liberal simply makes it that much easier for illiberal states to win great victories, and thereby destroy the liberal state that is to be maintained in the first place. As Waltz put it, "what sense does it make to preach laissez faire in international relations when not all states practice it? Those who do will find themselves at the mercy of those who do not."[20] The only way for a liberal state to survive is to contend with illiberal states, in the process becoming itself less liberal. A powerful liberal state could transcend this dilemma, hypothetically, by forcing all states to become liberal, by waging "perpetual war for perpetual peace." A nation waging such a campaign, Waltz presciently noted, is more likely to create enemies, hence returning to the first position, than to establish a liberal utopia.[21]

Waltz saw Marxism as more consistent here, since it foresees the abolition of states, rather than their preservation as peaceful entities.[22] Yet the history of socialist parties and movements at the outset of the First World War, as Waltz shows in a devastating fifth chapter, demonstrated how Marxists rapidly allowed their ideological consistency to become subordinate to the survival of their respective states. During the summer of 1914, socialist leaders confidently called upon the party faithful to refuse to participate in the looming capitalist war. Yet once war began, workers in all of the major belligerent nations, together with the vast majority of socialist figures, rallied to their respective flags. Were they simply coerced or manipulated into doing so by their repressive governments? On the contrary: socialist leaders quickly perceived that the policy of pacifism they had called for would, unless the working classes of all belligerent nations acted as one, doom their countries at the hands of a reactionary aggressor, thus destroying their own socialist movement, not to mention making them guilty of the worst sort of treason. The socialists faced the same dilemma as the liberals: adherence to principle invites defeat at the hands of the unprincipled. Thus European socialists

---

19. See Carr, *Twenty Years' Crisis*, chapter 4.
20. *Man, the State and War*, p. 108.
21. Ibid., p. 113. Waltz is therefore highly critical of contemporary American foreign policy. For a recent critique of U.S. policy that reflects Waltz's position, see Gore Vidal, *Perpetual War for Perpetual Peace* (New York: Avalon, 2002). Also see (for a more scholarly argument) Jack Snyder's compelling first chapter in *Myths of Empire: Domestic Politics and International Ambition* (Ithaca: Cornell University Press, 1991), esp. pp. 1–9.
22. Ibid,. p. 125.

distinguished between waging a war of defense, which was permissible for socialists to support, and wars of aggression. Of course, socialists in every nation at war identified their own war as defensive! The determination of left-wing movements to refuse to fight in 1914 crumbled completely.[23]

Both the liberal and Marxist cases reveal, according to Waltz, the systemic, structural impediments to a second-image solution of great-power conflict. Proponents of both ideologies cannot support conciliation in such a conflict, because to do so simply makes it easier for illiberal, or reactionary, regimes not hindered by such sentiment to prevail over them, thus destroying their liberal or socialist achievements, not to mention their homelands. This was the dominating political strategy, as Waltz readily pointed out, of Vladimir Lenin, who rapidly removed Marxian idealism from his new Soviet Union's foreign policy in favor of the sole objective of national survival.[24] Waltz stressed that the perception that pushes liberals and Marxists to support war when they ideologically oppose it derives not from the goodness or badness of the state in which liberals and Marxists reside, but from the anarchical nature of international relations, from the recognition of states that a policy of war-avoidance for idealistic reasons will only allow the enemies of that ideal to prevail.

It is here that Waltz's implicit critique of Niebuhr and Morgenthau progressed one level upward. Despite their initial political philosophies, by the 1940s and early 1950s Niebuhr and Morgenthau had adopted a normative view of the state. Unwilling to equate morally the United States with its totalitarian rivals, both Realists drifted toward the second image, which is to say that they came to regard the United States as a peaceful nation, and to blame the dangerous state of international politics upon the aggressive designs of bad states, namely Nazi Germany, and then the Soviet Union. From the Waltzian perspective, Niebuhr and Morgenthau had become, effectively, no different than the 1914 Socialists.

As a consequence, they once again faced the dilemma that Waltz's critique predicts. To avoid war, they had to choose between urging the United States to adopt an idealistic, war-averse policy, or to prepare to fight World

23. Ibid., chapter 5, esp. pp. 131–33.

24. A similar argument, examining the reaction of liberal regimes, might be made about the foreign policy of President Roosevelt in the late 1930s.

War Three, a process that would require shedding traditional American liberal values in the name of national security. Of course, they naturally chose the latter course, readily discarding their earlier condemnations of total warfare and militarization and accepting even the more extreme elements of early American Cold War policy. Having fallen into the trap of normative judgment, Niebuhr and Morgenthau were swept along by the Cold War, just as the socialists of 1914 were carried away by the Guns of August.

But there was one key difference, and this is a point Waltz did not raise. In supporting earlier great wars, the Marxists and Liberals could persuade themselves — however futilely, in Waltz's view — that by working for the survival of their state their universalist ideologies could live for another day. The scale of nuclear weapons technology prevented Niebuhr and Morgenthau from entertaining even this consolation, forcing them to ponder a new kind of political order at the international level.

If neither evil human nature nor the existence of bad states adequately explain the recurrence of major war, what does? As Waltz had suggested in his 1957 paper, war recurs not because of a normative fault in the behavior of people or nations, but because the structure of international politics possesses no mechanism to prevent it. No authority exists to regulate relations among states — as Niebuhr, Morgenthau, and many other contemporary writers had also argued. International relations are therefore anarchical. In a condition of anarchy, whether among people in a world before government, or among states in a world without supranational authority, actors find it difficult to rely upon cooperation. Because there is no entity to enforce cooperation, actors are disinclined to place their trust in the hands of another, the indispensable basis of any cooperative venture. Waltz had employed this idea to show how the socialist parties at the outset of the First World War came to support the war despite their ideological opposition to it; the socialists found themselves unwilling to call for resistance to the war because they could rely upon no authority to force other national parties to do the same.

To illustrate this problem, Waltz turned to the stag-hunt parable, which he borrows from Jean-Jacques Rousseau. In a world before government, a group of starving hunters come together in order to capture a stag, which will feed all of them. Poised to surround and trap the stag with his fellows, one of the hunters spies a hare nearby. If he leaps to catch the hare, which will allow him to survive rather than starve, he will alarm the stag, allowing it to escape. Rousseau, and Waltz, demonstrate why the hunter will always go for the hare.[25] If he catches it, his survival is assured. If he lets it pass by, he runs the risk not only of being unable in the end to capture the stag, but, and more profoundly, of giving another of the hunters the opportunity to catch it. Since he himself is tempted by the hare, he can assume that another hunter will be no less tempted. That means if he lets the hare go there is a strong chance that he will miss out not only on the hare, but also on the stag, which will end up being alarmed by the next hunter. Thus he faces a choice between certain survival and likely starvation. Because he cannot trust the other hunters any more than they can trust him, and because there is nothing to penalize the hunter who destroys cooperation for his own purposes, his choice becomes obvious.[26]

As Waltz says: "The story is simple; the implications are tremendous."[27] Without government, actors will always look after their own survival, will always pursue a policy of self-help, even when that means acting in a way that damages the collective welfare. At the most extreme point, a nation will choose war, even if it means unleashing a horrible great war, if its only alternative is to put its chances for survival in the hands of another whom it cannot trust. With no government to penalize those who act in their own interest, actors are impelled to look after themselves, and, crucially, to perceive that a gesture of cooperation is likely to be rewarded with betrayal. The defining moment in the stag hunt is the hunter's realization that others are likely to be tempted as he is; that one's own self-interest proves that others have it too, making cooperation futile. Everyone pursues self-interest, and everyone naturally has reason to mistrust the others. In an anarchical environment, reliable cooperation is impossible.

By locating the source of war in the anarchical nature of international

---

25. Rousseau's parable is very brief; Waltz develops these ideas from it. The original is in Rousseau, *Discours sur L'Inégalité* (Cambridge: Cambridge University Press, 1944), p. 69.

26. Ibid., pp. 167–68. A critique of the use of anarchy in parables and games like the Stag Hunt (and the "Prisoners' Dilemma") is Robert Axelrod, *The Evolution of Cooperation* (New York: Basic Books, 1984). Axelrod shows that "defectors" such as the hunter who chases the hare suffer over the long term by not being invited to future hunts; this process, he argues, indicates that cooperation becomes possible when defection can be reliably punished. But if the hunter is really starving, would he not seize the hare every time even if he knows perfectly well that he will be banned from later expeditions? Immediate, visceral need prevails over long-term reason.

27. Ibid., p. 168.

relations, rather than in the human condition or the policies of particular states, Waltz offered a static conception of international politics. Because the peaceful intentions of individual leaders or particular states are always outweighed by the structural forces that push nations toward war, conflict and war among great powers is inevitable until the structure changes — until a genuine supranational government able to exert true power over the states comes into being. Waltz concurred with Morgenthau that a stable balance of power might prevent conflict and war over the short term; Waltz did not reject, here, Morgenthau's belief that statesmen can act to try to maintain that balance.[28] But a perpetual peace — a permanent, assured end to major war — can never happen without the development of an authentic world state.[29] Waltz saw no reason to assume that the creation of such a state is somehow destined to occur, and indeed he points out — as had Morgenthau — how difficult it is to achieve.[30]

Waltz accepted the existence of an anarchical international structure as a fact of political life; like Rousseau, he wanted to regard it in an analytical, morally neutral way. Therefore, he was equally determined to avoid judging the actions of states caught within this structure in normative terms. In comparing the modern great power to the stag hunter, trapped within a system that forces him to act contrary to the common good, Waltz, again agreeing with Rousseau, maintained that his decision to seize the hare is neither good nor bad; it is simply a decision that an actor determined to survive is going to take. Thus it will not do to criticize actors, be they hunters or states, for acting "immorally" when they are caught in an anarchical environment. "Moral behavior is one thing in a system that produces predictable amounts and types of security," he argued; "another thing where such security is lacking."[31] Just as the stag hunter will feel entirely justified in devouring the hare, even as he incurs the loathing of his betrayed fellows, a nation will act to preserve its own security in ways it sees fit, and regard its actions as wholly justifiable for that very reason — no matter how offensive their policies may

---

28. In *Man, the State and War*, Waltz does not develop in any substantial sense a theory on when the structure is more peaceful and when it collapses into war. He does offer such a theory in his 1979 book *Theory of International Politics*, which is treated in chapter 7.
29. Ibid., p. 205.
30. Ibid., p. 228.
31. Ibid., p. 207.

appear to other states. There is no moral behavior in a condition of anarchy: anything a nation does to secure its survival goes.[32] Or as Thomas Hobbes put it: "where there is no common Power, there is no Law; where no Law, no Injustice."[33]

Total War in Waltz's Structuralism

Waltz used the word "war" in the title of his book to represent the third image of international relations because war is its inexorable outcome. "War in international relations," he stated, "is the analogue of the state in domestic politics."[34] The entity above states is not the United Nations, not the world economy, not a cosmopolitan mentality: it is the specter of great-power war. The anarchy that defines relations among great powers eventually pushes them toward a war of survival, barring the development of a world state, something Waltz saw (and sees) as highly unlikely. Nations are always justified in waging such war — "justified" in the morally neutral, almost biological sense that the stag hunter is justified in going after the hare. The conclusion to draw from this is straightforward: great powers shall, sooner or later, fight a major war, which at the time of Waltz's writing meant nuclear war.

If this was a problem for Waltz, he did not admit it. To maintain his argument, Waltz could not allow the thermonuclear dilemma to affect his analysis of international politics. The reasons are simple. First, the aversion to nuclear war is not a structural phenomenon. The fear of nuclear apocalypse is located in the hearts and minds of human beings, and, perhaps, in the policies of states; it cannot possibly be said to exist within the anarchical sphere of international relations. Waltz was perfectly clear on this point:

> Each major advance in the technology of war has found its prophet ready to proclaim that war is no longer possible: Alfred Nobel and dynamite, for example, or Benjamin Franklin and the lighter-than-air balloon. There may well have been a prophet to proclaim the end of

---

32. Ibid., pp. 181–83.
33. Thomas Hobbes, *Leviathan* part one, chapter 13 (New York: Viking Penguin, 1968), p. 188.
34. *Man, the State and War*, p. 96.

tribal warfare when the spear was invented and another to make a similar prediction when poison was first added to its tip. Unfortunately, these prophets have all been false. . . . The fear of modern weapons, of the danger of destroying the civilizations of the world, is not sufficient to establish the conditions of peace identified in our discussions of the three images of international relations.[35]

Perpetual peace can come only from the elimination of anarchy — from a change in the structure of international relations. Without such a change, great-power war is inevitable. Moral concerns expressed by intellectuals or even states play no part in this calculus.

A second factor kept Waltz from occupying himself with the nuclear dilemma. *Man, the State and War* is, as Waltz indicated in his subtitle, a "theoretical analysis." Dissatisfied with the normative interpretations of international politics undertaken by his predecessors, with the glaring inconsistencies that their shifting policy recommendations caused, and with their sloppy advancement of theoretical claims, Waltz was concerned throughout the book to maintain an analytical, descriptive view of his subject. By holding fast to the position of scholar as analyst, he sought to begin the process of transforming the study of international politics from an inexact medley of historical and philosophical interpretation into an authentic social science.[36]

Given this objective, the last thing Waltz could do was adopt a normative position on the question of thermonuclear war. By doing so, he would have undermined both the elegance of his methodological argument and also his own consistency as a theoretician interested in analysis rather than justification. The specter of nuclear war therefore had to play a subordinate role in *Man, the State and War*, even as it was dominating the actions of men and states in the world outside.

---

35. Ibid., pp. 235–36.

36. By this, he means a theoretical construct that proceeds from deductive reasoning rather than philosophical or historical generalization. Waltz, I think correctly, continues to argue that few alternative "theories" of international politics actually meet this definition. See Fred Halliday and Justin Rosenberg, "Interview with Ken Waltz," *Review of International Studies* 24 (1998), esp. pp. 379–86. On the lure of the natural sciences, particularly in order to avoid normative judgments, see F. Parkinson, *The Philosophy of International Relations: A Study in the History of Thought* (London: Sage, 1971), p. 186, 190–91.

The Waltzian Turn

At the end of the 1950s, the Realist school of thought in the United States was in turmoil. Reinhold Niebuhr and Hans Morgenthau, certainly the two most influential Realist scholars in America to that date, had failed to develop their normative interpretations of foreign policy into coherent theories of international politics. Both made half-hearted attempts — Niebuhr with his overwrought 1959 work *The Structure of Nations and Empires*, Morgenthau, with the third edition of *Politics Among Nations*, the Johns Hopkins lectures, and finally his abortive attempt to build a theory out of the nuclear revolution. Their unfamiliarity with modern social science methodology played a role here, together with their continuing inclination to offer policy advice (particularly on Vietnam) and the simple fact that they were getting old.

Far more important, however, was the unresolvable conflict between their normative understanding of Realism and international relations and the prospect of thermonuclear war. Niebuhr and Morgenthau had each developed a passionate case for Realism based upon the core demand that the United States engage in power politics, and therefore prepare to wage major war. To sell this case to American leaders and the wider public, they consistently made their demand in moral terms. The United States, they had argued, *must* confront Nazi Germany, and then the Soviet Union, because the evils entailed in allowing them to prevail are worse than the dangers and miseries of war. Great war is always the *ultima ratio*, the last resort, of a nation that would prefer peace. Their scholarship during the 1940s and through most of the 1950s stemmed from their determination to justify this claim.

The collapse of *ultima ratio* in the thought of Niebuhr and Morgenthau undermined their Realist worldview, or, to use Thomas Kuhn's famous terminology, their "paradigm."[37] As much as they tried, they could not reconcile their original Realist philosophy with the troubling, unavoidable fact of total thermonuclear war. Facing this inconsistency directly, Niebuhr and Morgenthau both concluded that some kind of world state was necessary to replace the international order. But neither of them made any serious attempt to show how such a world state might eventuate, preferring instead

---

37. Thomas Kuhn, *The Structure of Scientific Revolutions* (Chicago: University of Chicago Press, 1962).

in the twilight of their careers to oppose the idea of nuclear war generally and hope for an indefinite stalemate between the two superpowers.

As formal Realist scholars, Niebuhr and Morgenthau had little left to offer by the early 1960s. Their Realism was inconsistent, not rigorous, and unsystematically renounced by them in any event after the advent of the thermonuclear revolution. Their calls for a world state were desultory and unformed. They were Realists who had ruled out major war, provided no alternative to it, and found themselves simply hoping that the superpowers would avoid hostilities. That was not a practical research agenda.

One way around this Realist conundrum was to deny Niebuhr's and Morgenthau's leading assumption that nuclear war was unwinnable. Had the nuclear strategists managed to develop a more attractive solution to the thermonuclear dilemma, they might have succeeded in buttressing traditional Cold War Realism with war-winning military strategy. That would have changed the course of international relations scholarship, not to mention of world politics, in a profound and perhaps omnicidal manner. But the strategists did not succeed, brought down by unresolvable dilemmas of their own. The general revulsion in American society toward nuclear war, intensified by the Berlin and Cuban crises, prompted a backlash against nuclear strategy, particularly in the early 1960s. The scholarship of Herman Kahn, in particular, threatened to turn Realism into a macabre ideology of nuclear survivalism: a doctrine that regarded the killing of 50 million Americans and the destruction of the American economy for several decades as a military victory was not likely to rise to the top of American intellectual discourse.

American Realism around 1960, therefore, was in crisis. The traditional Realists were offering little besides banal endorsements of coexistence and anguished philosophical forays into the possibilities of a world state. Their rivals, the nuclear strategists, were uninterested in advancing the political philosophy of international politics; they focused upon the means of war rather than its ends, a topic that was initially attractive around 1957 and 1958 but by the early 1960s had come to be equated with the freakish personage of Dr Strangelove.[38]

It was in this intellectual context that Waltz put forward his structuralist interpretation of international politics. It was destined to prevail. The bril-

---

38. See Paul Boyer, *Fallout* (Columbus: Ohio State University Press, 1998), pp. 97–101.

liance and originality of the book would have made it influential in any
climate, and its employment of deductive reasoning and systemic theory
made it doubly appealing to theorists eager to apply the methodology of
microeconomics to other social realms. But the quiet foundation of *Man,
the State and War*'s appeal was its tacit promise to sustain the Realist paradigm while avoiding the thermonuclear pitfalls of the traditional Realists
and the strategists.

Realism had emerged in the twentieth century as an amalgam of analytical and historical treatments of international conflict and war, a body of
loosely affiliated scholarship written typically with the normative aim of in-
fluencing the thinking of high policymakers. Waltz was proposing that international relations depart from this tradition in two basic and interrelated
respects. First, the level of analysis must become structural and systemic:
that is, it should focus on the nature and dynamics of the interactions among
major powers, rather than upon the foreign policy of any particular nation.
Second, the approach of the analysis should be descriptive and positive: the
aim of the international relations scholar should be to assess the behavior of
great powers dispassionately and scientifically, with the aim of achieving a
deeper understanding of international relations rather than developing an
argument for the purposes of policy recommendation. By reasonably re-
sponding to the sphere of international politics as it is, rather than as it ought
to be, scholars could cultivate a new social science, a field which could
produce transcendent works of theory and prediction, rather than essays and
textbooks bound to the political circumstances of a particular time and place.
Structural Realism offered international relations scholars the opportunity
to become authentic social scientists — to develop a tradition of rigorous,
dispassionate, and scientific analysis along the lines of modern economics.
As Waltz wrote, on the last page of *Man, the State and War*: "A foreign
policy based upon this image of international relations is neither moral nor
immoral, but embodies merely a reasoned response to the world about us."[39]

Accordingly, Structural Realism offered scholars the opportunity to put
the vexing dilemma of thermonuclear war aside. By redirecting their focus
away from the day-to-day demands of national foreign policies, and toward
the deep nature of the international system, Structural Realism asked its
adherents to exclude the subjective, first-image, human fear of global ther-

---

39. *Man, the State and War*, p. 238.

monuclear holocaust from their enquiries. By demanding that scholars describe the structure of International politics as it is rather than devise schemes to change it, Structural Realism gave scholars a reason to step away from the morass of Realist agonizing and Strangeloveian nuclear strategy that had been characterizing the Realist study of international relations in the late 1950s. Waltz's message was crystal clear: both the structural *level* of analysis and the positivist, descriptive *method* of analysis not only allowed, but actually *required* Structural Realists to dismiss the moral problem of thermonuclear war from their field of study.

The methodological demands made by Waltz in *Man, the State and War* resemble in many respects the initial stages of a "paradigm shift." Revolutions in scientific thought occur, argues Thomas Kuhn, when traditional paradigms — scholarly worldviews — fail consistently to explain a particular phenomenon.[40] Scholars naturally cling to their preconceptions for as long as possible; their reputations are based upon them. Eventually, however, the inconsistency that cannot be accounted for by their old paradigm becomes too glaring to dismiss. The shift occurs when a younger scientist develops a new paradigm that explains things better: rapidly, other younger scientists recognize that the old paradigm is going to be dethroned, and they abandon it mercilessly, embracing the new paradigm and fomenting thereby a revolution in their field of inquiry. As Barry Barnes describes it:

> The group of scientists trained for normal research is at the same time a sensitive detector of anomaly. A strong set of expectations throws into relief whatever fails to confirm them, any puzzle which resists solution, any phenomenon which defies analysis as the familiar in unfamiliar form. Moreover, since scientists often manifest an intense and exclusive commitment to their paradigms . . . anomalies are often focused upon as things with no right to exist, insults to orthodox doctrine.

This stubbornness in the face of clearly anomalous phenomena, Barnes shows, is the opportunity younger scientists have been waiting for.

> The response to a crisis of this kind typically involves a change in the character of research. Speculation becomes more acceptable. Novel

---

40. Kuhn, *Structure of Scientific Revolutions*, pp. 77–83.

and radically deviant procedures and interpretations are tried. Paradigms, and the activities and judgements based upon them, are called into question.[41]

That is what happened after the publication of *Man, the State and War*. Thermonuclear war brought down traditional Realism, because Realists could not reconcile their normative justification of the *ultima ratio* with the prospect of a war that would utterly destroy the nation waging it. The strategists made a bid to replace the traditional Realists, but in the end they were brought down too by the Hobson's choice strategy offers between Cold War defeat and genocidal nuclear war, or perhaps both.

Waltz's solution to this problem was to eliminate the normative element — to explain, rather than justify. Rather than asking whether the United States, under certain circumstances, ought to wage thermonuclear war, he states: under certain circumstances, the United States is likely to wage thermonuclear war. Just like that, Realism could be maintained, and as a more rigorous, descriptive, and potentially theoretical field of inquiry at that.[42]

The paradigm shift Waltz initiated differs from the classic paradigm shifts in the natural sciences that Kuhn discusses in one fundamental respect. The heliocentric revolution Copernicus launched, to take a well-known example, did not remove anomalous astronomical phenomena from its scope of inquiry; it postulated a new explanation that suddenly showed why the anomalous phenomena now *made sense*. In the case of the Waltzian turn, thermonuclear war is not now made sensible, in the Copernican sense: rather, the methodology is changed so as to remove it from the subject of theoretical investigation. All of this would not have mattered, as Kuhn would argue, had the new Realism — neorealism — managed successfully to rid the anomaly suggested by the thermonuclear revolution indefinitely from its field of inquiry. But thermonuclear war was not done with Realism, as Waltz's return to the topic two decades hence would show.

---

41. Barry Barnes, *T. S. Kuhn and Social Science* (New York: Columbia University Press, 1982), pp. 53–54.

42. Guzzini argues (*Realism and International Relations*, pp. 109ff.) that the anomalies threatening the Realist paradigm were ideas posed by critics of structural realism that sought to undermine the Waltzian edifice. But Kuhn clearly shows that anomalies are not the new ideas introduced by younger scholars, but rather phenomena that give rise to these new ideas. An anomaly, in other words, must be an external problem, not an "internal" argument.

7   Retreat from Parsimony

In *Man, the State and War* Waltz put forward a Realist philosophy of international politics that departed from the earlier views of Niebuhr and Morgenthau in two general ways. Waltz rejected the normative brand of Realism, by which he meant the kind of Realist discourse that urged policymakers to adopt a particular course of action for explicitly normative ends. Such advocacy was antithetical to a genuinely scientific approach to international politics, not only because it interfered with the objectivity and dispassion of the scholar, but also because it detracted from the analytic enterprise. By describing his book as "a theoretical analysis," Waltz was distinguishing his work from his predecessors in precisely that sense. Theorists do not believe that events ought (or ought not) to occur; they seek to explain why they occur. By adopting a dispassionate view of international politics, a scholar could assess global affairs objectively, avoiding the inconsistencies and time-bound politicking that bedeviled the work of Niebuhr and Morgenthau. Such dispassion might allow the study of international politics to approach the rigor and descriptive power of other social sciences, such as microeconomics.

Deeply connected to Waltz's rejection of normative method was his rejection of the first image notion that human nature was the causative factor in international politics and great-power war. The human-nature argument, Waltz maintained, by pointing to human evil in its explanation of war, suffered from the reductionist fallacy that Durkheim had identified in the late nineteenth century. By defining human nature in a normative, universal way, the first-image adherents were unable to explain variation in history, to show why peace occurs as well as war. This very problem also led to the inconsistent and unrigorous writing of Niebuhr and Morgenthau.

People yearn for peace; yet great war recurs. By proposing a structural interpretation of international politics, Waltz aimed to show why both statements can be true. The wishes and fears of man are subsumed by the irreducible quest of states to survive, and the conflict that inevitably emerges among them, in an anarchical realm. The stag hunter may keenly and genuinely want to cooperate to catch the stag, but he will always leap for the hare if he can. The socialists in 1914 may have been resolutely determined to oppose war, but they all ended up supporting it. Structure, Waltz is saying, overcomes human will and desire; the theorist must explain peace and war first by looking at the structure of international politics rather than the desires and fears of individual peoples.

For both of these reasons, Waltz was determined in *Man, the State and War* to remain indifferent to the thermonuclear dilemma. Were he to take a normative view of nuclear war, regarding it, as Niebuhr and Morgenthau did, as a Hellish abomination that somehow had to be prevented, he would be abandoning the dispassionate stance that he believes is indispensable to the practice of theoretical analysis. One cannot easily claim to explain objectively why war recurs and at the same time demand that, this time, it must not; not only is this methodologically inconsistent, it also produces a bizarre kind of writing, as Morgenthau discovered in the late 1950s. Correspondingly, by adopting a normative view of nuclear war Waltz would be acknowledging that human desires and wishes might be able to have an effect upon international politics. Waltz's structural view relies upon the possibility that a great war, which in 1959 meant nuclear war, could occur even if everyone on the planet abhorred it. Unit-level factors cannot overcome structural forces; his own denunciations of nuclear war, no more than Niebuhr's or Morgenthau's, are not going to make a whit of difference to the systemic powers-that-be. This was an important claim, because while in previous periods crusaders and militarists, ideologues and nationalists openly welcomed the possibility of major war, making it possible to argue that wars begin because certain types of people want them to, almost nobody felt that way about major nuclear war. In other words, the possibility of a thermonuclear war epitomized Waltz's argument — the occurrence of such a war would validate his theory unlike any war in history.

Waltz's seminal redefinition of Realism in 1959 resembled a "paradigm shift," in that he would lead the transformation of the Realist study of international politics in the United States from a philosophically- and historically-oriented concern with normative policy ends into a theoretically rigorous social science. The Waltzian turn was not a true shift, however, because the inconsistency that brought down the traditional scholars — how to justify nuclear war as *ultima ratio* — was not *solved* by the new approach; rather, it was ignored by it. David Singer wrote, in an influential *World Politics* review of *Man, the State and War*, that Waltz's insistence upon the immutability of structure "seems to leave us with the feeling that World War III is inevitable," since neither human war-aversion nor a world state was possible.[1] To maintain the consistency of his new paradigm, Waltz was going to have to accept this. Yet he could not. The unauthentic nature of the Waltzian turn was demonstrated most clearly in Waltz's own writing toward the end of the period 1962–81, when, unable to resist reckoning with the problem of nuclear war, he abandoned the methodological strictures of *Man, the State and War*, turning toward a normative, first-image approach to international politics in order to contrive a means of avoiding nuclear holocaust.

Explaining Cold War Peace

During the period 1940–62, Reinhold Niebuhr and Hans Morgenthau developed, published, abandoned, and rewrote several major and innumerable minor works on international politics. In those two decades, they had somehow to assess and explain American entry into World War Two, wartime diplomacy with the British and Russians, Hiroshima, Nagasaki and the post-war settlement, the onset of hostilities with the Soviet Union, the invention of the hydrogen bomb, the Chinese communist revolution, the Korean War and its accompaning furor of anti-communism, the advent of the thermonuclear revolution, and several crises — Hungary, Quemoy-Matsu, Berlin, U-2, Berlin again, Cuba — any one of which might have escalated into World War Three. During this same period, they attempted to develop a political philosophical understanding of their subject in broader terms, even as these monumental events forced them to reconsider their most basic assumptions.

---

1. J. David Singer, "International Conflict: Three Levels of Analysis," *World Politics* 12 (April 1960), p. 459.

Their task was equivalent — intellectually, at least — to that a student of social revolution living in Paris would have confronted during the last decade of the eighteenth century, or a European scholar concerned with the connections between religion and war writing during the period 1618–48.

Waltz was able to refine and redevelop his understanding of international politics during a less tumultuous time. If the 1960s and early 1970s was a time of domestic upheaval in American society, it was — not coincidentally — also a time of settlement and relative calm in international politics. The Vietnam War was hardly a calm phenomenon, ripping layers of American society apart and unleashing insane destruction upon the Vietnamese people and countryside, but — as Waltz himself tirelessly pointed out — it was not nearly as important an event in the grand scheme of great-power politics as student radicals, or Henry Kissinger, liked to think. The major factor in international politics, the bipolar rivalry between the United States and the Soviet Union, remained unaffected by the war. The stability of international politics allowed Waltz to develop his ideas at a more leisurely pace.

Indeed, it is safe to say that Waltz's main subject during the two decades between the publication of *Man, the State and War* and *Theory of International Politics* was the increasing stability and routine of the Cold War international system. The two superpowers had become able to avoid not simply war but serious conflict as well, in Waltz's view, for the very fact that there were only two of them.

In 1962, a year in which the stability of the Cold War had not yet become obvious, Waltz elaborated upon some themes of *Man, the State and War* in a provocative article, "Kant, Liberalism, and War." Kant, Waltz began, may be "considered a theorist of power politics who hid his Machiavellian ideas by hanging 'round them the fashionable garments of liberalism." Kant had less faith in the possibility of moral international politics than widely believed, and indeed regarded states as "lawless savages" bound within a "nonjuridical condition."[2] Of course, Kant saw an escape from this condition in a classic "second image" sense, for he believed that liberal republics would not undertake aggressive war, using systems of peaceable international trade

---

2. "Kant, Liberalism, and War," *American Political Science Review* 56 (June 1962), pp. 331, 334. An interesting recent treatment of this piece, and of Waltz's Kantian influences, is Ewan Harrison, "Waltz, Kant and Systemic Approaches to International Relations," *Review of International Studies* 28 (April 2002), esp. pp. 149–50.

and the voluntary organization of global institutions to establish a perpetual peace among nations. Tellingly, Kant opposed the establishment of a more powerful world state, fearing the tyranny and repression that would inevitably accompany it.

Yet — as Morgenthau had shown — to rely upon the peacefulness of states rather than a serious world state was to forego the real possibility of perpetual peace. States, in Waltz's, and Morgenthau's view, could not remain liberal in their relations with other nations, for the very reason that they pursued liberalism at home. Liberalism at home required the survival of a strong state, which, in an international realm of anarchy and illiberal states — we have not attained the liberal utopia, we are only pursuing it — required war-like and confrontational foreign policies. In protecting the state from the dangerous world, the state acts illiberally abroad and becomes, in some ways, illiberal at home. Anarchy, therefore, places a Catch-22 in front of the idea of a democratic peace. International politics cannot become peaceful until all nations become peace-loving republics; yet nations cannot become peace-loving republics until international politics becomes peaceful.[3]

Waltz acknowledged that Kant perceived this difficulty — the Prussian philosopher "was not engaged in the puerile task of telling men of affairs to stop behaving badly."[4] Kant's solution to this impasse, therefore, was to rely upon the transformative effects of war. The horrors of war "might prepare a system based upon a moral basis," as Waltz paraphrased Kant. "It is the aim of his political philosophy," he continued, "to establish the hope that states may improve enough and learn enough from the suffering and devastation of war to make possible a rule of law among them that is not backed by power but is voluntarily observed."[5]

Waltz regarded this simply as "an act of faith." The imperfection of human morality which Kant bemoaned made it so. As long as moral behavior at the international level remained only a "possibility," then the possibility of perpetual peace had to be demonstrated despite that fact — it could not be "imperatively commanded." "Peace is possible," Waltz allowed. "This Kant has sought to prove. Its achievement remains an improbability."[6]

---

3. Ibid., pp. 336–40. Cf. *Man, the State and War*, pp. 107–13.
4. Ibid., pp. 339–40.
5. Ibid., pp. 335, 337.
6. Ibid., pp. 335, 339.

Taking Kant seriously, Waltz intended to show how even a formidable mind such as his trips up when trying to employ first- and second-image reasoning to argue for international peace. Kant's difficulties simply demonstrate "the causes of war and the difficulty of doing anything about them." Waltz's implication, though unstated in this article, was clear enough: the horrors of war are insufficient to establish perpetual peace, and that includes the prospective horrors of thermonuclear war. For peace to persist, at least over the short term, the international system must be stable. In his view, bipolarity made it so, and that — not the nuclear fear that would sweep the nation in October of 1962 — is what the United States should seek to maintain.

Waltz presented this argument formally in a major article in the summer 1964 issue of *Daedalus*. Many scholars of international politics, following Morgenthau's lead, believed that the bipolarity of the Cold War made it more unstable, more likely to explode into war. Waltz disagreed. While bipolarity, he allowed, does create a "nearly constant presence of pressure and the recurrence of crises," the simple means of communication and perception between each side, together with the relative unimportance of alliance gains or losses, actually makes it the most stable kind of international order. Great powers in a bipolar world need only concern themselves with the actions of the other: they do not have to monitor, simultaneously, the policies and power of several other states. This radically reduces uncertainty and miscalculation, making the waging of power politics easier: each side can keep its eyes steadily on the other, rather than having to look incessantly to and fro. Furthermore, the loss or gain of an ally does not throw the balance into chaos, as it can in a multilateral system. Superpowers can tolerate defections, like Yugoslavia or China, because these do not appreciably affect the balance. Whether Yugoslavia allies itself with the USSR or the United States, the two superpowers remain in either event far more powerful than any other nation, and roughly equivalent with one another.[7]

Much of Waltz's argument was dedicated not to showing why bipolarity is the main source of stability and peace, but rather to rejecting the idea that nuclear fear is. "Many argue," Waltz wrote, "that caution in crises, and resulting bipolar stability, is accounted for by the existence of nuclear weap-

---

7. "The Stability of a Bipolar World," *Daedalus* 93 (Summer 1964), pp. 881–83, 889–93.

ons, with the number of states involved comparatively inconsequent." Yet the bipolar nature of the Cold War also makes its two powers cautious, because the possibility of a limited war — of a peripheral war fought between some of the major powers, like the Crimean war of the 1850s — is ruled out. Any war between the great powers is likely to become a total war, since defeat can mean nothing else than the world domination of the victor.

Because of the all-or-nothing stakes of bipolar power politics, both nations arm to the teeth, nuclear weaponry or not. "Even had the atom never been split," Waltz maintains, "each would lose heavily if it were to engage in a major war against the other."[8] The fear of nuclear war, to be sure, "has reinforced" the stability caused by bipolarity, but it remains a secondary factor. Waltz repeated this argument in a 1965 review in *World Politics*: he rejected F. H. Hinsley's claim that nuclear deterrence has put an end to the possibility of war, and even more forcefully attacked Inis Claude's suggestion that global nuclear fear provides the impetus for a world state. World states require world societies, and if "there is practically no society upon which agencies of central control can be erected, then a manager possessed of great power is at once badly needed and impossible to find." Anarchy, Waltz repeated, trumps nuclear fear. "Consciousness of the nuclear danger may sharpen the desire to eliminate it, but it does not provide the means for doing so."[9]

In 1967, Waltz published his second book, *Foreign Policy and Democratic Politics* — a very interesting treatment of the respective effects of great-power status and second-power status upon the democratic formulation of foreign policy in the United States and Great Britain. Waltz's main objective was to apply his idea about the difficulties of great-power liberalism that he had expressed in *Man, the State and War* and the 1962 article on Kant to the experiences of Cold War America and Britain. Waltz showed in particular how British leaders, most notably Harold Macmillan, made up for their exclusion from the actual conduct of power politics by alternating between liberal condemnation of American excesses and futile attempts to foist great-power status back on to Great Britain.

---

8. Ibid., pp. 884, 885–86. For a similar argument, coming from a very different perspective, see John Mueller, *Retreat from Doomsday: The Obsolescence of Major War* (New York: Basic Books, 1989).

9. "Contention and Management in International Relations," *World Politics* 17 (July 1965), pp. 723, 733–37.

In this book he was critical of the British decision to acquire an independent nuclear force, and showed persuasively why such a force can add nothing to British security, and indeed have no bearing on the outbreak or outcome of a major war between the two superpowers and their allies. He added, however, that one point "can sensibly be made: building a small nuclear force, though an unpromising way of seeking to maintain the integrity of one's state, may enable that state to act positively against equal or lesser powers."[10] This was an interesting aside. Writing in 1967, Waltz here was not talking about the British using their weapons within the context of a Cold War dispute: as he had already shown, they were in no position to threaten or use their nuclear arsenal in that way other than to contribute to an American retaliation in World War Three. Rather, he was referring to the possibility of Great Britain using the threat of nuclear attack to act "positively" against non-nuclear states outside the realm of Cold War power politics. In this respect, he was foreshadowing an argument he would present in full bloom in 1981.

In developing his notion of bipolarity during the years 1962–67, Waltz did not ignore the question of nuclear war. In the wake of the Cuban Missile crisis, nuclear fear was widely perceived as the primary explanation of great-power peace: neither nation wanted to go through that again, and hence each avoided actions that might provoke the other. This was the explicit argument of Inis Claude, Stanley Hoffmann, and other scholars, as well of course the implicit belief of Niebuhr and Morgenthau in their last years.[11] Waltz rejected this line of thinking, but not as thoroughly as the logic of *Man, the State and War* dictated. Nuclear fear could not create a world state, this much was certain, but he did allow that it could play a reinforcing role in maintaining bipolar stability. "Some have believed," he wrote in 1967, "that a new world began with the explosion of an atomic bomb over Hiroshima. In shaping the balance of nations, the perennial forces of politics are as important as the new military technology."[12] This is a retreat; in 1959 he had stated that the fear of nuclear war was of no more importance in the prevention of war than earlier fears of balloons or poison-tipped spears had

---

10. *Foreign Policy and Democratic Politics*, (London: Longmans, 1967), p. 148.
11. See Hoffmann, *The State of War*, especially chapter 8, "Terror and Theory in Practice;
and Inis L. Claude, *Power and International Relations* (New York: Random House, 1962),
chapter 1.
12. "The Politics of Peace," *International Studies Quarterly* 11 (September 1967), p. 201.

been. Following the publication of *Foreign Policy and Democratic Politics*, Waltz turned his attention toward the development of a more systematic theory of international politics, one that could establish, in a more formal way than his philosophical writing in *Man, the State and War* had done, the role of structure as the dominant explanation of international war and peace. Yet the factor of nuclear fear would not go away, diluting his theoretical consistency even as he worked to purify it.

A *Theory of International Politics*

In *Man, the State and War* Waltz had put forth, as he called it, "a theoretical analysis": it was an attempt to evaluate explanations of the recurrence of major war by presenting a structural abstraction of international politics rather than pointing to the actions, beliefs, policies, and natures of men and states beneath. But his argument was not really a theory, in the common scientific meaning of the term, as it did not provide a model of international politics that could predict its future workings. To do that, Waltz needed to show not why first- or second-image thinking failed to explain great war and peace, but rather why, specifically, the anarchical structure of international politics could. How, exactly, can the idea of structure be used to explain formally why great-power war is more likely to occur at a particular time, and less at another? Precisely what elements of international politics are decisive in contriving such an explanation? Without applying it in this specific fashion, the third image is no less reductionist than the first or the second: to contend merely that international anarchy makes war inevitable is in that sense no different than to say that evil human nature makes it inevitable — indeed, these are perhaps simply two sides of the same metaphysical coin.

Waltz addressed this problem forthrightly during the years 1967–79, in so doing articulating several categories of analysis.[13] The realm to be ana-

---

13. International relations scholars routinely refer to Waltz's 1979 work, *Theory of International Politics*, as the source of his theorizing, when in fact, a great deal of what he published in book form in 1979 had been already written in various fora during the preceding twelve years. Indeed, to this day Waltz tends to re-use his writings, taking sections from an article or chapter and placing them in a later work, making the life of his

lyzed was international politics, defined as a bounded sphere of activity characterized by anarchy. The motivation of the actors within this realm — states, and in particular great powers — was self-preservation: to preserve their survival, states do whatever they think is best to look after themselves, a strategy of "self-help." The dynamic produced by these two phenomena was the balance of power, which changes according to the number of great powers and their respective military and economic capabilities — their ability to wield power and wage war. Using these suppositions, Waltz was able to put forth theoretical predictions about great-power war.

Waltz introduced this theoretical approach in a 1967 article in the *Journal of International Affairs*. In 1964, Waltz had claimed that bipolarity made for a more stable international order than multipolarity, and that it explained the peace between the two Cold war superpowers better than did nuclear fear. Here, he expands this argument, with the particular intention of showing how bipolarity lessens the chances of great-power war.[14]

"Balance-of-power theory assumes that the desire for survival supplies the basic motivation of states, indicates the responses that the constraints of the system encourage, and describes the expected outcome," Waltz began. Yet the traditional understanding of the balance of power suggests that it can be achieved only by a multipolar system, for this allows states to "balance" against others. How can one describe a bipolar rivalry as a "balance," when no balancing is taking place? Furthermore, other modern scholars were now arguing that the balance of power had been made obsolete by the onset of nuclear weaponry. The threat of war — the mechanism of the balance — had become too dangerous to execute. Both of these views, therefore, rejected the idea that a balance of power was operating during the Cold War at all. "A weird picture of the political world," Waltz wrote, "is thus drawn. The constraints of balance-of-power politics still operate: each state by its own efforts fends for its rights and seeks to maintain its existence. At the same time, the operation of balance-of-power politics is strangely truncated; for

---

intellectual historian especially difficult. Here, his earlier writings will be addressed as they were written, but I will not deal separately with his contribution to Nelson Polsby and Fred Greenstein's *Handbook of Political Science*, volume 8 (Reading: Addison-Wesley, 1975), reprinted as chapter 3 in *Theory of International Politics*, as it is less relevant to the theme of this chapter.

14. Sections of this article are reprinted in chapter 8 of *Theory of International Politics*.

one essential means of adjustment is absent, and the operation of the other is severely restricted."[15]

Waltz rejected both of these arguments. The balance of power continues to exist in a bipolar system, but the balance is maintained in a different fashion. Rather than using alliances and the possibility of war to preserve the equilibrium, great powers — the United States and the Soviet Union — balance against one another by increasing their power. Following the argument Morgenthau put forth in *Politics Among Nations*, Waltz regarded the arms race and the building of immense nuclear arsenals by each side as the means of balancing in the modern era of international politics.[16] Both superpowers constructed giant military complexes, to the dismay and envy of their allies, because this, rather than the cultivation of alliances, was the way to stay alive in a bipolar system. Superpowers can act flexibly and even irrationally — here, Waltz is alluding to Vietnam — in their relations with other states; what they must take seriously is the balance of military power between them.

But how can such a balance work when the power each side is developing is unusable as a means of war? "Is the use of military force," Waltz asked rhetorically, "so severely inhibited that the balance-of-power analysis has lost most if not all of its meaning?"[17] No. "It is highly important," Waltz wrote, "indeed useful, to think in 'cataclysmic terms,' to live in dread of all-out war, and to base military calculations on the forces needed for the ultimate but unlikely crisis." But the United States and the Soviet Union were able, unlike other, lesser, states, to wield their military power *beneath* the level of total nuclear war. That the United States was doing so purposelessly in Vietnam merely indicated its great-power status; unlike other nations, it could wage a costly, unsuccessful war without endangering its position in international politics. "To say that militarily strong states are feeble because they cannot easily bring order to minor states," Waltz insisted, "is like saying that a pneumatic hammer is weak because it is not suitable for drilling decayed teeth."[18]

This of course begged the larger question: if great war is "cataclysmic,"

---

15. "International Structure, National Force, and the Balance of World Power," *Journal of International Affairs* 21 (1967), pp. 215, 217.
16. *Politics Among Nations*, 1st ed., chapter 20.
17. "International Structure," p. 220.
18. Ibid., pp. 225, 227.

and minor wars like Vietnam — which Waltz attacks in this article as a senseless endeavor — are purposeless, almost whimsical, then what does the wielding of great power actually mean? Waltz seemed to evade this problem. "It
is not very interesting," he oddly argued, "to ask whether destabilizing events
will occur and disruptive relations will form, because the answer must always
be yes." The more interesting question, he believed, is what the vast power
of the two states produces in the realm of great-power conflict. Waltz suggested that it produces a high degree of stability. Indeed, the two superpowers
wield a kind of "hierarchical" control "that often goes unnoticed because
the means by which control is exercised are not institutionalized." Able to
control "destabilizing acts of third parties," indifferent to allies' complaints,
the United States and the Soviet Union comprise a rough substitution for a
world state. "What management there now is in international relations must
be provided," Waltz concluded, "singly and occasionally together, by the
duopolists at the top."[19]

Many of the arguments Waltz later presented in *Theory of International
Politics* are actually introduced, if in brief form, in this article. The most
striking one was Waltz's apparent shift regarding the uses of great power.
Great-power war is ruled out as a positive means of national advancement
in the realm of international politics; so, apparently, is peripheral war, as
neither victory nor defeat can alter the balance of power. The main function
of power, Waltz appeared to be arguing, is to give the two "duopolists" the
clout to manage international politics for the purposes of stability, which is
a less sentimental way of saying great-power peace. Indeed, Waltz suggested,
superpower management for the ends of peace can approach a hierarchical
form. His approval of this development suggests that underlying Waltz's theoretical assessment of the bipolar balance of power was a normative desire for
great-power peace.

The tension between Waltz's aims to construct a positivist theory of international politics and to suggest how great war might be avoided by bipolar
management was equally apparent in his 1971 essay, "Conflict in World
Politics." In this piece, Waltz introduced further elements of his theoretical
project. In the quest for self-preservation, states embark on a policy of "self-
help" within the "unalloyed anarchy of international relations." The dynamic created by this collective quest to look after oneself creates a structure

---

19. Ibid., pp. 229–31.

that pushes states away from cooperation and toward conflict. These structural constraints are not deterministic; they are "barriers, but men can try to jump over them," he stated. "Structure shapes and limits choices, it establishes behavioral tendencies without determining behavior."[20]

The structure created by the self-help policies of states in anarchy pushes states toward conflict and war. "Fortunately," Waltz pointed out, perhaps omitting the first half of the twentieth century from his analysis, "wars that shake the world order, or even a regional order, are rare." At least they are rare in the contemporary world: confrontations between the two great powers, he added, now "tend to be inconclusive. Their strategies are grounded on the principle that it is better to yield than to risk mutual destruction." The Cold War thus is a kind of passive peace, created by the "lessening" of contacts "among contenders." Does this suggest a gradual erosion of the anarchy of international politics? No. International conflict, he concluded, "is ultimately ended only by abolishing international relations." The difficulty of attaining this explains the "ubiquity of conflict and the recurrence of war among states."[21]

The nagging question here is even more difficult to ignore. Waltz was arguing that the anarchy produced by self-help policies of all states is a fact of international life. Conflict and war among states recurs, and Waltz was not speaking in the past tense. But is major war ubiquitous? Waltz claimed that it is not: great wars "that shake the world order" are rare, and we can take this to mean, following his earlier writing, that they are presently rare. This is so, clearly, because the fear of nuclear war and, more important, the ability of the two superpowers to avoid confrontation makes it so.

Should the leaders of the two superpowers then seek to keep war rare by sticking to the "principle" that yielding on minor issues is better than nuclear destruction, by managing their bipolar rivalry in a way that lessens conflict between the two sides? Anyone reading this article will reach the conclusion that Waltz's answer to this question is "yes." His emphasis upon the "management" of the bipolar rivalry, his reference to the "principle" of avoiding nuclear war — these are implicit endorsements of the proposition that subsystemic factors can play the most important role in international politics:

---

20. "Conflict in World Politics," in Waltz and Steven L. Spiegel, *Conflict in World Politics* (Cambridge, MA: Winthrop, 1971), pp. 460–61, 471.
21. Ibid., pp. 456, 461, 474.

they can determine whether great war occurs or not. It also suggests, no less significantly, that Waltz himself regarded this as a good thing, as a normative end.

If Waltz was aware of his move toward normative argumentation, he was not willing to acknowledge it. In a caustic 1976 review of Richard Sterling's book *Macropolitics*, Waltz rejected the notion that the objective of the academician — as Sterling had asserted — was to demand that things should change for the better; the real scholar avoids idealism, looking instead "for effective causes and ways of acting upon them." Sterling, Waltz concluded, can "do no more than describe problems and insist that the world's survival requires their solution."[22]

Yet in *Theory of International Politics*, a book which made him the undisputed dean of positivist theorizing about war and peace, Waltz quietly came close to doing just that. In this book he made the normative end of great-war avoidance even more explicit, a concession apparently lost on his supporters and critics alike.

Waltz brings together in his 1979 opus the theoretical ideas he had been expressing since 1964, and really, since 1954, the year he turned in his dissertation. To those who had been following his writing, therefore, *Theory of International Politics* contained nothing much new.[23] To those who had not, the book offered a *tour de force*. Waltz expressed in the book three main objectives: to define what theory is, and is not; to present his theory; and to suggest how his theory can apply to the current state of international affairs.

"Much pointless work is done," Waltz stated, because would-be theorists of international relations fail to grasp the basic rules of theorizing. The most basic rule of all, as Waltz had argued in 1959, is that reductionism is simply not allowed. To theorize about phenomena, such as the conflicts and wars among states, is not to describe conflicts, wars, and states, and then make

22. Review of Richard Sterling's *Macropolitics: International Relations in a Global Society* (New York: Knopf, 1974), in the *American Political Science Review* 70 (June, 1976), p. 297.
23. To summarize what has mostly been noted: chapter 2 derives considerably from chapters 3 and 4 of *Man, the State and War*. Chapter 3 is taken from the Polsby and Greenstein text. Chapters 7 and 8 include much from his 1964 article on bipolarity, and sections of chapter 8 repeat verbatim his 1967 *Journal of International Affairs* piece. Moreover, the first part of chapter 5 is borrowed from his 1967 book on foreign policy and democratic politics.

generalizations. True theory is based upon an abstract idea, a leap of logic, that explains the deep reasons for a phenomenon entirely apart from the elements involved within it. To theorize about a structure in international politics, Waltz insisted, one "must omit the attributes and the relations of the units," and instead concentrate upon the unique attributes of the structure itself. This distinction is revealed, as Waltz showed, in the difference between the two statements "He is a troublemaker" and "He makes trouble." The second statement relies upon the volition of the actor, and hence is not theoretical. The first statement, by postulating something essential about "him," indicates the theoretical leap: he may make trouble, or he may not, at any given moment, but there is something about "him" that inclines him toward the former.[24]

Waltz cited as a good example of social science theorizing the field of classical microeconomics. A theory of the market pays no attention to the particular desires, interests, or policies of firms. Rather, it seeks to predict their behavior based upon the one presumption that firms will always seek to survive, rather than go bankrupt. In a market of many firms competition will be fierce and chaotic, forcing firms which might have had objectives beyond mere survival to adapt or be destroyed. In an oligopolistic market, which Waltz saw as most comparable to the international system, firms have more room to maneuver, more room for minor errors. But if they do not continue to help themselves, by seeking to increase their market share, they will be eventually forced out by other firms that do.[25]

If the desire of firms in a market is survival, then so is the desire of states in the international system. "I assume," Waltz announced, in introducing his theory, "that states seek to ensure their survival."[26] Like stag hunters,

---

24. *Theory of International Politics*, pp. 5, 12, 60–61.

25. Ibid., pp. 71–72, 88–92. Waltz employs the microeconomic comparison more thoroughly here than he had in previous writings. As Charles Jones shows, Waltz's reliance upon the microeconomic model of an "anarchical" realm of market competition is flawed, because it is precisely the survival of the liberal state in the anarchy of global politics that allows for the perpetuation of market economics — as indeed Waltz implies in chapter five of *Man, the State and War*. Firms compete within a market economy provided for them by powerful liberal states. See Barry Buzan, Richard Little, and Charles Jones, *The Logic of Anarchy: Neorealism to Structural Realism* (New York: Columbia University Press, 1993), pp. 194–96.

26. Ibid., p. 91.

states seek to survive in a world where nothing above can protect them. International politics is therefore anarchical: this is the "ordering principle" of the structure of the international system. Like the stag hunt, this anarchy is a "bounded realm," which is to say that it can be analyzed in and of itself, without reference to other structures or systems. What is happening elsewhere cannot matter to the stag hunter, who finds himself within an enclosed realm that offers him two choices: survival or death. The same is (more obviously) true with states, which deal with one another exclusively within the anarchical realm of world politics.[27]

The second part of Waltz's theory, deriving from the first, is that because of the irreducible quest for survival among all states, they are "functionally undifferentiated" for the purposes of the theory. In other words, states can be regarded as "like units," survival-seeking entities, irrespective of their political and cultural characteristics. A microeconomist might see perfectly well that the firms within the market she is assessing have very different characteristics. But for the purposes of her theory, all that matters is their desire to survive. Because all firms, whatever their differences, possess this one motivation, it is sufficient to categorize them as alike. And indeed, the pressures of survival *force* them to become more alike, as struggling firms adopt the strategies of successful ones in order not to die.

As Waltz had shown in *Man, the State and War*, the same process occurs among states. States may differ in every imaginable respect, but they do share the one impulse of national survival. In the competition to stay alive, they begin to resemble one another, something that happens quickly and intensively during times of crisis and war. Thus the abandonment by the socialist parties of Europe of their ideological commitment in 1914; thus the enthusiastic adoption by the purportedly revolutionary Soviet Union of conservative, *Realpolitik* diplomacy. The first element of Waltz's theory is the bounded realm of anarchy; the second is the fundamental undifferentiation of states, all doing whatever they think is best to achieve survival.[28]

The dynamic of international politics, deriving from these first two theoretical propositions, is the balance of power. "If there is any distinctively political theory of international politics," Waltz wrote, "balance-of-power theory is it." States, Waltz reiterated, are undifferentiated actors "who, at a

---

27. Ibid., pp. 89–93.
28. Ibid., pp. 97–107.

minimum, seek their own preservation and, at a maximum, drive for universal domination." Because this is happening in an anarchical realm, states are terrified by the prospects of failure. This fear, Waltz continued, "stimulates states to behave in ways that tend toward the creation of balances of power." *Pace* Morgenthau — and in contradiction to his later argument — leaders need not deliberately pursue a balance; it will happen, whether they pursue it or not, because they are forced to contrive one by the dictates of the anarchical structure.[29]

The dynamics of the balance of power are affected by two objective criteria: the number of great powers in the system, and their military and economic capabilities. Just as a market with many firms, some weak and some strong, will be chaotic and convulsive, Waltz argues, an international system with many states struggling to maintain their power tends toward conflict and war. In chapter 8, Waltz reiterated his 1967 argument to show why bipolarity is the most stable kind of balance-of-power. The bipolar nature of contemporary international politics had established a "duopoly," a system run by two powers, comparable in this sense to a market dominated by two firms. Duopolistic systems are stable. Duopolists need not worry about appeasing their allies; this lessens the likelihood of a regional war escalating into great war, such as occurred in the summer of 1914. It is simple for duopolists to assess danger: they just have to monitor the military and economic power of one other nation. "In the great-power politics of bipolar worlds, who is a danger to whom is never in doubt."[30] The stability of bipolar politics diminishes the chances of great war and increases international order and routine, allowing states to pay more attention to domestic problems and peripheral foreign policy concerns.

In the latter part of *Theory of International Politics*, and especially in the concluding chapter, Waltz's affinity for the Cold War bipolar system becomes evident. Bipolarity allows the two superpowers to establish a regime of nuclear deterrence easily, making the outbreak of any major war between the two sides unlikely. It allows them to discourage their allies from embarking on provocative, destabilizing adventures, as both superpowers are strong enough to risk angering an ally without having to worry about upset-

---

29. Ibid., pp. 116–21.
30. Ibid., pp. 161–72. The quotation is from page 170.

ting the balance of power.[31] It gives them the time and energy to deal with transnational economic and environmental problems that a hard-pressed state within a convulsive multipolar system would never be able to worry about. All of these things are possible without the widespread rebellion and conflict that the imposition of a world state would invite.

In his concluding chapter, entitled "The Management of International Affairs," Waltz suggested that the bipolar is the best of all worlds. The range of possible international systems can be put onto a spectrum. At one end is an emerging array of many would-be great powers, which is the most dangerous international condition imaginable — as Waltz, following Hobbes, had noted in *Man, the State and War*. As the number of powers competing with one another decreases, the international system becomes more stable, more orderly. For one who regards international stability and order — i.e., the absence of great-power war — as paramount, the fewer great powers, the better. The ideal, according to this way of thinking, is indeed a powerful world state: a global Leviathan, falling at the other extreme of the international system spectrum.

Waltz stopped short of this. The risks involved in the continuing anarchy of a bipolar system are clear: "with competition unregulated," he admitted, "war occasionally occurs."[32] But Waltz finds the eventual war that will occur in an anarchical system to be less objectionable than the certain and immediate violence, possibly escalating into total war, that would accompany the formation of a world state. "The prospect of world government," he stated simply, "would be an invitation to prepare for world civil war."[33] Economic ideologies, ethnic grievances, religious missions, raw power lust — political impulses that the two superpowers had successfully repressed in the name of bipolar preeminence — would reemerge, intensified by the total stakes associated with the political and ideological orientation of a world state. The domination of the two superpowers led to injustice and the stifling of political aspirations around the world. In a thermonuclear age, this was a worthwhile price to pay. "If might decides," Waltz wrote, "then bloody struggles over right can more easily be avoided."[34] The management of world affairs,

---

31. An example here is the Suez crisis of 1956; Waltz's opinion here can be contrasted profitably to Morgenthau's criticism of U.S. policy.
32. *Theory of International Politics*, p. 195.
33. Ibid., p. 112.
34. Ibid.

made possible by the bipolar structure of the international system, could keep such bloody struggles in check indefinitely. In presenting a theory of international politics based upon a structural assessment of the balance of power, Waltz was at the same time articulating a plan for great-power peace and global management. His elegant conception of bipolarity allowed him to entertain both positions.

Waltz's advocacy of the bipolar system, together with his ominous critiques of alternatives to it, reflected his normative interest in the perpetuation of peace between the two superpowers. By explaining at some length why bipolarity makes for a stable international system, by warning of — not simply commenting upon — the dangers of both multipolarity and the world state, and by referring in his conclusion to the *management* of international affairs, Waltz revealed himself to have a decided normative interest in his subject. He was not merely explaining phenomena, as an astrophysicist might explain variations in planetary orbits: Waltz favored a particular outcome. The astrophysicist does not morally care whether the orbits of Neptune and Pluto intersect or not; he is exclusively concerned with the problem of explaining why they do. Waltz does morally care whether bipolarity leads to a stable international order, which is why he extolled bipolarity's virtues. Had Waltz concluded from his theorizing that bipolarity was unstable, more likely to lead to war, and in these respects inferior to multi- or unipolarity, he would have written a very different book.[35] Thinking about this possibility for more than a moment allows one to see how deeply normative concerns influence a social science occupied with the question of war and peace in the nuclear age.

"For the sake of stability, or peace, or whatever," Waltz wrote, the bipolar system is preferable to alternative orders.[36] No passage in *Theory of International Politics* reveals more clearly than this one how he had consciously moved away from the more dispassionate stance adopted in *Man, the State and War*. Waltz veered toward overt normative argumentation throughout his 1979 book, and understandably so: for his topic, the avoidance of great-power war in the thermonuclear age, is of the greatest moral importance.[37]

---

35. On this point, see Richard Rosecrance, "Reply to Waltz," *International Organization* 36 (Summer 1982), p. 684.

36. *Theory of International Politics*, p. 161.

37. On the tension between normative and analytical approaches to war, see Stanley

But he catches himself; he was careful to imply and suggest rather than to advocate outright. This balancing act became contrived, as is shown in the sentence above.[38] In considering Waltz's self-conscious struggle to avoid taking an overt normative position, the expression "for the sake of whatever" speaks for itself.

Further Retreat: The Spread of Nuclear Weapons

In *Man, the State and War* Waltz sought to advance beyond his predecessors' writing about international politics and war in two ways. He believed that the earlier Realists had taken a too atheoretical, normative approach to their subject, that they were too willing to advocate particular policies rather than analyze their topic objectively. It was time, he argued, to develop a social science of international politics that moved away from moral judgment and toward dispassionate explanation. Furthermore, he hoped to develop an understanding of international politics that could explain peace and war by referring to the structure of the international system rather than the desires and policies of individuals and states. Such an understanding would allow scholars to generalize about the main currents of power politics without resorting to reductionist causation or historical particularism.

In *Theory of International Politics*, Waltz tacitly reincorporated normative ideas into his writing, in particular the moral claim that bipolarity was better than multipolarity or unipolarity because it was less likely to foment great war. It was a heuristic more than a methodological concession: it had to do more with Waltz's own objectivity than with the merits of his theoretical argument. Still, it did signify an important departure from the strong position Waltz had taken in 1959.

It would be harder to claim, however, that with this move toward normative argumentation Waltz thereby also renounced his belief that structure plays a more profound role in establishing the conditions for war and peace than do the "sub-systemic" actions of individuals or states. He himself desired a bipolar world, and in this sense he must be asked what the reasons for

---

Hoffmann, "International Relations: The Long Road to Theory," *World Politics* 11 (April 1958), p. 376; Smith, *Realist Thought from Weber to Kissinger*, p. 143.

38. The Spread of Nuclear Weapons: More May Be Better," *Adelphi Paper number 171* (London: International Institute for Strategic Studies, 1981), p. 1.

writing a book extolling the virtues of bipolarity are if its readers are to do nothing about it. These objections, important as they are, do not disprove his structural thesis, however. Waltz is certainly entitled to argue that the structure of international politics is indifferent to his beliefs and the beliefs of his readers, even if this might lead to a certain intellectual pointlessness.

Any claim Waltz might have wanted to make about the predominance of third-image over first-image factors in *Theory of International Politics*, however, disappeared into thin air with the publication, in 1981, of his essay on the spread of nuclear weapons. In this work Waltz argued that the first-image factor of nuclear fear wields a profound effect upon international politics, even more profound, as will be shown, than the bipolar structure.

The International Institute for Strategic Studies, located in London, established its "Adelphi Papers" occasional article series in the 1960s. Waltz's Adelphi Paper number 171, titled "The Spread of Nuclear Weapons: More May be Better," published in 1981, continues to stand as the series' most famous piece. Waltz's spread argument sent the course of structural realism, now often called "neorealism," off into an unexpected direction. It also revealed how Waltz could not keep the discrepancy of nuclear war down forever. He had to deal with it, and in doing so he dismantled important philosophical elements of his Realist theory.

Waltz opened his argument not by contending that a spread of nuclear weapons ought to occur, but rather that it was going to occur. His case could then proceed from the question: "What will this do the world?"[39] By framing his article in this fashion, Waltz was ostensibly avoiding making a normative

---

39. This is a delicate point. Waltz may (and does) claim that the spread argument is simply analytical, that he takes as an assumption the spread of nuclear weapons and merely seeks to predict its likely effect upon international politics. To judge this claim one might put it within its broader intellectual history — in other words, we can assess Waltz's claim of moral neutrality by seeing how that fits in with his other writings. I believe that Waltz's normative advocacy of duopolistic management in *Theory of International Politics* suggests that he wants to see a spread of nuclear weapons, and is not simply interested in describing its effects, because the outcome of the spread, in his view, is international stability: the very goal he lauds in 1979. If he had concluded that the outcome of the spread of nuclear weapons would be international instability, Waltz's claim to be strictly descriptive would be more credible, though in my judgment had he reached this conclusion he would never have written the paper. My thinking on this point is heavily influenced by Robert Jervis, *System Effects: Complexity in Political and Social Life* (Princeton: Princeton University Press, 1997), pp. 118–24.

case for the spread of nuclear weapons, even though, as becomes apparent, that was precisely what he wanted to do.

The Cold War system, he stated, has shown a "high ability" to "absorb changes and to contain conflicts and hostility." Two factors explain this stability. First, of course, is the system's bipolarity. The second is the existence of nuclear weapons. The fear of nuclear war, a unit-level phenomenon, did not simply reinforce bipolarity, but in fact acted as an independent causal factor to discourage the great powers from going to war.

Nuclear weapons create stability primarily because they give a decisive advantage to a nation defending itself over a nation wanting to attack. Waltz listed three reasons why they make conquest difficult.[40] First, the existence of second-strike arsenals makes it risky to attack any nuclear-armed nation, for the simple, obvious reason that the possible benefits accruing from conquest are going to be outweighed by the unique costs of suffering a retaliatory nuclear attack. This immutable reality will make all states cautious when considering aggressive action. Second, the condition of nuclear deterrence between two nuclear-armed nations makes forward military strategies, for waging an offensive war to defeat a possible aggressor, unnecessary. Russia acted offensively in the opening days of the First World War for fear that Germany was about to overrun its weak forward defenses. Nations armed with many thermonuclear missiles never have to worry about that possibility. Third, nations fight harder to defend their own territory than they do to conquer another, which strengthens the nuclear deterrent. Because nuclear technology provides a very reliable form of retaliatory weapon, it intensifies the difficulties always inherent in conquest.

These observations led Waltz to a general claim about the effect of nuclear weaponry upon sub-systemic actors, i.e., people and states. The effect is existential, which is to say that it comes from the very existence of nuclear weaponry, rather than from the political situation of the moment or the strategies of the different countries involved. In the days before nuclear weaponry, nations could embark upon war "knowing that even in defeat their suffering would be limited. Calculations about nuclear war," he wrote,

> are differently made. Nuclear worlds call for and encourage a different
> kind of reasoning. If countries armed with nuclear weapons go to war,

---

40. He actually lists four, but numbers one and two appear to me as two ways of saying the same thing.

they do so knowing that their suffering may be unlimited. Of course, it also may not be. But that is not the kind of uncertainty that encourages anyone to use force. In a conventional world, one is uncertain about winning or losing. In a nuclear world, one is uncertain about surviving or being annihilated. . . .

The expected effect of the deterrent [he continues] achieves an easy clarity because wide margins of error in estimates of probable damage do not matter. Do we expect to lose one city or two, two cities or ten? When these are the pertinent questions, we stop thinking about running risks and start worrying about how to avoid them.[41]

For Waltz, the nuclear lessons of the Cold War are clear. The very existence of nuclear weapons discouraged the two superpowers from going to war, a condition that owed its success to no particular strategy, other than the blunt one of assured second strike retaliation. Nuclear deterrents give such tremendous advantages to the nation defending itself that a war of conquest is virtually unthinkable. "Contemplating the nuclear past," he concluded, "gives grounds for hoping that the world will survive if further nuclear powers join today's six or seven."[42]

Common wisdom, along with international policy, opposed the spread of nuclear weapons. That more and more states, many with belligerent foreign policies, would get their hands on thermonuclear bombs seemed an obvious recipe for disaster. Waltz carefully unveiled his response to this conventional view. Highly unstable states, he agreed, ought not to acquire nuclear weaponry — but such states, by definition, are the least likely to be able to do so. Developing a serious nuclear arsenal requires years of government planning, massive expenditure, and a political order stable enough to see the project through over decades. The kinds of states that ought not to have nuclear weapons, Waltz maintained — if a bit tautologically — are precisely those that are not going to able to get them.

What about stable, serious, but weak and militaristic states? Could not a small pariah regime dedicate all of its efforts to getting the bomb? Waltz also dealt with this, highly relevant, objection. States, whatever their ethnic or ideological makeup, seek to survive. Because of this, a weak state that de-

---

41. "Spread of Nuclear Weapons," pp. 6–7.
42. Ibid., p. 10.

velops nuclear weapons is going to be even more cautious than a strong state, for any misstep on its part will mean certain destruction. A non-nuclear nation like Vietnam could take on the United States for years, and eventually defeat it. A small nuclear nation would be running considerably higher risks by going to war against a nuclear superpower. "Nuclear weapons induce caution, especially in weak states."[43]

Finally, Waltz addressed the irrefutable argument that wars among nuclear states are not impossible. The spread of nuclear weapons, he maintained, makes wars among nuclear powers highly unlikely — yet anything is possible within the anarchical realm of international politics. But what would a nuclear war between two small nuclear states entail? The superpowers would, he claimed, have every reason to avoid becoming embroiled in it — as opposed to an escalating conventional war, for example. Other states would steer clear as well. Such a war would likely remain isolated to the two warring parties. "If such states use nuclear weapons," Waltz candidly asserted, "the world will not end."[44]

The development of several regimes of nuclear deterrence among smaller states, therefore, is likely to create a stable and peaceful world; or at least one more peaceful than a world characterized by many conventional rivalries. In the worst case, a nuclear war between two smaller parties would be immensely destructive for them but unlikely to trigger a global war. But the worst case was not necessarily the most likely one. The experience of the Cold War, Waltz insisted, ought to make students of international politics *more*, not less, optimistic about the future: what sense, he asked, does it make to point to the dread of war induced by nuclear fear as a reason to oppose a nuclear spread?[45] The spread of nuclear weapons would create defensive, conservative, and secure states, assured of their long-term survival and mindful of the extreme risks associated with aggression and conquest. International politics could thereby approach the "defensive ideal": a condition in which anarchy is not eliminated but rather adapted to by defensive-minded states so thoroughly as to make offensive wars exceedingly irrational and hence extremely unlikely.

---

43. Ibid., p. 10.
44. Ibid., p. 13.
45. Ibid., p. 3.

Two Levels of Consistency

In "The Spread of Nuclear Weapons" Waltz diluted even further the structuralist political philosophy he had articulated in *Man, the State and War.* What explains international war and peace? Previously, it had been the anarchical structure of international politics, a force that human aspirations and fears were, in the end, helpless to overcome. Now, it was also the aversion to nuclear war, a first-image phenomenon that resided in the hearts and minds of individual people.[46]

Indeed, implicit within Waltz's 1981 essay is the suggestion that nuclear fear plays a greater role in keeping the peace than bipolarity.[47] In his articles in the 1960s and early 1970s, and then in *Theory of International Politics,* Waltz consistently made a point of mentioning that bipolar stability was enhanced, or reinforced, by nuclear fear. If bipolarity was the driving force of great-power peace, the aversion to nuclear war pushed the bipolar relationship between the United States and the Soviet Union closer to a condition of duopolistic management, approaching even a kind of informal hierarchy. Yet when discussing the political effects of nuclear fear, Waltz did not incorporate bipolarity into his argument. His powerful case for "existential deterrence" relies not at all upon bipolarity, or, if it does, he does not say so. In lauding the possibilities of the "deterrent ideal," Waltz does not show how this ideal fits within the bipolar framework, and indeed toward the end of his essay he hinted at the notion of an absolute ideal: of a world populated entirely by secure nuclear states assured of their survival and uninterested in conquest. In such a world bipolarity, multipolarity — any kind of balance of power — would become much less important than the achievement of total nuclear security by all states.

This vision perhaps explains why Waltz did not consider what effect the spread of nuclear weapons might have had upon the Cold War bipolarity he had lauded in 1979. For it is certainly conceivable that the spread of

---

46. Students of Realism who have also emphasized this point include Jack Donnelly, *Realism and International Relations* (Cambridge: Cambridge University Press, 2000), pp. 110–11, Joseph Nye, "Neorealism and Neoliberalism," *World Politics* 40 (January 1988), p. 244, and Dale Copeland, "Neorealism and the Myth of Bipolar Stability," in Benjamin Frankel, ed., *Realism: Restatements and Renewal* (London: Frank Cass, 1996), pp. 31–32 n8.

47. See Donnelly, *Realism and International Relations*, p. 118 n20.

nuclear weapons to other states would give some of them, eventually, military and economic capabilities sufficient to aspire to great-power status. Indeed, as Waltz had pointed out earlier, the one thing keeping economic powers like Japan or (West) Germany from becoming great powers was the very fact that they did not possess the military capabilities that mattered in the modern world. Had such nations, or other nascent powers, acquired nuclear weapons, it is easy to imagine some of them challenging the bipolar system. Writing from a post–Cold War perspective, it is even easier to imagine.

This omission suggests that Waltz did regard the role of nuclear fear as more important than the bipolar structure in explaining the absence of great-power war, insofar as the logical conclusion of nuclear spread — total nuclear security of all states — trumped the stability established by bipolarity.[48] If this suggestion is accepted, then his departure from structuralism is not simply substantial, but complete. To make nuclear fear the dominant factor in questions of war and peace among great powers is to abandon the decisive role played by third-image structure.

In another respect, however, Waltz's "spread" argument was entirely consistent with his earlier writing. It was consistent, namely, with his ongoing attempts to apply his theoretical understanding of international politics toward the normative end of great-power peace. In *Man, the State and War* Waltz eschewed the normative tradition within the study of international relations in favor of a descriptive, positivist means of analysis. A policy based upon his new structural assessment of international politics, he wrote at the end of his first book, "is neither moral nor immoral, but embodies merely a reasoned response to the world around us."[49] Yet almost immediately Waltz began to retreat from this dispassionate position, implying regularly in his writings in the 1960s and early 1970s that bipolarity was not simply a "reasoned" conception of international politics for the purposes of academic understanding but rather the surest way to achieve great-power peace in the nuclear age. This retreat culminated in the concluding chapter to *Theory of International Politics*, in which Waltz straightforwardly argued that the bipolar management of international politics would more likely prevent great-power war than any imaginable alternative.

---

48. On this also see R. Harrison Wagner, "What was Bipolarity?" *International Organization* 47 (Winter 1993), pp. 83–84, 88, and Richard Ned Lebow, "The Long Peace, the End of the Cold War, and the Failure of Realism," *International Organization* 48 (Spring, 1994), p. 254.
49. *Man, the State and War*, p. 238.

If Waltz's fundamental aim as a scholar was to conceive of international orders most likely to preserve great-power peace, then his willingness to depart from his earlier political philosophy in his "spread" article becomes entirely explicable. Thinking normatively, Waltz contended (and still contends) that the political formation of a serious world state is likely to unleash severe and sustained conflict among societies eager to dominate — or avoid being dominated by — that state, leading to a kind of "international" civil war. In a world riddled with thermonuclear weaponry, global civil warfare could well mean planetary nuclear destruction. If that is so, then anarchy ought to be the fate of international politics for the indefinite future — it is to be preferred to the uncertain and volatile prospect of world-state formation in a thermonuclear context.

The dispassionate analyst of world politics might agree that anarchy will prevail over the foreseeable future, but he would stop there: whether anarchy leads to peace or war is outside his interest. For Waltz, on the other hand, the great objective was to ascertain how peace can be maintained *indefinitely* under such conditions. Bipolarity, especially if it is managed carefully, can make peace likely between the two great powers. Pervading Waltz's 1981 work, however, was the problem not of superpower peace *per se* but the danger that regional conflict might destabilize international relations. The greatest challenge to peaceful bipolar management is a major showdown between regional powers allied to one or the other superpower. This, Waltz showed, is a problem that can be best solved by the spread of nuclear weapons. Nuclear-armed states will be much less likely to go to war with one another, and, if they do, the superpowers will much more concerned to stay out of the war, and indeed perhaps cooperate to prevent it from escalating.

By advocating the spread of nuclear weapons to regional powers, therefore, Waltz further advanced his Realist agenda for great-power peace at the expense of theoretical consistency. His normative case for bipolar management signified an important departure from the political philosophy of *Man, the State and War*, insofar as it diluted Waltz's own claim for scientific dispassion and also suggested that unit-level action ("management") could have an important effect on the likelihood of great-power war. But Waltz really showed his cards when he came forward with the spread of nuclear weapons thesis. He discerned that a main threat to bipolar peace was the possibility of major regional war. He concluded that the best way to prevent such war over the indefinite future, given the problems associated with the world state, was for small states to acquire second-strike nuclear arsenals. To support this conclusion, Waltz had to accept not only the historical view that the first-image phenomenon of nuclear fear was decisive in keeping peace between the two superpowers, but also the more undermining idea that it would keep peace between other powers outside the realm of structural bipolarity. Placing before himself a choice between philosophical consistency and a program for great-power peace, in 1981 Waltz decisively opted for the latter.[50]

Recurrent Patterns

A basic pattern emerges from our consideration of how three political philosophers of American Realism adapted to the revolutionary implications of nuclear technology, one that transcends the distinctions drawn between "classical" and "neo" Realism. Niebuhr, Morgenthau, and Waltz all gravitated toward the normative goal of great-power peace in the thermonuclear age. They reached this conclusion in varying ways. Niebuhr rather suddenly determined in 1957 that nuclear war was unwinnable and hence no longer a just *ultima ratio*; thermonuclear war became for him the unambiguous moral evil of collective power politics, but he found no way to slay this evil other than muddling through the Cold War. Morgenthau, one senses, entertained the idea well before Niebuhr, but he remained ambiguous about it in his public writings until 1961. Once having made his decision, however, he announced in a more dramatic fashion the death of the nation state and the imperative of world government. Like Niebuhr, though, Morgenthau only hinted at the way such a state could develop.

Waltz's experience was different. Without the novel terrors of Cold War crises to move him, he tacitly advanced a normative program of nuclear peace by gradually incorporating it into his theoretical writings on neorealism. His "spread of nuclear weapons" article represented a more obvious departure from his original political philosophy, but such was Waltz's dominance in the field, following his 1979 opus, and such, perhaps, was the relative peacefulness of international politics at this time, that the departure

---

50. Steven Forde notes that Realists have traditionally believed that the pursuit of peace is an obvious goal of their work; he argues that their mission has been less idealistic. Waltz's experience then goes the other way around. See Forde, "International Realism and the Science of Politics: Thucydides, Machiavelli, and Neorealism," *International Studies Quarterly* 39 (1995), pp. 155–58.

seems to have gone largely unnoticed.[51] Waltz has never uttered the kind of things Niebuhr and Morgenthau were saying in the early 1960s, though. Niebuhr and Morgenthau came around to admitting that nuclear weapons had devastated their worldviews; Waltz has not.

But in a fundamental sense the same thing occurred to all three Realists. Each had become famous for articulating a political philosophy that regarded great-power war as a tragic inevitability of international power politics. Each of them came to reconsider this philosophy in the face of the overwhelming normative end of great-power nuclear peace. All three eventually chose to favor an atheoretical program for great-power war avoidance over philosophical consistency.

There was, then, no "paradigm shift." The specter of nuclear war that sapped the energy from the old realists never went away; Waltz tried to exclude it from *Man, the State and War,* but like a shadow it followed him wherever he went.[52] Unwilling to renounce the new worldview that had elevated him to the very top of his profession, working during a time when the prospect of nuclear war had become less immediate, Waltz tacitly returned to the position of his forefathers when it came to the question of great-power war. Niebuhr and Morgenthau combined a normative determination to avoid World War Three with a Realist pessimism about radical solutions to that problem. Waltz, as we have seen, has done just the same.

---

51. Though see Daniel Deudney, "Dividing Realism: Security Materialism vs. Structural Realism on Nuclear Security and Proliferation," *Security Studies* 2 (Spring/Summer 1993), pp. 7–36. Many of Waltz's severest critics — Barry Buzan, Richard Little, Richard Ashley, Richard Cox, Alexander Wendt — avoid the topic of nuclear weapons.

52. As Kuhn put it: "the defenders of traditional theory and procedure can almost always point to problems that its new rival has not solved but for their view are no problems at all." I think this insight explains Waltz's circuitous approach to nuclear weapons before 1981. See Thomas Kuhn, *The Structure of Scientific Revolutions* (Chicago: University of Chicago press, 1962), p. 156.

Conclusion

> . . . all the parties in a serious crisis have an overriding incentive
> to ask themselves one question: How can we get out of this mess
> without nuclear weapons exploding?
>
> — Kenneth Waltz[1]

      To advance his ideas about the establishment of great-power peace, Kenneth Waltz diluted the structural purity of *Theory of International Politics*, arguing that the careful management of bipolar politics by Cold War leaders could create a stable duopoly, one that indeed could approach a hierarchical order. This argument signified a retreat from his more rigorous thesis in *Man, the State and War* in two related ways: it indicated that Waltz himself believed that normative ideas (his ideas) ought to affect international politics; and it suggested that the actions of individuals, at the unit level, could determine whether the great powers went to war or remained at peace.

      As important as these concessions were, however, in the end they did not undermine his basic structural conception. Waltz might well admit that maintaining a completely disinterested approach to international politics was more difficult than he had imagined, and that he had tacitly incorporated a blueprint for stability and peace within his theoretical writings; he has admitted, frequently, that unit-level behavior can shape the course of international relations in the short term. Neither of these concessions, however, revoke the primary role of structure in determining the long-term fate of great powers. They are weaknesses in his case, weaknesses that will be shown, below, to have important implications, but they do not by themselves permit one to contend that Waltz's theory is not fundamentally structural.

---

1. "Nuclear Myths and Political Realities" *American Political Science Review* 84 (September, 1990), p. 740.

Much more damaging is the spread of nuclear weapons thesis. This is a major concession, because for the sake of contriving a long-term plan for international order, Waltz admits that a unit-level phenomenon, the fear of nuclear war, plays a *decisive* role in determining whether great powers, along with other states, go to war. As we have seen, the logic of Waltz's spread argument indeed suggests that nuclear fear plays a larger role in the maintenance of international peace than does the bipolar structure he had championed in 1979.

Waltz has continued to maintain that the controlled spread of nuclear weapons is a positive good, a force for international peace.[2] His argument is based upon two premises: first, that the spread of nuclear weapons is unlikely to increase the possibility of nuclear war, and in particular great-power nuclear war; second, that the spread of nuclear weapons is an optimal plan for international peace because more radical plans to establish international control over nuclear weapons, or even a world state to monopolize or abolish them, cannot be attained, because of the durability of international anarchy. The weakness of the first premise, a hypothesis about the future, can be shown by questioning the validity of its historical assumptions. The second premise is much harder to refute, because, for the reasons Waltz and his predecessors have enumerated, the building of a serious world state is an extremely difficult and dangerous prospect. But the logic of Waltz's argumentation does not rule out the attainment of a world state. Indeed, it points in the opposite direction.

Historical and Theoretical Weaknesses in the Spread of Nuclear Weapons Thesis

In his debate about the spread argument with Waltz, Scott Sagan reveals how organizational theory, buttressed by Sagan's seminal accounts of nuclear command and control failures during the Cold War, suggests that future nuclear states are unlikely to establish control over their nuclear arsenals as easily as Waltz assumes. Many recent works on the nuclear history of the Cold War bolster Sagan's thesis, as they show, contrary to Waltz's view, that

---

2. Waltz has stuck to his original argument in the second edition of his debate with Scott Sagan, defending in particular the decisions by India and Pakistan to acquire nuclear weaponry. See *The Spread of Nuclear Weapons: A Debate Renewed* (New York: Norton, 2003), pp. 109–24.

many military and civilian leaders in the United States, the Soviet Union, and China were willing, and even keen, to wage nuclear war despite the certainty of nuclear retaliation. Nuclear peace was not predetermined once the major Cold War powers acquired basic arsenals, as Waltz seems to imply. Both the accidental and deliberate waging of nuclear war came close to occurring on many occasions during the Cold War; the determined actions of a few leaders to prevent nuclear war, together with the simple luck that not one of the many false alarms precipitated a real attack, prevented nuclear holocaust. Waltz's contention that nuclear peace during the Cold War was easy to sustain has been shown by historians to be incorrect.[3]

This is a very serious blow, because, unlike Waltz's theoretical work, the spread argument is openly based upon his reading of Cold War history. While Waltz is rightly able to contend that his theory of international politics is a product of deductive reasoning, and hence not to be proven or disproven by a given historical episode, he can make no such claim about the spread thesis. As a "unit level" analysis, it depends upon the historical record, not upon deductive abstraction. If historians demonstrate, by pointing to a large amount of new archival evidence, that nuclear peace was more difficult to sustain than Waltz believed in 1981, then he is bound to revise his thesis, or, alternatively, he can assert that it was easy to avoid nuclear war whatever the historians have shown.

As Sagan has argued, the lessons of the Cold War suggest that future nuclear states will have a difficult time avoiding nuclear war indefinitely. The United States and the Soviet Union came close to intentionally starting a nuclear war on several occasions, seriously close in October 1962, and in several other instances a major accident in command and control almost led to the accidental outbreak of World War Three. Yet these two superpowers possessed the most modern means of command and control available. They were separated by large land masses and vast oceans. They were not, during the major nuclear crises, in contention over a piece of territory both

---

3. Scott Sagan and Kenneth Waltz, *The Spread of Nuclear Weapons: A Debate* (New York: Norton, 1995), pp. 56–61, 78–80. Dozens of recent historical works demonstrate the precariousness of nuclear peace during the Cold War, and in particular the crisis period 1957–62. Two representative works are Campbell Craig, *Destroying the Village: Eisenhower and Thermonuclear War* (New York: Columbia University Press, 1998) and Timothy Naftali and Alexandr Fursenko, *One Hell of a Gamble: Khrushchev, Castro, and Kennedy* (New York: Norton, 1997).

claimed as its own or an issue that threatened the basic political standing of one or the other power. How likely is it that rival nuclear states of the future, who may share highly disputed borders, who may struggle over core territories, who may not be able to afford elaborate command and control systems, will forever be able to avoid a deliberate or accidental nuclear exchange?[4]

The Myth of Immutable Anarchy

Underlying Waltz's endorsement of the spread of nuclear weapons is his presumption that anarchy will endure into the foreseeable future. Waltz might well admit that nuclear peace is harder to achieve than he had originally asserted, but still argue that a controlled spread of nuclear weapons systems remains the best means of preventing great-power war, because the serious world state one would require to prevent such war indefinitely is unattainable.

But Waltz's contention that anarchy is effectively immutable, like the spread of nuclear weapons proposal, is made unpersuasive by comparing his own arguments to the unfolding of recent events. Waltz's core philosophical presumption, the idea upon which his theory of international politics is based, was that the actions and intentions of people, at the unit level of analysis, cannot in the end *explain* the general course of great-power politics. "So long as one leaves the structure unaffected it is not possible," he stated, "for changes in the intentions and the actions of particular actors to produce desirable outcomes or to avoid undesirable ones."[5] The broad unfolding of great-power relations, the recurrence or avoidance of major, systemic war, is in the end determined by structural factors: the composition of the international system (the number of great powers); and the relative capabilities of each great power. This is the irreducible core of Waltz's theoretical understanding of international politics: take it away and there is nothing theoretical left.

This core presumption becomes, for Waltz, unsustainable when one considers his own retreats from it and then adds to these the unusual history of recent great-power politics. As has been shown, Waltz has conceded that

---

4. See Sagan, in *The Spread of Nuclear Weapons: A Debate Renewed*, pp. 168–77.
5. .*Man, the State and War*, p. 105.

unit-level phenomena affect international politics in three ways. The normative arguments underlying his own writing indicate that he believes that ideas, or at least his ideas, can have an effect upon questions of great-power war and peace. His case for the bipolar management of international politics also reveals that he thinks national leaders, by perceiving (or ignoring) the benefits of systemic stability, can wield a similar effect. The most important of these three concessions is Waltz's view that nuclear fear played a crucial role in preventing World War Three, and that it therefore can prevent other international rivalries from descending into war.

Until the early 1990s, Waltz would have been able to hold that these concessions were secondary to the enduring bipolar structure of international politics, the structure that had become, or so he argued in 1979, unusually stable and fixed. Indeed, he made this very point in a 1988 article, "War in Neorealist Theory."[6] But with the demise of the Soviet Union, and with it the bipolar structure of international politics, such an argument was no longer possible. Bipolar stability, as of 1991, was evidently not as stable and strong as he had contended: in fact, it had become so weak that it collapsed without triggering the great-power war that is supposed to accompany systemic changes in international politics.[7]

If bipolar stability was not as robust as Waltz (and everybody else) had assumed, then what else could have prevented the United States and the Soviet Union from going to war during their 45-year confrontation — and what, furthermore, stopped Soviet leaders from embarking upon aggression and war rather than simply allowing their nation to die? The answer is obvious and inescapable: nuclear fear must have played the primary role. The fear of nuclear war, and the corresponding determination to find some way to prevent one from happening, can manifest itself as popular sentiment, as an articulated scholarly argument, or as the underlying policy of national leaders. One can argue about the relative importance of each of these manifestations, but one point is irrefutable: they are all unit-level phenomena. Waltz stated before the end of the Cold War that the long peace was ex-

---

6. War in Neorealist Theory," *Journal of Interdisciplinary History* 18 (September 1988), p. 628.

7. The standard contemporary argument that great-power war accompanies systemic change is Robert Gilpin, *War and Change in World Politics* (New York: Cambridge University Press, 1981).

plained by the structural factor of bipolar stability and the unit-level factor of nuclear fear. After 1991, only nuclear fear remains.[8]

The primacy of nuclear fear in explaining the peaceful course and resolution of the Cold War undermines the claim made by Waltz, and other Realists, that anarchy cannot be overcome in the near term. Nuclear fear is a unit-level phenomenon, an idea that exists in the minds of people, yet, as we have seen, Waltz's own argumentation shows that it must have played the primary role in permitting a structural shift in international politics to occur without an accompanying great-power war. If a unit-level phenomenon is powerful enough to permit such an unprecedented occasion in the history of international politics, then it is difficult to see how the Realist can simply rule out as impossible the suggestion that it could be the impetus for overcoming anarchy. Attaining an effective global state remains an unimaginably huge task, not to mention an "invitation to global civil war," and it is easy to come up with any number of staggeringly difficult obstacles that would prevent its achievement. But the primary role of nuclear fear in facilitating structural change devastates the core neorealist implication that a world state is practically impossible. The debate becomes one of subsystemic conjecture: whether, in other words, the foreseeable problems associated with continuing anarchy are likely to be better or worse than those associated with the establishment of global governance. This is a serious argument, but one about which structural theory can say little.

What, according to the Realist, could facilitate the building of a serious world state? Niebuhr and Morgenthau agreed: the fear of nuclear war could do it. Nuclear fear could overcome anarchy because the outcome of a thermonuclear war threatens human survival, and the desire to be rid of this fear — the longing "innate in all men," Morgenthau wrote, "for self-

---

8. This is not to reject Waltz's bipolar stability argument *in toto*; I believe that his argument that bipolarity is more stable than multipolarity is a strong one, and would go further to say that it is probably the best theoretical explanation of why the two Cold War powers did not go to war before the late 1950s, and that it reinforced the primary factor of nuclear fear for awhile afterward. The peaceful demise of the USSR, however, disproves the claim of bipolar stability's preeminence in as obvious a way as can be imagined. I have yet to see how Waltz acknowledges this. A recent and comprehensive discussion of neorealism and the end of the Cold War is Margarita H. Petrova, "The End of the Cold War: A Battle or Bridging Ground Between Rationalist and Ideational Approaches in International Relations?"*European Journal of International Relations* 9 (March 2003), esp. pp. 117–129.

preservation" — is, in the traditional Realist understanding of political change, what establishes communities and forms states. If people can decide to act upon this fear, as Niebuhr, Morgenthau, and, effectively, Waltz believe they can, then the building of a world state, of a new Leviathan, in order to eliminate the threat of thermonuclear holocaust is a Realist possibility.

But the stakes of such a transformation are high. Why should anyone prefer the colossal risks of world-state formation over the familiar continuation of anarchical international politics? There are two answers to this question. The first is that simple statistical probability shows that the continuation of anarchy and of nuclear deterrence will sooner or later result in war, thermonuclear war. In the long term deterrence is bound to fail: to predict that it will succeed forever, never once collapsing into a nuclear war, is to engage in a utopian and ahistorical kind of thinking totally contrary to traditional Realist philosophy, as well to defy the irrefutable logic of infinite probability. When it fails, the ensuing war is likely to kill hundreds of millions of people, and possibly exterminate the human race.

The second is that the unipolar nature of international power politics today provides an unusually propitious opportunity for global state formation that may, if new powers arise to oppose U.S. hegemony militarily, disappear rather soon. It is difficult to think of any moment since the height of the Roman empire in which the establishment of a world state was more possible than it is now. There is no reason to believe, furthermore, that it will be easier in the near future.[9]

Many obstacles stand in the way of the formation of a genuine world state that can eliminate nuclear-armed international anarchy, not least of which is the apparent indifference to such concerns by the present United States government, or its possible desire to dominate a world state in such a way as to prevent a genuine one from developing. In the realm of ideas, however, a realm that, as we have seen, can play an important role in international politics, there are two key obstacles. The first is the idea that the spread of nuclear weapons is a positive development. For those who wish to see the emergence of an effective anti-nuclear world state, this is a very dangerous idea, because the more nations that attain nuclear weapons systems over the

---

9. As seems to be implied by John Mearsheimer, in his case for an Indian nuclear force. "Here We Go Again," editorial in *The New York Times*, May 17, 1998, section 4, page 17.

near term, the harder it will probably be to develop such a state. The second is the reification of anarchy: the odd idea that international anarchy is some kind of cosmic material force that cannot be overcome. These two ideas have a profound effect upon the thinking of world leaders today. They are inconsistent with a Realism aiming at long-term human survival.

Bibliography

Archival Collections and Unpublished Papers

Hans Morgenthau Papers, Library of Congress
Reinhold Niebuhr Papers, Library of Congress. (RNP)
Fromkin, David. "Hans Morgenthau: A Memoir." Unpublished paper presented to conference on American Realism, Bard College, February 1991.
Niebuhr, Reinhold. "The Problem of Nuclear Warfare." Unpublished essay (1957), RNP.
——. "Preventive War." Unpublished paper (c.1963), RNP.
——. "International Politics Under the Sword of Damocles." Unpublished paper (c.1963), RNP
Russell, Greg. "Hans J. Morgenthau's Political Realism and the Ethics of Evil," paper prepared for 1995 meeting of the International Studies Association, Chicago.

Books

Amis, Martin. *Einstein's Monsters.* London: Jonathan Cape, 1987.
Angell, Norman. *The Great Illusion.* London: Heinemann, 1913.
Aron, Raymond. *The Great Debate: Theories of Nuclear Strategy,* tr. Ernst Pawel. Lanham, MD: University Press of America, 1964.
——. *Peace and War: A Theory of International Relations.* Garden City, NY: Anchor Press, 1973.
Axelrod, Robert. *The Evolution of Cooperation.* New York: Basic Books, 1984.
Barnes, Barry. *T. S. Kuhn and Social Science.* New York: Columbia University Press, 1982.

Betts, Richard. *Nuclear Blackmail and Nuclear Balance*. Washington: Brookings, 1987.

Boyer, Paul. *Fallout*. Columbus: Ohio State University Press, 1998.

Brands, H. W. *What America Owes the World: The Struggle for the Soul of Foreign Policy*. Cambridge: Cambridge University Press, 1998.

Brodie, Bernard, ed. *The Absolute Weapon*. New York: Harcourt, Brace, 1946.

Brown, Michael E., et al., eds. *Theories of War and Peace*. Cambridge: MIT Press, 1998.

Buckley, John. *Air Power in the Age of Total War*. London: UCL Press, 1999.

Buzan, Barry, Richard Little, and Charles Jones. *The Logic of Anarchy: Neorealism to Structural Realism*. New York: Columbia University Press, 1993.

Cantril, Hadley and Mildred Strunk, eds. *Public Opinion 1935–1946*. Princeton: Princeton University Press, 1951.

Carr, E. H. *The Twenty Years' Crisis, 1919–1939: An Introduction to the Study of International Relations*. New York: Harper, 1984 (1939).

Claude, Inis L. *Power and International Relations*. New York: Random House, 1962.

Cochran, Thomas, William Arkin, and Milton Hoenig. *Nuclear Weapons Databook volume 1: U.S. Nuclear Forces and Capabilities*. Cambridge, MA: Ballinger, 1984.

Craig, Campbell. *Destroying the Village: Eisenhower and Thermonuclear War*. New York: Columbia University Press, 1998.

Crawford, Robert M. A. *Idealism and Realism in International Relations*. London: Routledge, 2000.

Danto, Arthur. *Nietzsche as Philosopher*. New York: Macmillan, 1965.

Divine, Robert. *The Sputnik Challenge*. New York: Oxford University Press, 1993.

Doenecke, Justus. *Storm on the Horizon: The Challenge to American Intervention, 1939–41*. New York: Rowman and Littlefield, 2001.

Donnelly, Jack. *Realism and International Relations*. Cambridge: Cambridge University Press, 2000.

Durkheim, Emile. *Rules of Sociological Method*. London: Macmillan, 1982.

Elman, Colin and Miriam Elman, eds. *Bridges and Boundaries: Historians, Political Scientists, and the Study of International Relations*. Cambridge: MIT Press, 2001.

Ferguson, Yale H. and Richard Mansbach. *The State, Conceptual Chaos and the future of International Relations Theory*. London: Lynne Riemmer, 1989.

Ferrell, Robert. *Woodrow Wilson and World War One*. New York: HarperCollins, 1985.

Fousek, John. *To Lead the Free World: American Nationalism and the Cultural Roots of the Cold War*. Chapel Hill: University of North Carolina Press, 2000.

Fox, Richard Wightman. *Reinhold Niebuhr, A Biography*. New York: Pantheon, 1985.

Fox, William T. R., ed. *Theoretical Aspects of International Relations*. South Bend: University of Notre Dame Press, 1959.

——. *The American Study of International Relations*. Columbia: University of South Carolina Press, 1968.

Frankel, Benjamin, ed. *Realism: Restatements and Renewal*. London: Frank Cass, 1996.

Freedman, Lawrence. *The Evolution of Nuclear Strategy*. New York: St Martin's, 1981.

Frei, Christophe. *Hans J. Morgenthau: An Intellectual Biography*. Baton Rouge: Louisiana State University Press, 2001.

Freud, Sigmund. *Civilization, War, and Death* ed. John Rickman. London: Hogarth Press, 1939.

Fussell, Paul. *The Great War and Modern Memory*. New York: Oxford University Press, 1975.

Gaddis, John Lewis. *The Long Peace: Inquiries into the History of the Cold War*. New York: Oxford University Press, 1987.

Gauthier, David. *The Logic of Leviathan: The Moral and Political Theory of Thomas Hobbes*. London: Oxford University Press, 1969.

Gerth, H. H. and Mills, C. Wright, eds., *From Max Weber: Essays in Sociology*. London: Routledge, 1991.

Giddens, Anthony. *Politics and Sociology in the thought of Max Weber*. London: MacMillan, 1972.

Gilpin, Robert. *War and Change in World Politics*. New York: Cambridge University Press, 1981.

Gray, Colin. *Nuclear Strategy and National Style*. Lanham, MD: Hamilton Press, 1986.

Guzzini, Stefano. *Realism in International Relations and International Political Economy*. London: Routledge, 1998.

Hamby, Alonzo. *Man of the People*. New York: Oxford, 1995.

Haslam, Jonathan. *No Virtue Like Necessity: Realist Thought in International Relations Since Machiavelli*. New Haven: Yale University Press, 2002.

Herken, Gregg. *Counsels of War*. New York: Knopf, 1985.

Herz, John. *International Politics in the Atomic Age*. New York: Columbia University Press, 1959.

Hobbes, Thomas. *Leviathan*. New York: Viking Penguin, 1968.

Hobson, J. A. *Imperialism: A Study* 3rd ed., rev. London: Allen & Unwin, 1938.

Hoffman, Stanley. *The State of War: Essays on the Theory and Practice of International Relations*. New York: Praeger, 1965.

Hollingdale, R. J. *Nietzsche: The Man and His Philosophy*. London: Routledge, 1965.

Holsti, K. J. *The Dividing Discipline: Hegemony and Diversity in International Theory*. London: Allen and Unwin, 1985.

Iriye, Akira. *Cambridge History of American Foreign Relations* vol. III. Cambridge: Cambridge University Press, 1993.

Jervis, Robert. *The Illogic of American Nuclear Strategy*. Ithaca: Cornell University Press, 1984.

———. *Perception and Misperception in International Politics*. Princeton: Princeton University Press, 1976.

———. *System Effects: Complexity in Political and Social Life*. Princeton: Princeton University Press, 1997.

———. *The Meaning of the Thermonuclear Revolution*. Ithaca: Cornell University Press, 1989.

Johnson, James Turner. *The Just War Tradition and the Restraint of War*. Princeton: Princeton University Press, 1981.

Jones, Charles. *E.H. Carr and International Relations: A Duty to Lie*. Cambridge: Cambridge University Press, 1998.

Kahn, Herman. *On Thermonuclear War*. Princeton: Princeton University Press, 1960.

Kaplan, Fred. *The Wizards of Armageddon*. New York: Simon & Schuster, 1984.

Kennan, George. *Russia, the Atom and the West*. New York: Harper, 1957.

Kennedy, David. *Freedom From Fear*. New York: Oxford University Press, 1999.

Kennedy, John F. *The Strategy of Peace*. New York: Harper, 1960.

Keohane, Robert, ed. *Neorealism and its Critics*. New York: Columbia University Press, 1986.

Knutsen, Torbjørn. *A History of International Relations Theory*. 2nd ed. Manchester: Manchester University Press, 1997.

Kuhn, Thomas. *The Structure of Scientific Revolutions*. Chicago: University of Chicago Press, 1962.

LaFeber, Walter. *The New Empire: An Interpretation of American Expansion, 1860–98*. Ithaca: Cornell University Press, 1963.

Lasch, Christopher. *The New Radicalism in America,1889–1963: The Intellectual as a Social Type*. New York: Norton, 1965.

Lebow, Richard Ned and Janice Gross Stein. *We All Lost the Cold War*. Princeton: Princeton University Press, 1994.

Levin, N. Gordon. *Woodrow Wilson and World Politics*. New York: Oxford University Press, 1967.

Mandelbaum, Michael. *The Nuclear Revolution: International Politics before and after Hiroshima*. Cambridge: Cambridge University Press, 1979.

Mearsheimer, John. *The Tragedy of Great Power Politics*. New York: Norton, 2001.

McCormick, Thomas. *China Market*. Chicago: Ivan Dee, 1990.

Messenger, Charles. *'Bomber' Harris and the Strategic Bombing Offensive, 1939–1945*. London: Leventhal, 1984.

Morgenstern, Oskar. *The Question of National Defense*. New York: Random House, 1959.

Morgenthau, Hans. *Scientific Man vs. Power Politics.* Chicago: University of Chicago Press, 1946.

———. *Politics Among Nations.* 1st edition. Chicago: University of Chicago Press, 1948.

———. *In Defense of the National Interest.* New York: Knopf, 1951.

———. *The Purpose of American Politics.* New York: Knopf, 1960.

———. *Politics in the 20th Century,* 3 vols. Chicago: University of Chicago Press, 1962.

Mueller, John. *Retreat from Doomsday: The Obsolescence of Major War.* New York: Basic Books, 1989.

Naftali, Timothy and Alexandr Fursenko. *One Hell of a Gamble: Khrushchev, Castro, and Kennedy.* New York: Norton, 1997.

Newhouse, John. *War and Peace in the Nuclear Age.* New York: Knopf, 1989.

Niebuhr, Reinhold. *Leaves from the Notebook of a Tamed Cynic.* Louisville: John Knox Press, 1980 [1929].

———. *Moral Man and Immoral Society.* New York: Scribner's, 1932.

———. *The Nature and Destiny of Man* 2 vols. New York: Scribner's, 1941, 1943.

———. *The Children of Light and the Children of Darkness.* New York: Scribner's, 1944.

———. *The Irony of American History.* New York: Scribner's, 1952.

———. *The Structures of Nations and Empires.* New York: Scribner's, 1959.

Nietzsche, Friedrich. *Basic Writings of Nietzsche.* tr. and ed. Walter Kaufmann. New York: Random House, 1968.

———. *Daybreak, Thoughts on the Prejudices of Morality,* tr. R. J. Hollingdale. Cambridge: Cambridge University Press, 1982.

O'Brien, William. *The Conduct of Just and Limited War.* New York: Praeger, 1981.

Osgood, Robert. *Limited War: The Challenge to American Strategy.* Chicago: University of Chicago Press, 1957.

Parkinson, F. *The Philosophy of International Relations: A Study in the History of Thought.* London: Sage, 1971.

Polsby, Nelson and Fred Greenstein. *Handbook of Political Science,* vol. 8. Reading: Addison-Wesley, 1975.

Rhodes, Richard. *The Making of the Atomic Bomb.* New York: Touchstone, 1986.

———. *Dark Sun: The Making of the Hydrogen Bomb.* New York: Simon and Schuster, 1995.

Rice, Daniel F. *Reinhold Niebuhr and John Dewey: An American Odyssey.* Albany: SUNY Press, 1993.

Roman, Peter. *Eisenhower and the Missile Gap.* Ithaca: Cornell University Press, 1995.

Rosenthal, Joel. *Righteous Realists: Political Realism, Responsible Power, and American Culture in the Nuclear Age.* Baton Rouge: Louisiana State University Press, 1991.

Rousseau, J. J. *Discours sur L'Inégalité*. Cambridge: Cambridge University Press, 1944.

Russell, Greg. *Hans J. Morgenthau and the Ethics of American Statecraft*. Baton Rouge: Louisiana State University Press, 1990.

Sagan, Scott. *The Limits of Safety: Organizations, Accidents, and Nuclear Weapons*. Princeton, Princeton University Press, 1993.

Sagan, Scott and Kenneth Waltz. *The Spread of Nuclear Weapons: A Debate*. New York: Norton, 1995.

——. *The Spread of Nuclear Weapons: A Debate Renewed*. New York: Norton, 2002.

Schell, Jonathan. *The Fate of the Earth*. New York: Avon, 1982.

Schlesinger, Arthur, Jr. *A Life in the 20th Century: Innocent Beginnings, 1917–1950*. New York: Houghton Mifflin, 2000.

Schmidt, Brian. *The Political Discourse of Anarchy: A Disciplinary History of International Relations*. Albany: SUNY Press, 1998.

Sherry, Michael. *The Rise of American Air Power: The Creation of Armageddon*. New Haven: Yale University Press, 1987.

Skinner, Quentin. *The Foundations of Modern Political Thought, Vol. 1* Cambridge: Cambridge University Press, 1978.

Smith, Michael Joseph. *Realist Thought from Weber to Kissinger*. Baton Rouge: Louisiana State University Press, 1986.

Snyder, Jack. *Myths of Empire: Domestic Politics and International Ambition*. Ithaca: Cornell University Press, 1991.

Spykman, Nicholas J. *America's Strategy in World Politics*. New York: Harcourt, Brace, and Co., 1942.

Stammer, Otto, ed. *Max Weber and Sociology Today*. Tr. Kathleen Morris. Oxford: Blackwell, 1971.

Stevenson, William R. *Christian Love And Just War: Moral Paradox And Political Life In St. Augustine And His Modern Interpreters*. Macon: Mercer University Press, 1987.

Trachtenberg, Marc. *History and Strategy*. Princeton: Princeton University Press, 1991.

Tucker, Robert C. *Stalin in Power: The Revolution from Above, 1928–1941*. New York: Norton, 1990.

Vidal, Gore. *Perpetual War for Perpetual Peace*. New York: Avalon, 2002.

Waltz, Kenneth. *Man, the State and War*. New York: Columbia University Press, 1959.

——. *Foreign Policy and Democratic Politics*. London: Longmans, 1967.

——. *Theory of International Politics*. Reading: Addison-Wesley, 1979.

Weart, Spencer. *Nuclear Fear: A History of Images*. Cambridge: Harvard University Press, 1988.

Wendt, Alexander. *Social Theory of International Politics*. Cambridge: Cambridge University Press, 1999.

Werrell, Kenneth. *Blankets of Fire: US Bombers over Japan during World War II*. Washington: Smithsonian Institution, 1996.

White, Morton. *Social Thought in America: the Revolt Against Formalism*. New York: Viking, 1949.

Williams, William Appleman. *The Tragedy of American Diplomacy* 2nd ed. New York: Delta, 1959.

Wolfers, Arnold. *Discord and Collaboration*. Baltimore: Johns Hopkins Press, 1962.

Articles

Ahrensdorf, Peter. "The Fear of Death and the Longing for Immortality: Hobbes and Thucydides on Human Nature and the Problem of Anarchy," *American Political Science Review* 94 (September 2000).

Aron, Raymond. "Max Weber and Power Politics." In Otto Stammer, ed., *Max Weber and Sociology Today* tr. Kathleen Morris. Oxford: Blackwell, 1971.

Barkawi, Tarak. "Strategy as a Vocation: Weber, Morgenthau, and Modern Strategic studies," *Review of International Studies* 24 (1998).

Barkdull, John. "Waltz, Durkheim and International Relations: The International System as an Abnormal Form." *American Political Science Review* 89 (September 1995).

Bennett, John. "Niebuhr's Ethic: The Later Years." *Christianity and Crisis* 42 (April 12, 1982).

Bull, Hedley. "International Theory: the Case for a Classical Approach." *World Politics* 18 (April, 1966).

Copeland, Dale. "Neorealism and the Myth of Bipolar Stability." In Benjamin Frankel, ed., *Realism: Restatements and Renewal*. London: Frank Cass, 1996.

Craig, Campbell. "The New Meaning of Modern War in the Thought of Reinhold Niebuhr." *Journal of the History of Ideas* 53 (October–December 1992).

———. "The Not-So-Strange Career of Charles Beard." *Diplomatic History* 25 (Spring 2001).

———. "The (Il)logic of Henry Kissinger's Nuclear Strategy," *Armed Forces and Society* 30 (2003), forthcoming.

Deudney, Daniel. "Dividing Realism: Security Materialism vs. Structural Realism on Nuclear Security and Proliferation," *Security Studies* 2 (Spring/Summer 1993).

———. "Nuclear Weapons and the Waning of the *Real*-State." *Daedalus* 124 (Spring 1995).

———. "Geopolitics as Theory: Historical Security Materialism," *European Journal of International Relations* 6 (Winter, 2000).

———. "Greater Britain, or Greater Synthesis," *Review of International Studies* 27 (2001).

———. "Regrounding Realism: Anarchy, Security, and Changing Material Contexts," *Security Studies* 10 (Autumn 2000).

Deutsch, Karl. "Discussion." In Otto Stammer, ed., *Max Weber and Sociology Today* tr. Kathleen Morris. Oxford: Blackwell, 1971.

Drell, Sidney. "Nuclear Weapons." In John Whiteday Chambers II et al, eds., *The Oxford Companion to American Military Military History*. New York: Oxford University Press, 1999.

Easton, David. "An Approach to the Analysis of Political Systems." *World Politics* 9 (April, 1957).

Evera, Stephen Van. "Offense, Defense, and the Causes of War." In Michael E. Brown, et al, eds., *Theories of War and Peace*. Cambridge: MIT Press, 1998.

Feaver, Peter D. "Neooptimists and the Enduring Problem of Nuclear Proliferation" *Security Studies* 6 (Summer 1997).

Forde, Steven. "International Realism and the Science of Politics: Thucydides, Machiavelli, and Neorealism." *International Studies Quarterly* 39 (1995).

Gaddis, John. "International Relations Theory and the End of the Cold War." *International Security* 17 (Winter 1992–93).

Halliday, Fred and Justin Rosenberg. "Interview with Ken Waltz." *Review of International Studies* 24 (1998).

Harrison, Ewan. "Waltz, Kant and systemic approaches to international relations." *Review of International Studies* 28 (April 2002).

Herz, John. "Rise and Demise of the Territorial State." *World Politics* 9 (July 1957).

Hoffmann, Stanley. "International Relations: The Long Road to Theory." *World Politics* 11 (April 1958).

———. "An American Social Science: International Relations." *Daedalus* 106 (Summer 1977).

Holsti, K. J. "Retreat from Utopia: International Relations Theory, 1945–70." *Canadian Journal of Political Science* 4 (June, 1971).

———. "Scholarship in an Era of Anxiety: The Study of International Politics During the Cold War," *Review of International Studies* 24 (1998).

Honig, Jan Willem. "Totalitarianism and Realism: Hans Morgenthau's German Years." *Security Studies* 5 (Winter 1995/1996).

Jervis, Robert. "Cooperation under the Security Dilemma." *World Politics* 30 (January 1978).

———. "Deterrence Theory Revisited." *World Politics* 31 (January 1979).

———. "Hans Morgenthau, Realism, and the Scientific Study of International Relations." *Social Research* 61 (Winter 1994).

Kindleberger, C. P. "Scientific International Politics." *World Politics* 11 (October 1958).

King, James. "Nuclear Plenty and Limited War." *Foreign Affairs* 35 (January 1957).

Lebow, Richard Ned. "The Long Peace, the End of the Cold War, and the Failure of Realism." *International Organization* 48 (Spring 1994).

Little, Richard. "International Relations and the Methodological Turn." *Political Studies* 39 (1991).

Mearsheimer, John. "Nuclear Weapons and Deterrence in Europe." *International Security* 9 (Winter 1984/85).

———. "The Case for a Ukrainian Nuclear Deterrent." *Foreign Affairs* 72 (Summer 1993).

———."Here We Go Again." Editorial in *The New York Times*, May 17, 1998.

Morgenthau, Hans. "The H-Bomb and After." *Bulletin of the Atomic Scientists* (1950). Reprinted in *Politics in the 20th Century* vol. 3. Chicago: University of Chicago Press, 1962.

———. "The Unfinished Business of United States Foreign Policy." *Wisconsin Idea* (Fall 1953). Reprinted in *Politics in the 20th Century* vol. 2. Chicago: University of Chicago Press, 1962.

———. "Will it Deter Aggression?" *New Republic* 137 (March 29, 1954).

———. "The Political and Military Strategy of the United States." *Bulletin of Atomic Scientists* (October 1954). Reprinted in *Politics in the 20th Century* vol. 2. Chicago: University of Chicago Press, 1962.

———. "Diplomacy." Originally published in *The State of the Social Sciences*. Reprinted in *Politics in the 20th Century* vol. 2. Chicago: University of Chicago Press, 1962.

———. "Has Atomic War Really Become Impossible?" *Bulletin of Atomic Scientists* 11 (January 1956).

———. November 13, 1956, letter to *The New York Times*. Reprinted in *Politics in the 20th Century* vol. 2 (Chicago: University of Chicago Press, 1962).

———. "The Decline and Fall of American Foreign Policy." *New Republic* 139 (December 10, 1956).

———. "The Paradoxes of Nationalism." *Yale Review* 46 (June 1957).

———. "The Revolution in United States Foreign Policy." Originally published in *Commentary* (February 1957). Reprinted in *Politics in the 20th Century* vol. 2. Chicago: University of Chicago Press, 1962.

———. "Atomic Force and Foreign Policy: Can the 'New Pacifism' Insure Peace?" *Commentary* 23 (June 1957).

———. "Decline of American Power." Originally published in *The New Republic* (December 9, 1957). Reprinted in *Politics in the 20th Century* vol. 2. Chicago: University of Chicago Press, 1962.

———. "A Reassessment of United States Foreign Policy." Lecture at Dartmouth College, February 10, 1958, in *Politics in the 20th Century* vol. 2. Chicago: University of Chicago Press, 1962.

——. "The Last Years of Our Greatness?" *New Republic* (December 29, 1958).

——. "What the Big Two Can, and Can't Negotiate." Originally published in the *New York Times Magazine*, September 20, 1959. Reprinted in *Politics in the 20th Century* vol. 3. Chicago: University of Chicago Press, 1962.

——. Review of Niebuhr's *The Structures of Nations and Empires. Christianity and Crisis* 20 (February 8, 1960).

——. "International Relations." Entry originally published in *Encyclopedia Britannica* (1961). Reprinted in *Politics in the 20th Century* vol. 3. Chicago: University of Chicago Press, 1962.

——. University of Maryland address, March 1961, originally reprinted in *Politics in the 20th Century* vol. 3. Chicago: University of Chicago Press, 1962.

——. "Death in the Nuclear Age." *Commentary* 32 (September 1961].

——. "Truth and Power." *Commentary* 32 (January 1962).

——. "The Four Paradoxes of Nuclear Strategy." *American Political Science Review* 58 (1964).

——. "The Ethics of War and Peace in the Nuclear Age." (Interview with Niebuhr and Morgenthau.) *War/Peace Report* (February 1967).

Niebuhr, Reinhold. "The Crisis." lead editorial in *Christianity and Crisis* 1 (February 10, 1941).

——. "The Christian Faith and the World Crisis." *Christianity and Crisis* 1 (February 10, 1941).

——. "Whosoever Will Save His Life . . ." *Christianity and Crisis* 1 (February 24, 1941).

——. "Fighting Chance for a Sick Society." *Nation* 152 (March 22 1941).

——. "Pacifism and America First." *Christianity and Crisis* 1 (June 16, 1941).

——. "New Allies, Old Issues." *Nation* 153 (July 19, 1941), p. 50.

——. "American Doldrums." lead editorial in *Christianity and Crisis* 1 (September 22, 1941).

——. "Armistice Day 1941." lead editorial in *Christianity and Crisis* 1 (November 17, 1941).

——. Lead editorial in *Christianity and Crisis* 2 (March 9, 1942).

——. "The Anglo-Russian Pact." *Christianity and Crisis* 2 (June 29, 1942).

——. Lead editorial in *Christianity and Crisis* 2 (August 10, 1942).

——. "Plans for World Reorganization," *Christianity and Crisis* 2 (October 19, 1942).

——. Lead editorial in *Christianity and Crisis* 3 (October 4, 1943).

——. "We are in Peril." *Christianity and Crisis* 3 (October 18, 1943).

——. "Politics and the Children of Light." *Christianity and Crisis* 3 (November 29, 1943).

——. "Our Relations to Japan." *Christianity and Crisis* 5 (September 17, 1945).

——. "The Atomic Issue." *Christianity and Crisis* 5 (October 15, 1945).

——. "The Fight for Germany." *Life* (October 21, 1946).

———. "For Peace, We Must Risk War." *Life* (September 20, 1948).

———. "Editorial Notes." *Christianity and Crisis* 10 (February 6, 1950).

———. "The Christian Conscience and Atomic War." *Christianity and Crisis* 10 (December 11, 1950).

———. "The Two Dimensions of the Struggle." *Christianity and Crisis* 11 (May 28, 1951).

———. "The Case for Coexistence." *New Leader* 37 (October 4, 1954).

———. "The Dismal Prospects for Disarmament." *Christianity and Crisis* 17 (September 16, 1957).

———. "Editorial Notes." *Christianity and Crisis* 17 (November 11, 1957).

———. "The Moral Insecurity of Our Security." *Christianity and Crisis* 17 (January 6, 1958).

———. "Editorial Notes." *Christianity and Crisis* 18 (April 28, 1958).

———. "Coexistence Under a Nuclear Stalemate." *Christianity and Crisis* 19 (September 21, 1959).

———. "The Long Haul of Coexistence." *Christianity and Crisis* 19 (November 30, 1959).

———. "A Christian View of the Future: A Conversation with Reinhold Niebuhr." *Harper's* 221 (December, 1960).

———. "Rising Hopes for Arms Control." *Christianity and Crisis* 21 (March 6, 1961).

———. "The Resumption of Nuclear Testing." *Christianity and Crisis* 21 (October 2, 1961).

———. "Nuclear Dilemma." *Union Seminary Quarterly Review* 17 (March 1962).

———. "Editorial Notes." *Christianity and Crisis* 22 (November 26, 1962).

———. "The Cuban Crisis in Retrospect." *New Leader* 45 (December 10, 1962).

———. "History's Limitations in the Nuclear Age." *New Leader* 46 (February 4, 1963).

Niebuhr, Reinhold and Bishop Angus Dun. "God Wills Both Justice and Peace." *Christianity and Crisis* 15 (June 13, 1955).

Nye, Joseph. "Neorealism and Neoliberalism," *World Politics* 40 (January 1988).

Petersen, Ulrik Enemark. "Breathing Nietzsche's Air: New Reflections on Morgenthau's Concepts of Power and Human Nature." *Alternatives* 24 (1999).

Petrova, Magarita H. "The End of the Cold War: A Battle or Bridging Ground Between Rationalist and Ideational Approaches in International Relations?" *European Jouranl of International Relations* 9 (March 2003), pp. 117–129.

Pichler, Hans-Karl. "The Godfathers of 'Truth': Max Weber and Carl Schmitt in Morgenthau's Theory of Power Politics," *Review of International Studies* 24 (1998).

Rosecrance, Richard. "Reply to Waltz." *International Organization* 36 (Summer 1982).

Singer, J. David. "International Conflict: Three Levels of Analysis." *World Politics* 12 (April 1960).

Speer, James P. II. "Hans Morgenthau and the World State." *World Politics* 20 (June 1968).

Suri, Jeremi and Scott Sagan, "The Madman Nuclear Alert: Secrecy, Signaling and Safety in the October 1969 crises," *International Security* 27 (Spring 2003), forthcoming..

Wagner, R. Harrison. "What was Bipolarity?" *International Organization* 47 (Winter 1993).

Waltz, Kenneth. "Political Philosophy and the Study of International Relations." In William T. R. Fox, ed., *Theoretical Aspects of International Relations*. South Bend: University of Notre Dame Press, 1959.

——. Review of Morgenthau's *Dilemmas of Politics* in *American Political Science Review* 53 (June 1959).

——. Review of Niebuhr's *The Structure of Nations and Empires* in *International Journal* (1959).

——. "Kant, Liberalism, and War." *American Political Science Review* 56 (June 1962).

——. "The Stability of a Bipolar World." *Daedalus* 93 (Summer 1964).

——. "Contention and Management in International Relations." *World Politics* 17 (July 1965).

——. "The Politics of Peace." *International Studies Quarterly* 11 (September 1967).

——. "International Structure, National Force, and the Balance of World Power." *Journal of International Affairs* 21 (1967).

——. "Conflict in World Politics." In Waltz and Steven L. Spiegel, *Conflict in World Politics*. Cambridge, MA: Winthrop, 1971.

——. Review of Richard Sterling's *Macropolitics: International Relations in a Global Society*. New York: Knopf, 1974, in *American Political Science Review* 70 (June 1976).

——. "The Spread of Nuclear Weapons: More May Be Better." *Adelphi Paper number 171*. London: International Institute for Strategic Studies, 1981.

——. "War in Neorealist Theory." *Journal of Interdisciplinary History* 18 (September 1988).

——. "Nuclear Myths and Political Realities." *American Political Science Review* 84 (September 1990).

——. "The Emerging Structure of International Politics." *International Security* 18 (Fall 1993).

——. "Realism after the Cold War." An address to American Political Science Association, Boston, MA, 1998.

Wolin, Richard. "Reasons of State, States of Reason." *New Republic* (June 4, 2001).

Woods, Matthew. "Reflections on nuclear optimism: Waltz, Burke and proliferation," *Review of International Studies* 28 (2002).

Woodward, C. Vann. "The Age of Reinterpretation." *American Historical Review* 66 (October 1960).

Index